Remainders of the American Century

Remainders of the American Century

Post-Apocalyptic Novels in the Age of US Decline

BRENT RYAN BELLAMY

WESLEYAN UNIVERSITY PRESS Middletown, Connecticut

Wesleyan University Press
Middletown CT 06459
www.wesleyan.edu/wespress
© 2021 Brent Ryan Bellamy
All rights reserved
Manufactured in the United States of America
Designed by Richard Hendel
Typeset in Miller and Klavika by Integrated Publishing Solutions

Library of Congress Cataloging-in-Publication Data
Names: Bellamy, Brent Ryan, author.
Title: Remainders of the American century : post-apocalyptic novels in the age of US decline / Brent Ryan Bellamy.
Description: Middletown, Connecticut : Wesleyan University Press, [2021] | Includes bibliographical references and index. | Summary: "A literary study of mainstream and science fiction novels shows the contest between the reactionary impulse of the post-apocalyptic mode and the progressive impetus for a new world"— Provided by publisher.
Identifiers: LCCN 2021000704 (print) | LCCN 2021000705 (ebook) | ISBN 9780819580313 (cloth) | ISBN 9780819580320 (trade paperback) | ISBN 9780819580337 (ebook)
Subjects: LCSH: American fiction—20th century—History and criticism. | American fiction—21st century—History and criticism. | Science fiction, American—History and criticism. | Dystopias in literature. | Apocalypse in literature.
Classification: LCC PS374.D96 B45 2021 (print) | LCC PS374.D96 (ebook) | DDC 813/.509372—dc23
LC record available at https://lccn.loc.gov/2021000704
LC ebook record available at https://lccn.loc.gov/2021000705

5 4 3 2 1

Dedicated to family, immediate, extended, and found; and to Alex and George, partners in thought and deed

The study of post-apocalypse is a study of what disappears and what remains, and of how the remainder has been transformed.
—JAMES BERGER, *After the End*

Contents

Acknowledgments — ix

Introduction:
   Post-Apocalyptic Novels in the Age of US Decline — 1

PART ONE
THE POST-APOCALYPTIC MODE

1. Post-Apocalypse Tropes — 31
2. Reduced Futures — 52
3. Remaindered Books — 74

PART TWO
THE CONTESTED POLITICS OF US DECLINE

4. Old and New Americas — 103
5. Segregated Futures — 130
6. The Reproductive Imperative — 154
7. Automobility Regression — 172

Conclusion:
   Remainders of the American Century — 201

Notes — 209
Bibliography — 241
Index — 263

Acknowledgments

This intellectual project had its inception in 2008 as I completed my graduate studies in English (Public Texts) at Trent University. Rather than writing about something I was a fan of (the work of William Blake and Bruce Springsteen, respectively, had been the topics of my bachelor's and master's of art theses), I was compelled to ask a critical question: why did the apocalyptic mood seem to dominate popular culture? Several mentors offered guidance as this question became my proposal for future research and then a doctoral dissertation, a book proposal, a manuscript, and finally this book. At Trent, Michael Epp guided my intellectual curiosity. At the University of Alberta, Imre Szeman introduced me to the wonders of academic community. At Memorial University of Newfoundland, Danine Farquharson helped me navigate academia as a professional. At Trent once more, Veronica Hollinger advised me on my approach to the science fiction courses she pioneered, which I was teaching for the first time. These brief notes only dimly illuminate my gratitude: thank you.

Academia produces hurdles one has to jump through only once: writing a dissertation, defending it, writing a first book proposal, publishing a first book, and so on. My academic colleagues guided me through such hurdles and pointed out other, less-obvious challenges: at the University of Alberta, Karyn Ball, Jaimie Baron, Kim Brown, Dianne Chisholm, Odile Cisneros, Jonathan Cohn, Elena Del Rio, Cecily Devereux, Mary Marshall Durrell, Nat Hurley, Eddy Kent, Sha LaBare, Natalie Loveless, Michael O'Driscoll, Mark Simpson, Terri Tomsky, Marcie Whitecotton-Carroll, Sheena Wilson, and Teresa Zackodnik; at Memorial University of Newfoundland, Jennifer

Lokash, Christopher Lockett, Andrew Loman, and Fiona Polack; at Trent University, Jessica Marion Barr, Rita Bode, Sally Chivers, Rosemary Devlin, Patricia Heffernan, Hugh Hodges, Aishwarya Javalgekar, Ihor Junyk, Katrina Keefer, Andrew Loeb, Kelly McGuire, Liam Mitchell, Catherine O'Brien, and Joshua Synenko. You have each supported this work directly and indirectly through input or conversation and kindness: thank you.

With an eye for its potential and relevance, Marla Zubel, then at Wesleyan University Press, offered me an advance contract for this book. My editor, Suzanna Tamminen, saw the book through peer review (twice!) and to the finish line. My anonymous readers showed me what was not coming across and did so in a gregarious and thoughtful manner. I specifically appreciate the fact that my readers returned to the material once I had revised it; this kind of return is no small feat. There is one other person who comes close to having spent as much time as me on this project: my substantive editor and dear friend Justin Sully. Justin, you are a brilliant, careful, and incisive reader. You made this book immeasurably better. Full stop. To Ann Brash, Jeanne Ferris, Stephanie Elliott Prieto, and Jaclyn Wilson, who oversaw the production and integrity of this manuscript: thank you.

A version of chapter 6, "The Reproductive Imperative," first appeared in volume 16, issue 1, of the *Cormac McCarthy Journal* as "The Reproductive Imperative of *The Road*." A version of chapter 7, "Automobility Regression," is included in *Transportation and the Culture of Climate Change: The Accelerating Ride to Global Crisis* (West Virginia University Press, 2020), edited by Tatiana Prorokova-Konard. as "Remainders of the Fossil Regime: Automobility Regression in Three Post-Apocalyptic Novels." Thanks to Stacey Peebles of the *Cormac McCarthy Journal* and Derek Krissoff of West Virginia University Press.

I would like to thank the librarians of the Merril Collection of Science Fiction, Speculation and Fantasy who helped me find key references early in my doctoral research on post-apocalyptic texts and again late during my revisions of this book. Thank you to those on Science Fiction Research Association listserv who answered my questions in July 2020, especially Jeremy W. Brett, Michael Page, Rikk Mulligan, and Lauren Wallace.

As it is the convention to say, please credit me with everything that does not make sense and blame the following people who provided feedback on this work for anything thoughtful I have written: Stacy Balkan, Gerry Canavan, Jeff Diamanti, Jessica Hurley, Thomas Laughlin, Sean O'Brien, Stacey Peebles, Shama Rangwala, Benjamin Robertson, Michael Rubenstein, Kaitlyn Schoop, David Thomas, Myka Tucker-Abrhamson, and Priscilla Wald. I want to mention in particular my writing-group comrades Ryan Brooks, Julie Fiorelli, Lindsay Marshall, and Jen Phillis. Additionally, Jen Phillis produced the index for this book and assures me that there are one or two good goofs in there. To those who read and commented on this work: thank you.

I presented part of this work at conferences such as meetings of the American Comparative Literature Association, the Association for College and University Teachers of English, the Marxist Literary Group, and the Modern Language Association. I also received feedback in workshops and conversations. Here is a terrifyingly incomplete list of those who engaged with this work in progress in some such venue: Eric Beckman, Brett Benjamin, Beverly Best, Mark Bould, Sarah Brouillette, Maria Elisa Cevasco, Brad Congdon, Andrew Culp, Ryan Culpepper, Ashley Dawson, Sharae Deckard, Caroline Edwards, Rebecca Evans, Lai-Tze Fan, Jacob Goessling, Meghan Gorman-Darif, Dan Hartley, Christian Haynes, Michael Horka, Rob Imes, Fredric Jameson, Leigh Claire La Berge, Stephanie LeMenager, Graeme MacDonald, Courtney Maloney, Jessica McDonald, Geordie Miller, Kristin Moriah, Mathias Nilges, Oded Nir, Chuckie Palmer-Patel, Jon Parsons, Emilio Sauri, Leif Schenstead-Harris, Matthew Schneider-Mayerson, Rebekah Sheldon, Mark Soderstrom, Julianna Spahr, Anne Stewart, Michael Truscello, Tony Vinci, Jennifer Wenzel, Rhys Williams, and Daniel Worden. For raising a question or recommending a resource: thank you.

I suspect a great many people from the Marxist Literary Group will find ways to thank the incomparable Kevin Floyd in passages such as this one. He deserves every bit of the love and the praise that we voice, think, and feel. Kevin passed away too soon for anyone's good, but his presence still encourages me to think precisely and express my thoughts eloquently. You left an empty space, Kevin, though your earnest care still radiates through us. To Kevin and those who love him: thank you.

Friends and comrades Adrienne Batke, Sarah Blacker, Rebecca

Blakey, Adam Carlson, Marija Cetinic, Amy De'Ath, Jonathan Dyck, Trevor Chow-Fraser, Michael Granzow, Lisa Haynes, Rob Jackson, Eva-Lynn Jagoe, Jason James, David Janzen, Robert Janzen, Jordan Kinder, Marcelle Kosman, Kate Lawless, Norman Mack, Katie Lewandowski, Derritt Mason, Hannah McGregor, Andrew Pendakis, Joseph Ren, Valerie Savard, Jana Smith-Elford, and Sylvie Vigneux, I am grateful for your friendship and terribly distraught that we live so far apart. Barbara, Brent, Wendy, Leigh Ann, Josten, William, Rebecca, Clyde, Lindsay, Adrienne, and Dion, I love you. I will indulge in a special mention of my stalwart writing companion, George, who once bodily languished over my keyboard. When I composed these acknowledgments I had playfully added "thankfully not at this precise moment" in parentheses, but most days I long for him to be in the way of my writing. I find these words offer a sadly fitting acknowledgment for a book about the force and presence of remainders. To loved ones, far and near: thank you.

Metaphors of debt do disservice to the grateful, but it seems there is a paucity of ways to express gratitude without phrases such as "I owe everything to those who supported me." Let me say this instead: this work would not be the same—in fact, would not be possible—without Alexandra Carruthers. Alex, you taught me new ways to think about social spaces, encouraged me every step of the way, helped me to recover from setbacks, grieved for our incomprehensible losses, and insisted we celebrate successes. Perhaps I do owe you something, but it is a kind of gratitude beyond debt and guilt, from a realm of freedom: thank you.

Remainders of the American Century

Introduction
Post-Apocalyptic Novels in the Age of US Decline

Post-apocalyptic novels are not about the end of the world. Instead, they represent fictional endings that may be interpreted with a sense of urgency or of history.[1] For me, such stories recently produced in or about the United States express cultural anxiety about the end of US hegemony and the long, slow, and painful acclimatization to life under neoliberalism, especially for those who up to this point have enjoyed a relatively high standard of living. This book finds that post-apocalyptic storytelling tendentially veers toward political reaction: such tales feature characters who respond to fundamental changes in their storyworld, often through a winnowing out of various social possibilities.[2] Characters in a post-apocalyptic situation must resort to eking out subsistence, often at the expense of other survivors and their pre-apocalyptic habits. In gruesome mimicry, such narratives play out the less dramatic, yet no less impactful, adjustments that many people around the real world have had to make in response to the expansions and then contractions of US power and capital. *Remainders of the American Century* selectively covers the period from the end of World War II to the wake of the 2007–8 financial crisis, or from the height of US hegemony to a present that is largely characterized by uncertainty over the standing of the United States in the world. The book traces the outlines of the structural forces that have made such stories into a coherent and pervasive cultural form.

A core premise of this book is that the techniques of storytelling that post-apocalyptic novels evolved after World War II lend themselves remarkably well to the exploration of geopolitical anxiety in the twenty-first century. Before the multimedia explosion of the post-apocalyptic mode, it was incubated in the novel form.[3] The first post-apocalyptic stories were found in novels, and it was as short stories and novels in the mid-twentieth century that the tradition was transformed into the mode we recognize today.[4] By imagining a future without enough material wealth to be shared among the survivors, despite massive reductions in the population, post-apocalyptic novels describe a situation uncannily like the one that capital's ideologues would have people believe they live in today. In the uncertain present, these novels offer a way of describing the management of anxiety—personal, corporate, governmental, and planetary—at the sunset of the American century. From the worries of those with little of what they will need to get by to the technocrats watching with concern as capital reverses its flow, it is important to recognize that such anxiety comes in many forms. The anxieties expressed across the mode of post-apocalyptic storytelling offer crucial information about what people fear and how they might respond to the realization of such concerns. Meanwhile, eventful stories of survival often obscure the sources of such anxieties. This fact gets further complicated by the emerging variety and changing character of fear-inducing historical realities. As the focus of cultural anxiety changes, the fictional worlds of post-apocalyptic stories expand.

Yet a dominant trend can be found in the post-apocalyptic novels examined in this book: they treat crisis as opportunity and encourage an understanding of history that counterintuitively valorizes the individual over the collective and seeks a return to the way things were. Such texts express a profound form of wish fulfillment that, in many cases, stages the imaginary collapse of the United States to narrate its return to the days of promise. While some texts wholeheartedly embrace this vision, others stage this narrative move to show it in a critical light. For instance, in Octavia E. Butler's *Parable of the Talents*, first published in 1998, the presidential candidate Andrew Steele Jarret implores everyone to join him "to make America great again" (20). Butler's work inspires a core thesis of this book: post-apocalyptic remainders fuel the US cultural imaginary. The repetition compulsion of US politics speaks to Butler's capacity for not so much a kind of oracle-esque prescience as a clear-eyed assessment of the machinations and trajectories of US power and capital. The reemergence of that rallying cry in 2016 evinces the degree to which the playbooks of Butler's character and Donald Trump can both be traced to a shared manner of operating.[5] US post-apocalyptic novels develop a fantasy of the possibility that the United States could return to the height of its power. The valorization of the individual and the desire for a return to the previous status quo resonate with long-established tendencies in the US political imaginary and with the individual-focused, anticollectivist ethos that emerged to become America's most significant export during the period under examination here.

This book proceeds from an assessment of what it calls the post-apocalyptic mode, drawing on what the science-fiction critic Veronica Hollinger describes as a mode—which "implies not a kind but a method, a way of getting something done" ("Genre vs. Mode," 140). Building on this discussion, the introduction begins with the argument that historically dominant US post-apocalyptic writing is a symbolic mode of storytelling, rather than a genre in and of itself. I then return to the motif of the opening: the American century. I draw on world-systems theory to situate the historical and national dimensions of my reading of post-apocalyptic novels. Following that account of this book's historical underpinning, I discuss the term "remainders" as its central, mediating concept. As a literary term, "remainder" offers a point of contact between post-apocalyptic writing and its often unspoken political commitments. Finally, I comment on the organization of the book and provide an overview of its contents.

THE POST-APOCALYPTIC MODE: ALLEGORIC OR SYMBOLIC?

The post-apocalyptic mode has long been associated with contemporary real-world crises. In 1890, Ignatius Donnelly published a left-leaning, populist novel titled *Caesar's Column*. The novel may well be the first US example of post-apocalyptic fiction, even if it could more properly be considered postrevolutionary.[6] It is named for a constructed edifice, a monument that is also a symbol of the sacrifices made by the men and women whose labor built the nation. The climax of the novel describes a working-class revolt that overthrows the oligarchic dictatorship of the United States. The infamous column is built of human bodies covered with concrete. Alexander Saxton, writing in *American Quarterly*, describes the power of this symbol as associative:

> A reader contemporary with Donnelly would have thought of Atlanta and Richmond; perhaps of Haymarket Square; certainly of the Paris Commune. An American reader today might think of Coventry or Dresden, of the German death camps; and then thanks to the curious and ghastly coincidence of visual imagery, he [*sic*] would come to the column of white cloud that towered over Hiroshima. But clearly the symbol has a life of its own; it demands the associations. ("*Caesar's Column*," 224)

The capacity of the symbol of the towering horror in Donnelly's novel to resonate over time reveals a critical tendency: to treat the post-apocalyptic mode's tropes, images, and settings as exchangeable for any given crisis, fashionable and horrific, of the present. One can easily update Saxton's list: my contemporary readers might have thought of the billows of smoke from Kuwaiti oil fields set on fire by retreating Iraqi troops, the collapse of the World Trade Center buildings in 2001, a wall whose construction was promised to win an election. or other walls built to hold at bay rising tides. Your contemporary readers will undoubtedly have fresh disasters ready to mind. The meaning of Donnelly's tower is mutable in readers' minds and critics' hands. Even a brief look at *Caesar's Column* demonstrates that apocalyptic novels can be readily cross-referenced with events in the present, even if they predate the present by over a century.[7]

Though some post-apocalyptic stories certainly respond to singular events, they have significance across a broader symbolic domain. Even texts that are from markedly different moments in the development of the post-apocalyptic mode and that tell different stories share distinguishing characteristics. For instance, Judith Merril's *The Shadow on the Hearth* (1950) offers a realistic look at human survival after the atomic bomb; Paul Auster's *In the Country of Last Things* (1988; first published in 1987) depicts the temporality of homelessness; and Carola Dibbell's *The Only Ones* (2015) imagines the future of a clone's reproductive rights. These three novels are separate, though for their characters, a temporality of the moment holds sway: Merril's Gladys Mitchell waits to hear from her husband, who gets trapped in the city when the air-raid siren announces a nuclear strike; Auster's Anna Blume's letter details the dysphoria she experiences as she searches an unnamed city for her brother; and Dibbell's Inez Kissena Fardo moves from job to job, accepting life as a courier, host, and egg donor. These characters try to make some sort of meaning out of the disconnected moments of their lives after apocalyptic change. Such works do not lend themselves to allegorical reading. If as Brenda Machosky claims, allegory is for "saying or showing one thing and meaning another" (*Structures of Appearing*, 1), then it seems an ill-suited interpretive model for the task of reading the post-apocalyptic mode. These stories are about the end of the state, capitalism, and modernity; allegory is not required. Reading symbolically offers a chance to read narratives en masse. In a pivotal piece on the relation of allegory and symbol, the literary critic Umberto Eco suggests that the symbolic mode appears "not at the level of rhetorical figures but at the level of a more macroscopic textual strategy" ("At the Roots of the Modern Concept of Symbol," 392). *Remainders of the American Century* employs such a "macroscopic textual strategy" to read post-apocalyptic novels together. Rather than treating these novels on their own, this book aims to aggregate the whole set of texts that constitute the post-apocalyptic mode of storytelling as worthy of comparison to works from the longer cultural period of the decline of US hegemony.[8] It finds the hinge for such a project in the literary concept of mode.

Not every post-apocalyptic story is about surviving a nuclear bomb strike, but most nuclear-holocaust stories are post-apocalyptic. What do readers look for when they search for a post-apocalyptic story? The science fiction critic John Rieder writes: "The pressures of the market, the dynamics of prestige, and the construction of genealogies are intrinsic features of the web of resemblances that constitute a genre. Genres are best understood by way of the practices that produce these resemblances and the motives that drive those practices" (*Colonialism and the Emergence of Science Fiction*, 18).[9] Drawing on the French sociologist Pierre Bourdieu's concept of the field of cultural production, Rieder offers a capacious sense of genre as the practices—and motives behind them—that form a "web of resemblances," yet the conventions that define genres may ultimately limit what they can be and do. Since a particular genre exceeds any individual text, generic elements that appear in one example need not reappear in another. I follow Hollinger's argument about science fiction in treating the post-apocalyptic as a mode of writing.

Modes can be critically organized by their effects, rather than necessarily by their "web of resemblances." Yet there is also a historical distinction at play in Hollinger's elaboration of the concept of mode. While genres rise and fall in rhythm with specific social forms, modes correspond to longer cultural periods. To elaborate on this point, Hollinger draws on a 1971 essay by the literary critic Alastair Fowler titled "The Life and Death of Literary Forms." Eventually genres outgrow their potential to evolve, while modes, according to Fowler, have the potential to create many newer generic forms. Fowler's punctual example is "pastoral eclogue is dead: long live pastoral" (ibid., 214, quoted in Hollinger, "Genre vs. Mode," 143). Though a particular generic form may no longer obtain, it gives storytellers the capacity to channel it in new, perhaps unexpected, directions. Following Fowler's logic, modes are the abstracted, dehistoricized cores of generic convention that have then been redeployed in a new historical context.[10] This understanding of the relationship between genres and modes bears particular import for the post-apocalyptic mode of writing in the period under consideration here, and to look ahead, it anticipates the idea that remainders can be repurposed and redeployed or cast off to rest.

For Hollinger, reading narratives in aggregate as genre produces a "particular kind of narrative complex," which literary scholars would file in an archive of stories with "particular themes, motifs, and figures," whereas thinking through modes—with an emphasis on function—offers critics a way of imagining and describing contemporary reality ("Genre vs. Mode," 140).[11] Post-apocalyptic writing is not only a sort of generic category. It is also a way of dividing texts based on the literary and cultural effects they produce. The post-apocalyptic text envisions how characters might respond to world-destroying events; the post-apocalyptic mode imagines how a culture, nation, or people might respond to having their way of life suddenly transformed in the most dramatic of ways. Post-apocalyptic stories, then, respond to larger, fundamental, though sometimes misinterpreted changes. Such responses to world-shattering crises provoke an emphatically political injunction to imagine the consequences of the historical present—this future is where we could end up if we continue to behave as we do today—and what might be possible, or become impossible, were this world to be wiped away and a new one created in its place.

The science fiction critic Eric S. Rabkin succinctly identifies the essentially political work of comparison that post-apocalyptic storytelling elicits: "In tales of the end of the world as we know it, crucial judgments arise by comparing the world destroyed with the world for which it makes room" ("Introduction," ix). Two examples illustrate this process of comparison. Alan DeNiro's *Total Oblivion, More or Less* (2009) presents a storyworld that is transformed from a primary world (that is, a storyworld based on the real world) to a secondary one (one that establishes new landscapes and geographies). DeNiro's book displaces the object of its critique through a cascade of apocalyptic events. Macy, the teenage protagonist, longs for a return to normalcy—including the availability of electricity, the retreat of the antagonistic horse warriors and the Nueva Roman empire, cars could run again, and a cure for the plague—and hopes that "we'll all go back to St. Paul and I'll start my senior year, none the worse for wear" (ibid., 3). The goal, for Macy, is already set at a continuation of how life is supposed to be. Judging by her long list of apocalyptic effects, one would be hard pressed to begrudge her desire to return to normalcy. She longs for a return to the pre-apocalyptic world that she has come to expect after sixteen years of life in the American midwest, now suffocated and blocked off as she is by a cascade of apocalyptic events. The book asks readers to compare its storyworld with the real world and, in so doing, to question the stability they once took for granted.[12] Such comparisons are an integral part of post-apocalyptic storytelling.

The Canadian author Margaret Atwood's 2003 novel *Oryx and Crake* evaluates the real world by relaying its narrative in two distinct modes: the dystopian and the post-apocalyptic.[13] Its critique of factory farming and genetically modified organisms occurs in the dystopian past and ultimately leads to the post-apocalyptic present. This holds true for the novel's focal character, Snowman (also known as Jimmy), who has somehow managed to survive a pandemic disease and now wanders the wastes, being careful to avoid gene-hacked pigoons and other strange beasts. *Oryx and Crake* reflects on the consequences of organizing the food supply through a mass culture of meat production, logistics, and consumption. Each of the novel's modes has separate critical aims. Whereas its dystopian past shows corporate dominance, mass consumption, and generalized misogyny, the unfolding of events after its apocalyptic moment suggests that even if such market-driven industries were to collapse, their legacies would be long lasting. In this way, Atwood's novel explores both the limitations of the dystopian criticism of a steady state and the false promise of the rupture of such a present. *Oryx and Crake* demonstrates that the post-apocalyptic can readily be used as a way of accomplishing particular narrative ends that exceed the limitations of genre.[14]

Both DeNiro's and Atwood's novels deploy a satirical, tongue-in-cheek tone that further develops the criticality of their narrators' tales. On the one hand, *Total Oblivion* presents wildly improbable geological and political changes only to have Macy shrug them off, adapt to the new reality, and carry on. On the other hand, *Oryx and Crake* depicts Jimmy facing reconfigurations that originate from two sources: corporate bioscience and apocalyptic chaos. DeNiro does not explain the origins of the new reality, while Atwood shows how a dystopian storyworld produces catastrophe, which slides into postcatastrophe. Neither storyworld is desirable, yet both seek to test how characters respond to changing situations, whether totally incomprehensible or utterly discernible. In these examples, the post-apocalyptic mode produces a relationship between turbulent social change and legibility, on the part of characters and readers. At its best, it might even give us an opportunity to discern real historical change, while, at its worst, it argues for further fragmenting and dividing of the social fabric.

The post-apocalyptic mode is an actor shaping and a symptom shaped by the American century. According to the cultural critic Fredric Jameson's influential account, the symbolic act "begins by generating and producing its own context in the same moment of emergence in which it steps back from it, taking its measure with a view toward its own projects of transformation" (*The Political Unconscious*, 81). In this sense, history precedes the text, and our apprehension of history is shaped by the text. Jameson recasts this first dialectical formulation, offering another approach to understanding how the role of interpretation is bound to the text: "The whole paradox of what we have here called the subtext may be summed up in this, that the literary work or cultural object, as though for the first time, brings into being that very situation to which it is also, at one and the same time, a reaction" (ibid., 81–82). The seeming impossibility of this proposal—that a text reacts to a situation of its own creation—makes sense when considered in terms of the interpretive act. Someone must be reading this text, and that someone brings a whole set of assumptions, experiences, and habits to the text. Their interpretive position is such that an experience of a text's generative capacity and reactive character could be described simultaneously. This form of apprehension, which could be described as a temporal embeddedness in the plot, is a crucial part of the story of interpretation in general and the interpretation of the post-apocalyptic mode in particular. To put my methodology in philosophical terms, this book reads the diachronic unfolding of the post-apocalyptic plot from the synchronic vantage point of an aggregated mode. What it detects there are the cultural tremors that signal and make way for hegemonic change.

This centering of interpretation on hegemonic uncertainty produces a focus on the historical present and a search for the moment when things changed. One foremost thinker of the contemporary, Lauren Berlant, describes crisis as a genre that calls for interpretation. For instance, Berlant strives to locate personal and collective attachments historically and to negotiate the record of crisis they produce: "The genre of crisis is itself a heightening interpretive genre, rhetorically turning an ongoing condition into an intensified situation in which extensive threats to survival are said to dominate the reproduction of life" (*Cruel Optimism*, 7). Crisis quickens the interpretive act. To put it differently, what was once a feature of life becomes an all-determining state of things wherein one feels one must take a defensive stance and treat any setback as life threatening. Berlant's words could easily describe the interpretive situation produced by the post-apocalyptic mode. The difference is Berlant's focus on the ongoingness of crisis, which she describes as "the state's withdrawal from the uneven expansion of economic opportunity, social norms, and legal rights that motored so much postwar optimism for democratic access to the good life" (ibid., 3). Berlant accounts for what I will describe as the decline of US hegemony and the end of the American century. She focuses on the effects of duress on the social programs of the state. Her further observation of how individuals and groups respond to crisis in the real world holds true, in many ways, for characters as well: "People's styles of response to crisis are powerfully related to the expectations of the world they had to reconfigure in the face of tattering formal and informal norms of social and institutional reciprocity." She continues, "People born into unwelcoming worlds and unreliable environments have a different response to the new precarities than do people who presume they would be protected" (ibid., 20).[15] Who experiences crisis as ongoing, and who regards it as a momentary lapse?

Crisis shapes and transforms expectations about rights and freedoms. In its ongoingness it alters normative understandings about daily life and the eligibility for a life lived free from hardship. Indeed, the ongoingness of crisis instantiates protracted states of emergency. People caught within such elongated states may experience them differently, but the interests of the individual—as a protagonist in the triumphalist narrative of neoliberalism—galvanizes the ongoingness of crises in a manner that benefits few to the detriment of many. I think that crisis might thus be productively reconsidered along the lines I am proposing for post-apocalyptic writing—as a mode, rather than a genre. Crisis already operates as a way of getting something done, and the post-apocalyptic mode stages the real-world work of crisis in narrative terms as the unfolding relationship of a plot to a story.[16] Thus, the representation of storyworld crises also works to establish a benchmark for the kind of life one might expect in the wake of real-world catastrophic events.

Remainders of the American Century elaborates the relationship of the post-apocalyptic mode to its literary form and ideological underpinnings. The themes of this book—family, nation, hegemony, publishing, nuclear warfare, and energy—do not form a mode of their own accord. Instead, post-apocalyptic novels contain and shape these components of my analysis. My conceptualizing of the post-apocalyptic as a mode, distinct yet related to post-apocalyptic genre and setting, integrates discourses germane to American studies today: from the development of the atomic bomb and the ecological threats of a carbon-based economy to white supremacy; from the state of the publishing industry to the decline of US hegemony; and from the space of the frontier and ways that human beings traverse it to forms of community and family. The book reads the literary history of post-apocalyptic US storytelling as a mode that represents the political economy, ecology, and social forms of the postwar period. It seeks to convey a sense of historicity to the writing that is both constituted by and constitutive of the structures that shape the fate of the American century.

THE END OF THE AMERICAN CENTURY?

Backlit, the motif of surviving the apocalypse develops against the brilliance of the meteoric rise and fading certainty of future US fortunes. Whether understood as demarcating a historical frame (the post-1945 world system) or as a field of study itself (post-1945 US literature and culture), the phrase "the decline of the American century" implies a beginning and an end.[17] The international relations scholar Mary Manjikian draws a parallel between the sorts of speculative fiction created in fin de siècle Britain and those created in the present-day United States. She suggests that "strong nations seem to have a monopoly on the creation of this type of [post-apocalyptic] literature" (*Apocalypse and Post-Politics*, 7). Indeed, the American century begins as the United States takes the center stage from Great Britain in the early twentieth century. The American magazine magnate Henry Luce's popular critique of US isolationism, "The American Century," provides 1941 as the date for the recognition of America's hegemonic status and the height of the American century.[18] The end date of the decline from that status is far from certain.

Taking a global perspective in *The Long Twentieth Century* and subsequent works, the sociologist Giovanni Arrighi describes the century as a repetition of the cyclical development of the capitalist mode of production.[19] Arrighi identifies a shift starting in the 1970s from the peak of US hegemony to what he calls its autumnal phase, drawing on the work of the historian Fernand Braudel. Arrighi describes this movement as a two-step development, involving the increasing mobility of capital and a protracted transition to a new center of accumulation. In previous cycles, this phase signaled the rise of a new hegemony. But financial expansion's "sign of autumn" (Braudel, *Civilization and Capitalism*, 3:246, quoted in Arrighi and Silver, introduction, 31) for the United States has heralded little but uncertainty in the world system. As the cultural critic Marija Cetinic puts it,

> the growth of speculative capital or financialization is not a sign of the increasing strength of the economic order, but is rather

symptomatic of a development percussive to the onset of terminal decline.... Autumn, then, means something different now; it functions a-seasonally. It does not foreshadow the brutal discontent of winter nor anticipate the emergence of the cruel optimism of spring. ("House and Field," 35–36)

The uncertainty of the form and direction of the future implied by Arrighi's model clearly raises questions about the end of the long twentieth century. What remains clear in Arrighi's analysis, and has been mirrored in innumerable accounts since, is that the story of the long twentieth century is the story of the rise and fall of the United States as the central player in the world system.

If the end of the American century remains uncertain, its start is, at least for my present purpose, less ambiguous. According to the US history scholar Bruce Cumings, "by the turn of the last century the United States was the most productive industrial economy in the world, and everyone knew this by the early 1920s as American firms pioneered mass production and consumption and its banks became the effective centre of global commerce" ("Still the American Century," 281). The United States led the industrialized world with an alliance between mass production, mass consumption, and US banks as the driving force of global commerce. During the years from 1914 until its entrance into World War II, the United States perfected its engine for hegemony. Cumings locates the rise of the United States in the 1920s as coinciding with the birth of American-style consumerism, which featured a synthesis of new technologies, cheap credit, and cheap energy with the automobile industry.[20] Debts began to accumulate from this consumption-heavy lifestyle.[21] Though its production and revenue generation soared, the United States had a small military.

World War II galvanized US military research and spending.[22] The number of people in the military grew from less than half a million in 1940 to twelve million in 1945.[23] Alongside the rise in US military spending, the US cultural historian H. Bruce Franklin notes that US superweapons would become "leading characters in a horror story of a nation terrorized into committing itself to perpetual warfare" (*War Stars*, xi). Franklin tracks what happened to the US cultural imaginary once it apprehended the idea of weapons capable of mass destruction: "the main purpose of the government became to achieve 'defense' not against the forces that actually threaten and wound our lives—such as poverty, disease, ignorance, climate change, polluted air and water, and addictions to alcohol, nicotine, and other drugs—but against a shifting roster of 'enemy' nations and forces" (ibid., 4).[24] Franklin's central claim, which I reiterate here, is that US weapons and US culture cannot be understood in isolation from each other. With increased military spending and the development of weapons of mass destruction, the United States continued its ascension as global hegemon.

After World War II, US military bases were maintained in Germany and elsewhere.[25] As the Cold War dawned, the United States began engaging on the world stage in countries such as Korea, Iran, and Guatemala.[26] Aided by the move to a world financial order as laid out in the Bretton Woods Agreement, the tendrils of US influence stretched across the globe. US foreign policy and economic investment became a determining force on the world stage. During this period, production and consumption on US soil came to form a vast spatial dialectic with military advances and foreign development projects abroad, feeding the growth of US capital and hegemony. The American century reached its zenith after World War II, with US economic activity and political prowess at an all-time high. According to Arrighi, the high-water mark of the American century was not due to the success of the state's formula that mixed political power with national identity but was instead a result of the contingent historical development of capitalism in the twentieth century. In other words, the United States rode the wave of history as it surged.

In the 1970s, the wave broke. The United States faced a mounting energy crisis and was piling up debts and deaths in Vietnam, and the productive boom that had followed World War II ground to a halt. Moving off the gold standard, the United States effectively ended the Bretton Woods Agreement. What the historian and social theorist Robert Brenner has called the "long downturn" had begun.[27] Brenner argues that

> Between 1973 and the present, economic performance in the US, western Europe, and Japan has, by every standard macroeconomic indicator, deteriorated, business cycle by business cycle, decade

by decade (with the exception of the second half of the 1990s). (*The Economics of Global Turbulence*, quoted in Clover, *Riot. Strike. Riot*, 23)[28]

In the 1980s and 1990s, the United States, along with many other nations, faced the continuing decline of industrial employment, while largely agricultural and resource-bound countries were hit even harder by the downturn (Benanav and Clegg, "Misery and Debt," 598). From the 1970s on, the United States maintained its hegemony through covert military operations and securities schemes masquerading as financial prowess.[29] Literary critic Maxine Lavon Montgomery critiques the 1991 Gulf War, when President George Bush described the so-called new world order as a governmental response to crisis. In Montgomery's terms, this new world order was "a multinational one ... built upon militaristic aggression, political strength, and world domination cloaked in the guise of democracy," and these catchwords validate "the notion of manifest destiny present in the national psyche" (*The Apocalypse in African-American Fiction*, 1). The way Bush described his response to crisis varies wildly from Montgomery's characterization of the responses made by African American leaders who instead emphasized "America's hypocrisy in intervening in a foreign country's dilemma while neglecting the most pressing social, economic, and political problems confronting black citizens at home" (ibid.). In spite of such activity and neglect, the stagnation of wages and rising unemployment, in the United States and abroad, were momentarily relieved during the 1990s.

Between the end of the Cold War and the invasion of Iraq in the George W. Bush administration, there was a decade a potential and uncertainty. The US cultural critic Phillip Wegner describes the long 1990s as "the place 'between two deaths'" (Slavoj Žižek, *Sublime Object of Ideology*, 135, quoted in Wegner, *Life between Two Deaths*, 28). The first death, the fall of the Berlin Wall in 1989, finds new meaning in the second death:

> September 11 enabled the United States, in ways impossible in the immediate, uncertain aftermath of the Cold War, to assume a global mantle, giving rise to the so-called Bush doctrine of unilateralism and preemptive military violence ... thereby

marking the final closure of the world historical situation of the Cold War and the opening of the new period in global history. (Wegner, *Life between Two Deaths*, 25)

The ramifications of the fall of the Berlin Wall became intelligible only after the fall of the World Trade Center in 2001, which gave the United States license to unleash its military forces openly once more—something it had not undertaken since the Korean War. Much relied upon by the United States, there is a definitional slippage here between war (a formally declared military engagement) and conflict (the low-intensity conflict that occurred in the Bay of Pigs, Vietnam, Nicaragua, and Iran). By using the term "conflict" rather than "war," the United States could push its geopolitical agenda and claim that it was not engaged in any active wars. It engaged in a game of smoke and mirrors that was not difficult to see through but incredibly tough to stop. Even in the invasion of Iraq in 2003, though the smoke had become thin and the mirrors tarnished, the United States wielded military clout in a failed bid for economic dominance. This form of hyperextension simultaneously marks the incredible power and wealth amassed by the economic center and signals that flows of capital are no longer predominantly US bound.

From the late 1990s onward, apprehensions of the future of the United States have ranged from denial and melancholy to revanchist belligerence. An impetus for survival and progress is apparent, for example, in the policy of organizations such as the Project for the New American Century (PNAC). The PNAC's "Statement of Principles" critiques the incoherence of the administration of President Bill Clinton, while resisting the lure of conservative isolationism. It trumpets the accomplishments of the administration of President Ronald Reagan, arguing for a renewed focus on a strong military and purposeful foreign intervention and declaring that "we cannot safely avoid the responsibilities of global leadership or the costs that are associated with its exercise" (Elliott Abrams et al., "Statement of Principles"). In a nigh-apocalyptic outlook, it posits that "the history of the 20th century should have taught us that it is important to shape circumstances before crises emerge, and to meet threats before they become dire." The PNAC position essentially argues for more defense spending as a path to ongoing US hegemony. Yet rather than a well-proven path to prosperity, such spending is better understood as an anomalous opportunity of the American century. The PNAC envisions the unimpeded march of progress. In a separate document, it suggests that "the United States faces no global rival," arguing that "America's grand strategy should aim to preserve and extend this advantageous position as far into the future as possible" (Thomas Donnelly et al., i). Conceptually the PNAC connects US power to good global standing, presenting the prospect of a ruinous future as the result of declining military capacity. In this manner, it presents the threat of an apocalypse at home if the contingencies of global relations are not managed with military expenditure and economic development.[30] In presenting such arguments it lays bare a core truth of the American century: apocalyptic policies in the United States have long produced post-apocalyptic situations elsewhere.

Over the course of the first decade of the twenty-first century, US actions at home and on the world stage reflected the destructive struggle of the country to retain its dominance by whatever means necessary. To understand the position of the United States in a global capitalist economy, one could look to the debt-driven crisis of the United States in the early twenty-first century and particularly to the US failure to transform a hegemonic order in crisis. For Arrighi, the failure of the US military action in Iraq signals the terminal crisis not of a narrowly geopolitical hegemony but also of a specifically American regime of accumulation founded on an economic symbiosis of war and debt.[31] In effect, the turbulent political economy of the late twentieth and early twenty-first centuries can be described as a struggle between the goal of limitless accumulation of wealth and the interests of a hegemonic power wishing to remain in charge. "The true novelty," writes Arrighi, "is the attempt of the declining hegemonic power to resist that decline by turning itself into a world state" (*Adam Smith in Beijing*, 253). Characterized not only by its aggressive foreign policy and military actions but also by the increased role of finance in the US economy, the United States has reached the limits of its capacity to be the center of capital accumulation—as Britain, Holland, and Genoa did before it. If expanded financialization is a sign of the autumnal phase of a given regime of accumulation and the marker of capital shifting its global center of operations, then the 2007–8 financial crisis signaled that the cycle of accumulation now, in Cetinic's provocative phrase, "functions a-seasonally" ("House and Field," 36).[32]

When it comes to the question of what comes next for the hegemon, most people would agree with Cetinic that profound uncertainty best characterizes the future. The world imagined by advocates of the new American century is one in which the remainders of that century can be put to work to rebuild the level of prosperity and wealth enjoyed by the affluent and certain portions of the working class on the rise after World War II. Such remainders can also be seen in the legacies of the war economy, ongoing military spending at the expense of social programs, the difficulties facing the development of alternative energy sources, and so on.[33] Yet this moment is one that cannot return.[34] The dividends of the industrial boom can be paid only once, and developments such as highway infrastructure and nuclear energy programs are proving to have decisive ecological and environmental impacts. Moreover, the mid-century economic relationship between industry and labor in the United States was riddled with inequalities and problems. A bargain for working men had repercussions for women, and though desegregation was on the horizon, the racial dynamics of mid-century production are similarly unsuitable for any properly antiracist politics today. This breakneck recap of US power seeks to establish the centrality of such mass-scale military developments to the cultural imagination, especially through what I term the remainders of the American century.

THE TRACE, AFTERMATH, AND REMAINDERS

Texts written in the post-apocalyptic mode stage their plots against the backdrop of growing US militarization, expanding financialization, and declining hegemony. Post-apocalyptic writing casts nearly everything into the diegetic flames of a world-destroying event. The imaginary post-apocalyptic interregnum is the realm of historical and generic holdovers, but it is just as clearly an opening to a discourse of the political. The apocalyptic event of the story creates a new fictional plotline that branches off from reality toward an imagined future. This future is littered with the remainders of the pre-apocalyptic world. For instance, these might include the real-world infrastructure established when the United States was the global hegemon. Highways, shopping malls, and apartment towers fall into disuse in the post-apocalyptic storyworld. Remainders, as a concept, gathers the ill fitting and the residual into a complex reordering of social structures—of value, matter, and historicity. Though remainders are recognizable from their previous context, they now work in new ways. The way characters interact with such remainders signals their merit as survivors through qualities such as savviness or moral fiber.

Alongside such a social-economic understanding of remainders, I enrich their conceptual dynamic by turning to poststructuralist thought. In an account of radical atheism, the philosopher Martin Hägglund presents a useful formulation for unpacking the imaginary traumas of post-apocalyptic scenarios: "To survive is never to be absolutely present; it is to remain after a past that is no longer and to keep the memory of this past for a future that is not yet" (*Radical Atheism*, 1). With these words, Hägglund invokes the Derridean logic of the trace.[35] As with remainders, the trace carries forward something of the past despite the passage of time. On Haggluund's account, the trace is integral to the persistence of being. He argues that the trace "can only live on, however, by being left for a future that may erase it" (ibid.). This openness to the possibility of usefulness and uselessness characterizes both the trace and remainders. This trace and these remainders may or may not be entirely discernible.

Jacques Derrida develops a comparison between the remainder and the trace in an interview with Antoine Spire. Of the remainder, Derrida says, "Often, like the trace, I associate it with ashes" (Derrida and Spire, "'Others Are Secret Because They Are Other,'" 151). Ashes left after a fire make a fitting image for remainders in the sense that I use in this book, even if ashes are (mostly) useless. Derrida describes such ashes as "remains without a substantial remainder, essentially, but which have to be taken account of and without which there would be neither accounting nor calculation" (ibid., 151–52). For Derrida there is here an important marking of a thing that was, but can no longer be, recognized. The remainder, like the trace, indicates a passage, yet neither the trace nor the remainder is forthcoming about what is no longer. The remainder conceptualized in this way sheds light on Derrida's description of nuclear catastrophe as "dealing hypothetically with a total and *remainderless* destruction of the archive" ("No Apocalypse, Not Now," 20). Atomic war was imagined to leave no ashes, trace, or remainder. Though implausible, the total destruction of the archive by nuclear war offers a vision of the antithesis of post-apocalyptic storytelling.[36] For a story to be a post-apocalyptic one, there must be remainders. Here the difference between remainders, in my sense, and the trace, in Derrida's, is the clearest: remainders are the story elements not completely destroyed by the world-destroying event. They offer legible information about the storyworld—indeed, about the real world as well—compared to that offered by the trace.

The story of the post-apocalyptic mode is a story of remainders, elements of form, style, and thematic preoccupations that persist beyond their historical context and are reworked and revalued. As may be true of any mode of writing over time, the internal transformation of the US post-apocalyptic mode of writing is in many ways the story of how old tendencies operate in new frameworks. For my argument, the term "remainder" operates in distinct registers, and when it comes to the post-apocalyptic mode, it has at least three descriptive senses. It identifies diegetic things (objects, people, and places), literary concepts (forms, plots, and styles), and real-world materials (remaindered books) as components and markers of a single process of abandonment, failure, and ruin. Across each of the term's uses, it operates in accordance with a larger shift in context—whether narrative, market, or historical. In this sense, it may be instructive to think of remainders as objects available for some form of salvage or repurposing. How the remainder is treated provides a good indication of what sort of transformation has taken place. Knowing who takes up a particular remainder and how they do so could reveal something of the potentially missing context. From the origin of the world-destroying event to the shifting predilections of the publishing market, what gets remaindered and how that remainder comes to be used offer critical information.[37]

Some of the worlds imagined in post-apocalyptic stories could accurately be described as bastions of rugged masculinity and whiteness as neutral categories. Many of the novels described in this book depict futures in which white men form new communities—in some instances, at the exclusion or expense of racialized characters. Any study of the archive of US post-apocalyptic writing encounters a critical tendency to identify this mode of storytelling with whiteness on the level of characters and in terms of who writes these books. Though the archive could be characterized as written predominantly by white men about white men, this is not entirely the case. Beginning with Leigh Brackett and Judith Merril in the late 1940s and early 1950s, women have written stories in the post-apocalyptic mode. In the 1970s writers such as Samuel R. Delany, Marge Piercy, and Suzy McKee Charnas introduced sexually and racially dynamic characters in their apocalyptic and post-apocalyptic storytelling. In the demographics of the mode and its characters, a racially diverse substrate emerged that has become a consistent and prominent feature of the mode in the twenty-first century.[38]

There are at least two ways of accounting for the twentieth-century post-apocalyptic mode's racial and gender dynamics. The first is structural. White men dominated the field of genre publishing in the mid-twentieth-century United States. There were financial, social, and cultural barriers to others' entry into the field.[39] Moreover, the editorial practices of magazines and series editors also meant that certain types of story dominated.[40] The second looks at the cultural role played by post-apocalyptic storytelling. These stories focus on the contingencies that characters face in terms of their relative affluence. In sociological terms, the post-apocalypse world could be seen as the realm of mostly white, middle-class people. The struggles facing people of color—including blacks, Asian Americans, Latinx, and Indigenous peoples—already resemble the post-apocalyptic challenges described by these novels. Peter Fitting describes the post-apocalyptic mode "as the scandalous images of a disaster that has already happened and in whose ruins we can already walk, although only if we are prepared to visit the collapsing inner cities of the great metropolises of the United States" ("You're History, Buddy," 123). The post-apocalyptic mode offers, in Fitting's haunting words, "temporally dislocated images of a present of which we are only dimly aware."[41]

Whether we look at the recent history of US dominance or its colonial past, humanity lives with the still-reverberating consequences of many apocalyptic ruptures. As James Berger puts it, "For American Indians, the worst catastrophe imaginable has already happened" (*After the End*, 31). Moreover, Indigenous scholars have long been arguing that Indigenous people have already experienced an ongoing apocalyptic event.[42] Meanwhile, Rieder writes:

> Environmental devastation, species extinction, enslavement, plague, and genocide[,] . . . these are not merely nightmares morbidly fixed upon by science fiction writers and readers, but are rather the bare historical record of what happened to non-European people and lands after being "discovered" by Europeans and integrated into European political and economic arrangements from the fifteenth century to the present.
> (*Colonialism and the Emergence of Science Fiction*, 124)

Berger and Rieder vividly illustrate the ways in which apocalyptic writing, especially by white authors, tends to recast colonial histories in the image of future fears.

This book attempts to walk a line between, on the one hand, accurately portraying an archive of US post-apocalyptic novels to establish its dominant though contested characteristics and, on the other hand, making room for those authors and stories that historically have been not represented, underrepresented, or represented poorly. To characterize the post-apocalyptic mode as exclusively the domain of white men does an unforgiveable disservice to those who have long been using world destroying as a narrative device.[43] Butler is foremost among the authors who deploy the post-apocalyptic genre against its dominant tradition, and thus I will draw heavily on her writing to continue my elaboration of remainders.

Remainders need not always be massive: they can be small, too. Starting from within the post-apocalyptic storyworld, things are a first kind of remainder. The canned goods that offer satiation, the cash money that has become useless, the gasoline that goes bad in the gas tank—these things belong in this first grouping. So too do the survivors forming loose communities and the loners wandering the wastes on their own. To the survivors (fictional or otherwise), remainders might not seem to be left behind at all. They might seem new, or at least novel, especially when these characters forget what life was like before people, objects, and landscapes were torn from their sphere of intelligibility. In post-apocalyptic novels, at times remainders act as a resource: some characters repurpose coins as arrowheads, others use the highways as track beds; and a shopping cart can carry a tramp's bindle (an innovation long used by the homeless). Characters might be imagined to act more or less as they had before the apocalyptic event and its immediate aftermath. As remainders, habits of thought and action often persist despite the absence of the world that once afforded these habits meaning. Rounding out remainders in this first sense are places left unscathed by destruction, cities crumbling from the lack of repairs, and swaths of land obliterated by aerial assaults.

The remainders at this level make up the diegetic portion of the concept, and they serve as signposts for other kinds of remainders as well. In one sense, they act as component parts. The discarded noncontent of the apocalypse, they are part of what makes the post-apocalyptic mode recognizable. Remainders represent the imaginary relationship of characters to their pre-apocalyptic conditions of existence, conditions that no longer obtain in the post-apocalyptic storyworld. Early in Butler's *Parable of the Sower* (first published in 1993), Lauren Oya Olamina asks her stepmother about city lights. Her stepmother responds, "Kids today have no idea what a blaze of light cities used to be—and not that long ago" (6). When Olamina says that she would "rather have the stars," her stepmother responds, "The stars are free.... I'd rather have the city lights back myself, the sooner the better. But we can afford the stars." This brief exchange encapsulates the question of remainders in Butler's novel. Some characters cope by wishing for a return, as the stepmother does: though she would like the city lights back, she also rejects at least a part of the past world. The idea that they could "afford the stars" suggests they could not afford electric lights, although whether this collective pronoun refers to the family or the community is left ambiguous. Other characters acclimatize themselves to, and even affirm, the changes that have taken place, as Olamina does. The infrastructure for delivering electric energy remains, though it goes unpowered. Houses still stand and provide shelter. The book opens with a scene in which characters ride their bikes away from their community to engage in target practice.[44] New modes of social life and protocols for its stewardship emerge from the old ways of doing things. Things are different from what they were, but not that different—at least for some.

The second kind of remainder is found in the treatment of the tropes of post-apocalyptic storytelling. An exemplary case of a bricoleur literary discourse, post-apocalyptic novels collect the remainders of other kinds of storytelling. They do so in a manner that inverts the practice of science fiction. If science fiction tends to borrow its plots from other genres, the post-apocalyptic mode borrows its settings from other fictions or from the author's real, historical world. Butler's Xenogenesis trilogy, collected under the title *Lilith's Brood*, offers an extreme example of generic remainders as it blends science fiction with the post-apocalyptic mode. The trilogy is set in a postnuclear future in which aliens capture or rescue humanity, depending on one's reading. Known as the Oankali, the benevolent yet manipulative aliens interact with humans through the use of hormones and neural stimulation. Some characters cannot abide the aliens' meddling, while others embrace their way of life. Structurally, what this relationship illustrates, regardless of how characters or readers might feel about it, is the manner in which the Oankali make the humans' capacity to feel pleasure central to their mutual integration with the earth, its more-than-human inhabitants, and its ecosystems.

The first novel in the series, *Dawn* (first published in 1987), invites a reading in terms of an allegory of colonization, in which the power of the Oankali in their new world is enforced by the same mixture of unfamiliar technology and civilizing projects that characterized European imperialism.[45] However, casting *Dawn*'s central character, Lilith, as a black woman immediately troubles such familiar allegorical mapping, which is then turned on its head with the revelation that the Oankali exist by genetically mixing with other species—a mixing that raises the ire of segregationist humans. The remainder comes to the fore as a critical category when the trilogy is read in terms of its generic tendencies, with the distrustful humans acting in accordance with a post-apocalyptic script and the Oankali acting out a science-fictional alien encounter narrative. Each novel features a new generation of children resulting from the mixture of humans and Oankali who are ever more capable of relating, understanding, and imagining what both sides want and need. The novels ultimately describe a storyworld without a precise analog.

The Xenogenesis trilogy shows the complex way in which the alien encounter trope of science fiction might be transformed when presented in a post-apocalyptic context. Similarly, post-apocalyptic tropes of insular attitudes and mistrust of outsiders are revealed as stubborn, conservative, and reactionary in such a science-fictional context. This is ultimately proven to be the case in the trilogy when the Oankali unveil their ultimate plan. Human cancer rates have skyrocketed since the nuclear war, and the Oankali counterintuitively see cancer as a remarkable capacity of human cells and want to integrate human physiology into their own. With the correct deployment of human cancer cells in the offspring of the Oankali, who are much more attuned to their bodies, they could gain regenerative powers to regrow any damaged or destroyed cells of the body.[46] Here the science-fictional trope provides a counterweight to the post-apocalyptic one, allowing Butler to tell an alien encounter story in the post-apocalyptic mode that advances the latter's inherent narrative possibilities. In this sense, remainders in the post-apocalyptic storyworld often overlap with generic remainders that litter the canon of post-apocalyptic fiction. Such stories give symbolic shape to the concern with what is left behind, what has been forever changed, and what may return in time. Cancer cells are the remainder of humanity put to new use by the gene-hacking Oankali.

Given its place within the field of popular fiction, I expand the conceit of the remainder beyond narrative discourse to encompass even the publication and print history of post-apocalyptic novels. In this latter case, the remainder assumes its most literal sense in the archive of printed and remaindered books. In the third sense, the term "remainder" is transformed from a noun to a verb. To remainder a book means to decide that it will not sell. It means that after careful accounting, a book has proven incapable of achieving future sales. To remainder a book is to lift it from a shelf where it might be recognized as having future possibilities and set it on one where its possibilities have been radically constrained or place it in a pile where such possibilities have been revoked altogether. The act of remaindering books describes the state of the publishing industry today: whether a book ends up in a bargain bin or a recycling center, the practice of remaindering titles is yet another step in the long-standing and thoroughgoing commoditization of the novel.

The relation of remainders to the act of remaindering reveals a logic of accounting, cost cutting, and the quantifying of human activity. One lesson of remaindering in post-apocalyptic writing, the publishing industry, US politics, and US decline is that people can rely on no one but themselves. This experience is that of the long crisis in each domain, the shifting of responsibility from the state, the press, the world, or one another to the individual—a move that reproduces the logic of the market in each instance. Letting the market decide in publishing, politics, the management of personnel and resources, and so on places incredible limits on people's ability to accomplish anything but mere survival. Remainders—what we imagine might persist and even flourish after the apocalyptic, storyworld ending—point to complex ways of imagining the economic, environmental, social, and political limits facing the United States today.[47]

THIS BOOK

Read as a mode, US post-apocalyptic novels reveal a layered stratigraphy of cultural and political contests over the transforming meanings of apocalypse and survival. Understanding how and why stories about surviving the end of the world became so popular as to be ubiquitous by the early twenty-first century necessitates different critical approaches and interpretive strategies. This book engages with the fields of American studies, science fiction studies, and print culture studies, taking on a range of methodologies from critiques of nationalism to those of petroculture and a range of frameworks from critical race theory to feminist and queer studies critiques of reproductive futurity. The breadth of the analysis here, and my endeavor to include as many post-apocalyptic texts as possible in each chapter, follows multiple paths to understand the political unconscious of post-apocalyptic writing.

The first part of the book seeks to define the post-apocalyptic mode. As it takes up literary remainders—tropes, narrative, and physical books—this part can be understood as an account of the emergence of the post-apocalyptic mode in the long 1950s and its path to prominence in the 1970s and 1980s.[48] The second part addresses more particular remainders of the American century through case studies. It opens where the first part ends, in the 1980s. Part 2 elaborates scenes of US decline through national communities, racial politics, gendered futurity, and energy imaginaries.

Chapter 1 describes the emergence of post-apocalypse tropes in the postcatastrophe novels of the long 1950s. Reading representative works by Pat Frank, Leigh Brackett, Richard Matheson, Walter Miller Jr., and George R. Stewart, alongside other titles, "Post-Apocalypse Tropes" presents the post-apocalyptic mode as part of a tradition of writing riddled with remainders in the form of narrative tropes. Chapter 2 compares the process of world building as it has been theorized in relation to fantastic literature and science fiction to that of world destroying, which I argue is the way post-apocalyptic novels create their fictional worlds.[49] It assesses the narrative consequences of post-apocalyptic storytelling by reading Sherri S. Tepper's *The Gate to Women's Country* (first published in 1988) with Stephen King's *The Stand* (first published in 1978; the unabridged version was published in 1990). Though the books have opposing politics, each presents a storyworld in which future possibilities have become limited by both apocalyptic events and characters' actions—in narratives bound by the necessities of what remains, only certain possibilities remain available. Chapter 3 develops the third sense of remainder, discussing the post-apocalyptic publishing industry. In the chapter, I argue that as much as the post-apocalyptic mode coheres around a tradition of writing and an ideological reduction of future possibilities, the book market has also shaped it through developments in book retail, publishing, and the field of science fiction writing.[50]

While part 1 defined the post-apocalyptic mode, part 2 elaborates particular scenes of its development. If the threat of nuclear war and concerns over social protests dominate the post-apocalyptic writing of the mid-century, the 1980s provides a new set of anxieties for post-apocalyptic fiction to extrapolate. Part 2 includes four case studies that focus on particular remainders of the American century. First, in "Old and New Americas," the nation provides a focal point for my reading of David Brin's *The Postman* (1985) and Kim Stanley Robinson's *The Wild Shore* (first published in 1984). The return to the fictional spaces of the frontier in these novels provides a complex and indirect representation of US activity at home and abroad during the 1980s. Second, in "Segregated Futures," I argue that Robert A. Heinlein's *Farnham's Freehold* (first published in 1964) and LeVar Burton's *Aftermath* (1997) use opposed techniques to critique the whiteness of the post-apocalyptic mode. Heinlein attempts a critical inversion of race relations by sending a suburban white family traveling through time into slavery, but he cannot shake himself of his own residual assumptions about race. Burton's extrapolation of a United States after a race war contests the whiteness of the mode.[51]

Third, "The Reproductive Imperative" presents the role of family in Cormac McCarthy's *The Road* (2006) as a remainder. The book banishes from its pages the person whom both central characters rely on: the woman. Engaging the vision of a solely masculine future, chapter 6 strives to disentangle the ways McCarthy's novel is caught between projecting a blasted storyworld and one in which the potential for redemption exists. Finally, chapter 7 engages with a number of texts—Butler's *Parable of the Sower*, Emily St. John Mandel's *Station Eleven* (2014), Pat Frank's *Alas, Babylon* (first published in 1959), Peter Heller's *The Dog Stars* (2012), James Howard Kunstler's *World Made by Hand* (2008) and John Varley's *Slow Apocalypse* (2012)—for the ways they imagine the future of energy. Differentiating between oil apocalypse novels and energy apocalypse novels, I argue that the remainders in the case of the latter confront humanity as an unrecognizable force of our own forgotten creation in the form of the massive build of carbon dioxide in the atmosphere and material structures across the planet. Post-apocalyptic stories imagine these remainders of the fossil regime as either worthy of destruction or completely alienated components of our daily lives.

I close the book by pivoting to Colson Whitehead's and N. K. Jemisin's recent apocalyptic storytelling. Whitehead's *Zone One* (2011) closes discussions about apocalyptic survival opened by W.E.B. Du Bois in his 1920 short story "The Comet." *Zone One* gestures to apocalypse tropes of the enclave and the last man, even as it engages in a metacommentary on post-apocalyptic publishing. Jemisin's much-lauded Broken Earth trilogy provides rich ground upon which to further consider remainders, though its fantastic setting distances it as a symbol of the post-apocalyptic United States. While the trilogy's storyworld may be a representation of the earth in the distant future, Jemisin produces a thoroughly fantastic and science-fictional secondary storyworld that cannot be mapped so directly and easily to the real world. Both authors diverge from the post-apocalyptic mode as it is described here. However, they do not leave it completely behind, and some remainders persist. In closing the book, I reflect on the archive of post-apocalyptic novels under consideration here and offer these texts as possible bookends to the archive of post-apocalyptic novels in the age of US decline.

You might read this book as a resource to help frame compatible or divergent interpretations of other post-apocalyptic stories. It could also serve as a tool for understanding other genres adjacent to science fiction or modes that flood the book market at present. Alternatively, you might wish to read about specific titles. Whatever has brought you here, welcome. I am pleased to provide the opportunity for us to think together about what I am calling the post-apocalyptic mode and the remainders of the American century.

Part One
The Post-Apocalyptic Mode

1
Post-Apocalypse Tropes

The mid-twentieth century is a crucial turning point for the post-apocalyptic mode, especially for emerging tropes that become the mode's standards.[1] The development of the post-apocalyptic mode fundamentally rests on a problem that is best understood as historiographical. Post-apocalyptic novels of the 1950s are preoccupied with the interruption of technological and industrial progress. Such texts fixate on imagining historical change through breaks in the time line and ruptures in the trajectory of human possibility. Post-apocalypse tropes arise from authors' attempts to make sense of the fundamental conceit of the mode: namely, a story of humans surviving the cataclysmic destruction of their world and all of the systems that had sustained it.

The novels at the core of this chapter—George R. Stewart's *Earth Abides*, first published in 1949; Leigh Brackett's *The Long Tomorrow*, first published in 1955; Walter Miller Jr.'s *A Canticle for Leibowitz*, first published in 1959; and Richard Matheson's *I Am Legend*, first published in 1954—privilege the subject of the post-apocalypse (the protagonist and sometimes the narrator) as the one who can understand the changes that have taken place in the world. They explore communities' varying responses to their respective post-apocalyptic worlds. They express anxieties symptomatic of a number of endings and beginnings: these titles were published after Auschwitz and the atomic bomb, but before free speech movements and antiwar demonstrations and at the birth of civil rights movements. Finally, they hold to the apocalyptic thesis that the truth is clear only in a kind of secular revelation, and it arrives only after the final echoes of civilization have died away. In other words, these books claim that only after the end can humanity truly reckon with its social actions, technological developments, and political accomplishments.

THE EFFECT OF THE BOMB ON POST-APOCALYPSE TROPES

The calcification of post-apocalypse tropes occurs in the 1940s and 1950s, a period during which speculative fiction in general responds to the cataclysmic possible futures unleashed by atomic weapons. The destructive potential of atomic war had an indelible impact on the way post-apocalyptic storytelling took place from the 1940s on. While science fiction writing described the effect of the atom bomb well before it was unleashed in the desert or on Hiroshima and Nagasaki, in the 1950s post-apocalyptic writing brought nuclear holocaust into focus as a concrete apocalyptic event.[2]

The cultural imagination of the bomb supplanted both biblical and naturalistic apocalyptic visions of the future with nightmares of the total annihilation of life on Earth or less-extreme fever dreams of radioactive wastelands and mutated wildlife. Both nightmare images are depicted in Mordecai Roshwald's satirical critique of the Cold War, *Level 7* (first published in 1959). The book takes place miles underground in a military complex that was built to withstand a nuclear strike and keep survivors alive long enough for surface radiation levels to decrease. Long after the bombs have been dropped by both sides in the war, a couple of people go out of the bunker. They broadcast portions of their journey to their colleagues:

> She: No birds are singing in the world today, no flowers are blooming. There are no trees, there are no fields.
> He: Just débris.
> She: Man is gone, and woman too. No children play around.
> He: Just bare earth.
> She: The world is like a ship abandoned by her crew. Like the moon, it is arid and dreary.
> He: Another planet. (ibid., 154)

In their earlier broadcasts, the man and the woman described themselves as doves leaving Noah's ark, but they come to agree that the metaphor does not hold sway in the world they find. In the story of Noah, the return of the doves to the ark signaled failure, since the doves would not return if they had found dry land. The man and the woman cannot return because they become sick as they traverse the irradiated countryside. In the above passage, they find more fitting metaphors from the world of space exploration and science fiction: the face of the earth has been so altered that it appears to be another planet altogether. This move from biblical myth to the secular tales of the space age signals a shift in apocalyptic tropology in the wake of the atomic bomb. The spaces of bomb shelters and radioactive wastelands, the concern over mutation and mutants, and the descriptive phrases "nuclear winter" and "nuclear holocaust" are all tropes that did not exist before the development of the bomb and its attendant technologies and effects.

Post-1945 publications compete to provide the soundest explanations of nuclear winter and how people might be imagined to survive it. Since the unleashing of the atomic bomb, post-apocalyptic novels have appeared with greater frequency and describe ever more advanced (and credible) threats. Pat Frank's *Alas, Babylon* (first published in 1959) and Roger Zelazny's *Damnation Alley* (first published in 1969) stand out as two strikingly different tales of postnuclear survival in the early Cold War period, when the threat of atomic war was most troubling to US citizens. Frank's novel is set in the quiet town of Fort Repose, Florida, which—unlike the rest of the country—is mercifully spared from atomic explosions and fallout. The apocalyptic event happens in the night as the protagonist sleeps: "What had jolted Randy from sleep—he would not learn all the facts for a long, a very long time after—were two nuclear explosions, both in the megaton range, the warheads of missiles lobbed in by submarines" (*Alas, Babylon*, 82). One hits the Homestead Strategic Air Command base; the other targets the Miami International Airport. The narrator describes what the character can only assume has happened. In relative safety, Randy sees only the explosions illuminating the night sky. Rather than focus on the immediate impact of the bomb and its effects on the natural landscape, as Roshwald's *Level 7* had done, *Alas,*

Babylon explores the results that the devastation of so many US cities would have on the people and places left physically and radioactively unscathed.

Zelazny's novel is quite different. Using what might now be labeled a proto–George Miller aesthetic, it follows Hell Tanner, the last Hells Angel, as he attempts a desperate crossing of the nuclear wastes between Los Angeles and Boston in a weaponized tanklike vehicle. On his journey, Tanner is confronted by mutant scorpions, bad weather, and even rival motorcycle gangs. The thrilling ride of this action-packed novel does not leave much room for the kind of social analysis found in either Roshwald's satire or Frank's postnuclear thought experiment. Instead, its pace makes it a story about trajectory and speed rather than one about the destruction and reconstruction of the social order. The chain reaction unleashed by splitting the atom was both atomic and cultural.[3] Addressing the central question of how historical change happens in the wake of the bomb, new postnuclear, post-apocalyptic tropes changed the face of the genre. Whether set in a small community such as Fort Repose or on the road as in *Damnation Alley*, post-apocalyptic novels published in the early part of the Cold War intensified the post-apocalyptic mode's new emphasis on survival. Through the tropes discussed in this chapter, survival becomes a core premise of post-apocalyptic mode.

THE EMERGENCE OF POST-APOCALYPSE TROPES

Stewart, Brackett, Matheson, and Miller wrote post-apocalyptic texts between the end the Golden Age of science fiction (1930s to late 1940s) and the New Wave (1960s).[4] Addressing different concerns than Golden Age science fiction did, post-apocalyptic novels gained readership between these periods. Whereas Golden Age science fiction followed daring explorers on fantastic voyages, post-apocalyptic stories focused on new relationships between characters and their world. It also exhibited a logic that is paradigmatic of a number of texts from the postwar period: Stewart's *Earth Abides*, Brackett's *The Long Tomorrow*, Matheson's *I Am Legend*, and Miller's *A Canticle for Leibowitz* begin to deploy the tropes that post-apocalyptic novels use today. They introduce readers to the idea of surviving apocalyptic events and present plausible scenarios for their characters' struggles. These texts adopt what are now recognized as the central tropes of the post-apocalyptic novel: sole survivors navigate a less complex storyworld; society rebuilds, but with a difference; or small groups struggle to maintain ways of belonging to a world that no longer exists.

Earth Abides imagines a scenario in which the survivor of an epidemic disease travels across the United States documenting the subtle changes in a world nearly without people. Stewart's interest in the environment anticipates Rachel Carson's *Silent Spring* (first published in 1962), which is often credited with raising the public's ecological consciousness. Brackett's *The Long Tomorrow* explores post-apocalyptic communities separated by their different ideas about the pre-apocalyptic world and its technologies. Brackett's novel introduces nuclear technology as a problem. In the novel, a secret community with a nuclear reactor places everyone at risk, even those who assume they have avoided the threat posed by nuclear technology. Even an acute case of technophobia cannot save a community from what its neighbors are doing. Using narrative shifts in time, Miller's *A Canticle for Leibowitz* plays out the rebuilding of society after the near total destruction of humanity and with it all knowledge of technology, engineering, and science. Each of these novels exemplifies a particular apocalypse trope as it emerges in the development of the post-apocalyptic mode. Finally, one of the more widely known titles of this period, Matheson's *I Am Legend*, imagines the response of an individual to the threat of a virus that turns humans into vampire-like creatures. Taking the motif of the sole survivor to an unanticipated conclusion, *I Am Legend* perfects a critical inversion of the post-apocalyptic mode's gathering community trope by singling out an antihero outsider.

Together these tropes informed the development of post-apocalyptic storytelling from the middle of the twentieth century on. On the one hand, post-apocalypse tropes arose from the arrangement of the setting, as scenarios created by the apocalyptic events invited certain authorial responses. On the other hand, authors of post-apocalypse fiction sometimes added a particular flourish that later became a consistent feature of the mode. These processes of invention developed in tandem. Further iterations of post-apocalyptic plots and settings presented opportunities to preserve different features of modern life and to test old reactions in new scenarios.[5] As the genre developed, these early iterations formed a foundation for what was to come. Like so many other textual remainders, post-apocalypse tropes have been taken up or cast aside by post-apocalyptic authors. The four that follow have had a great impact on the evolution of the post-apocalyptic mode.

CATALOGUING THE POST-APOCALYPSE

Earth Abides has surprisingly little to say directly about the nuclear threat; instead, it catalogues apocalyptic changes to the world in the near total absence of humans. Retrospectively, *Earth Abides* stands out due to its narrative difference from the post-apocalyptic novels that follow it. Across the literature of critical engagement with the novel, *Earth Abides* is consistently singled out for its ecological focus as well as its approach to narrating the cleared spaces of a depopulated United States.[6] It follows a doctoral student as he explores the United States after an epidemic disease has killed most of the population. The focal character, Isherwood Williams, survives because of a luckily timed snake bite. After describing Williams's mourning for his family, the narrator delights in a new sense of open space: "man was gone, certainly for a while, perhaps forever. Even if some survivors were left, they would be a long time in again obtaining supremacy. What would happen to the world and its creatures? *That* he was left to see!" (ibid., 24–25). *Earth Abides* treats survival as an exciting social-scientific opportunity to explore the United States in the absence of humans. In one of Williams's many cross-country drives through the abandoned, now pastoral landscape of the United States, he must clear several fallen trees from the road: no one maintains the roads, and humans are apparent only in their more or less conspicuous absence. The old roads that Williams travels in *Earth Abides* are those of the United States at the time of the book's publication, prior to the Federal Aid Highway Act of 1956 and the creation of the interstate system that readers today might imagine that he uses. Alongside the dominant conceit of travel is an equally forceful impulse to catalogue.

The cataloguing narrative discourse of *Earth Abides* distinguishes itself by taking larger descriptive steps forward through story time: In "Part I: World Without End," a full year is narrated in detail, followed by a section aptly dubbed "Quick Years" that covers the following twenty-one years. "Part II: The Year 22" drops back to a closer narration and is followed by another series of "Quick Years," which cover the course of Williams's lifetime through fragments. The book ends with "Part III: The Last American," which slows the pace of the narrative as Williams lives out his final year.[7] He is the last American, not because he is the last one left alive but because he is the last one who remembers modern—that is, pre-apocalyptic—life. While other characters seem ready to forget that life, Williams is haunted by modernity's remainders.

This cataloguing impulse undoubtedly serves as an efficient and unobtrusive tool for world building. It is perhaps most obvious in moments of direct commentary by the narrator, which are formally separated from the thoughts and actions of the protagonist. The narrative apparatus interrupts first-person narration with objective interstitial sections that describe unpopulated scenes of the deteriorated US infrastructure. Stewart places these sections, which are in italics, in the middle of chapters. The sections are reminiscent of John Steinbeck's *The Grapes of Wrath* (first published in 1939), in which mass migration is narrated from a distance in between the chapters that narrate the Joad family's journey.[8] In *The Grapes of Wrath* such sections are sometimes written in the third person and sometimes in the first, and they never use proper names to identify the people described, as in this passage: "The doors of the empty houses swung open, and drifted back and forth in the wind. Bands of little boys came out from the towns to break the windows and pick over the debris, looking for treasures" (116). Here is another example: "One man, one family driven from the land; this rusty car creaking along the highway to the west. I lost my land, a single tractor took my land. I am alone and I am bewildered. And in the night one family camps in a ditch and another family pulls in and the tents come out" (ibid., 151). These passages are from what Steinbeck called interchapters. The interplay between interchapters and Joad chapters does not situate the Joads as an exceptional family capable of surviving the dust bowl's devastation of their farmland and the inhospitable welcome of California fruit farmers but as one family among many consigned to face environmental catastrophe and subsequent migration. As the literary critics Lewis Owens and Hector Torres explain, "The result of Steinbeck's narrative experiment is a pattern of expansion (interchapters) and contraction (Joad chapters) that runs throughout the novel from beginning to end, creating a powerful dialectic between regional disaster and intimate pathos as [readers] move between macro- and microcosm" ("Dialogic Structure and Levels of Discourse in Steinbeck's *The Grapes of Wrath*." 76). In effect, Steinbeck maps the social layer (class) alongside the psychological one (family).

In *Earth Abides*, however, the interstitial sections are clearly not about people and, indeed, could not occur in the presence of humans. For instance, "*As with dogs and cats, so also with the grasses and flowers which man had long nourished. The clover and the blue-grass withered on the lawns, and the dandelions grew tall*" (40; emphasis in the original). These descriptions continue, lamenting the loss of the asters, camellias, wisteria vines, and rose bushes and replete with imagery of an imperial fall: "*as once, when the armies of the empire were shattered and the strong barbarians poured in upon the soft provincials, so now the fierce weeds pressed in to destroy the pampered nurslings of man*" (ibid.). These sections appear, unlike the interchapters in *The Grapes of Wrath*, within chapters that follow the protagonist.[9] They intensify the sense of world and environment as a force, even an agent, in the narrative. Here, Stewart offers an ecological mapping alongside a geographical one, but Williams and the narrator make separate yet intertwined progress across the empty spaces of North America.[10] The catalogue functions as a kind of stitching device within the narrative discourse, suturing together the impact of the absence of human activity, the journey of the observer-explorer, and the commentary of the narrator.

The novel does place Williams crucially at the center of its narrative project, despite the introduction of other characters such as his eventual life partner, Emma, and the interchapters that focus on the slow deterioration of the built world. Though Williams is separate from the backdrop of the post-apocalyptic setting, his impulse to catalogue maintains his link to the time before the end and his intellectual investment in the post-apocalyptic world. At one point, the narrator remarks, "The more [Williams] thought about it, the more fundamental he considered [Emma's] idea of keeping track of time. After all, time was history, and history was tradition, and tradition was civilization. If you lost the continuity of time, you lost something that might never be recovered" (Stewart, *Earth Abides*, 113). The catalogue is of prime importance for the protagonist's cultural endeavors, and at the same time, it begins to document remainders.

Earth Abides differs from earlier US post-apocalyptic novels, such as Jack London's *The Scarlet Plague* (first published in 1912). Whereas an old man who tells the story of how he survived the apocalypse to a few youngsters in London's novel, Stewart's follows Williams's first-hand experience of the apocalypse and its aftermath. In *Earth Abides*, no character looks back to make sense of what has taken place; narrative time moves only forward. Moreover, because the novel ends when Williams dies of old age, the future of that particular storyworld is left radically uncertain. Using Williams's movements as a cipher and the free indirect discourse of the interstitial sections, Stewart writes a detailed account of how human culture and society might transform itself, what it might retain, and what it might lose. Stewart places the conceit of the remainder at the novel's heart. The threat of nuclear war on Earth may have been behind his cataloguing impulse: faced with the possibility that plants and animals could be wiped off the face of the planet, Stewart's book can be read as a catalogue of how an earlier mode of apocalypse might have left the earth without quite so many humans but with much of the natural world still in place—a remainder of the apocalyptic imagination from a pre-irradiated world.

FORMING COMMUNITIES

Brackett's *The Long Tomorrow* charts the ways communities develop and devolve in the aftermath of a far-from-total nuclear war. Len Coulter narrates the novel. Hailing from the New Mennonite pastoral community of Piper's Run, he dreams of a different kind of life in a hidden city of which he has only heard the whispered name "Bartorstown." He comes from a background of Mennonite communalism, yet he dreams of commerce and trade. Coulter longs for self-possessed individuality as though through it he might escape the constraints of Piper's Run. Despite the warnings he receives from his father about the dangers of technology, he longs to learn more of the world. In this sense, he is an able-bodied, driven, and intensely curious person who can act as a middle-of-the-road hero, though his post-apocalyptic storyworld is structured not by "two opposing camps" (Lukács, *The Historical Novel*, 37), but rather by different forms of self-contained social organization.[11] The critical medical anthropologist Matthew Wolf-Meyer describes Coulter as "symbolic of his culture (roots in neo-Luddite religion, but striving towards technological integration)" and argues that "his development metonymically describes the development of all of post-apocalyptic America" ("Apocalypse, Ideology, America"). Along with his cousin, Coulter uncovers a radio and some old books—a discovery that eventually leads to their escape from Piper's Run.

The two travel to a different settlement, a new social space. Founded around a small steam-engine manufactory and some warehouses along the river, Refuge is about as big a city as can legally be. According to the thirtieth amendment to the US Constitution, "No city, no town, no community of more than one thousand people or two hundred buildings to the square mile shall be built or permitted to exist anywhere in the United States of America" (Brackett, *The Long Tomorrow*, 7). Judge Taylor offers Coulter a chance to stay in Refuge and learn the law, while at the same time cautioning him against the evils of cities—which either aligns with or thinly veils a segregationist attitude. "They were dying even before the destruction," says Taylor. "Megalopolis, drowned in its own sewage, choked with its own waste gases, smothered and crushed by its own population. 'City' sounds like a musical word to your ear, but what do you really know about them?" (ibid., 70). The unclear pronoun "they" in Taylor's speech could stand for black people just as easily as it could mean city dwellers. Brackett's established use of different communities to represent different post-apocalyptic attitudes and with her use of Taylor as the speaker present a question for critical interpretation: is this veiled racist language critical, or is it merely symptomatic of contemporary racist attitudes toward the inner city? Coulter's insistence on returning to modernity pushes against Taylor's veiled racism, but not explicitly or directly. People in Refuge are not worried about more advanced social forms, but as Taylor's words make clear, they are afraid of the perceived evils of modernity in the form of the modern city. Here competition is regulated and geographically constrained, as if the evil of the mode of production comes from its scale, if not from a racially integrating workforce.

When trouble starts to brew with the neighboring town of Shadwell, Coulter and his cousin join a band of men reportedly heading for Bartorstown. For many, the whispered legend and hushed mystery that surround the spot keep the idea of cities and civilization alive. Yet their arrival there rends the veil of the town's legendary name, which allows it to hide in plain sight a greater secret than its supposed shady mercantile dealing. The small mountain village of Bartorstown also conceals a secret government installation that houses a nuclear reactor power station and a computer (Brackett, *The Long Tomorrow*, 150).

Ultimately, the position of the novel on the question of nuclear power is deeply ambivalent. With the move into the cloistered environment of Bartorstown, the novel shifts its secondary characters' political discourse from one that disparages cities and moral decay to one that defends the virtues of nuclear power. While introducing Coulter to the nuclear reactor that powers Bartorstown, one of the scientists says, "Listen.... You're thinking of the bomb. This isn't a bomb. It isn't hurtful. We've lived with it here for nearly a hundred years. It can't explode, and it can't burn you. The concrete makes us safe. Look.... See? There's nothing to fear" (Brackett, *The Long Tomorrow*, 151). During the same tour of the high-tech facilities, the narrator says, "the Power entrapped behind the concrete wall gave off its strength silently, untiringly, the deathless heart beating and throbbing in the rock" (ibid., 172). The scientist offers a defense of nuclear energy, while the narrator gives it an otherworldly dimension. Finally, Coulter provides a third position, neither defensive nor uncertain, when he pragmatically muses, "The bomb is a fact. Atomic power is a fact. It is a living fact close down under my feet, the dreadful power that made these pictures. You can't deny it, you can't destroy it" (ibid., 155). This realization leads Coulter to plan an escape from the town.

In Swiftian fashion, as when Gulliver moves from island to island, or even perhaps like the ancient Ulysses, Coulter maps the world both geographically and ideologically. He identifies the divergent visions of different communities, as he is able to live with them for a time. *The Long Tomorrow* puts Coulter in a position to reveal different kinds of post-apocalyptic persisting and, crucially, to connect them. Despite the knowledge gained by the protagonist, the novel is a version of the hero quest with no return to its starting point—there is no return to Piper's Run at the end. This world is caught in stasis, waiting for the time when history might begin again. The novel offers much in a critical reading: with its alignment and comparison of Piper's Run, Refuge, and Bartorstown, the novel pulls apart religion, commerce, and science and reveals each to have its own means of production and form of social life. Crucial too is the different mode of analysis offered in each area: in Piper's Run, larger communities that rely on technology are a threat; in Refuge, the letter of the law regarding city size is a threat for some, while for others steam power is a boon for manufacturing and boat travel; in Bartorstown, the threat is of technophobic people discovering their secret nuclear reactor and computer lab. *The Long Tomorrow* establishes the trope of community so frequently used in later post-apocalyptic novels. It is in this way that Brackett's novel reaches toward a form of meta-analysis of the quickly solidifying post-apocalyptic mode: the communities within a given text may be read as standing in for other texts, each with its own version of the origins of the apocalypse, response to the post-apocalyptic world, and plans to keep something similar from ever happening again. In novels such as Brackett's, post-apocalyptic world building begins to produce critical reflexivity and to model the contested character of the post-apocalyptic mode.

BUILDING ENCLAVES

Miller's *A Canticle for Leibowitz* offers a synthesis of the distinctive tropes of Brackett's and Stewart's novels—namely, cataloguing the post-apocalypse and forming communities. Consisting of three connected novellas, the book follows separate characters and plots that unfold centuries apart after a nuclear holocaust. Each novella works through the diverse conflicts arising from the pursuit of survival, the protection of knowledge, and the rebirth of society, all unified by their shared setting: the monastery of the order of St. Leibowitz. The novellas follow the order of brothers who guard the scraps of a destroyed civilization as they work to rediscover technology—here, Brackett's religious and scientific community are united. The plot begins when one brother discovers a series of precatastrophe writings that the reader recognizes as engineering blueprints and designs for computer hardware. In the novel, the cultural significance of these artifacts belongs in the realm of the sacred, and some are even rendered in stained glass by brothers of the order. A deep distrust of learning has developed, since the intellectual class is blamed for the catastrophe, so in the wrong hands the blueprints might also appear to be profane. The order of St. Leibowitz creates an eddy amid a rushing river of ignorance, swirling around forbidden knowledges. It obscures information-laden relics of the past from the outside world. Although this novel appears to be about societal retrogression, it does not depict a uniform movement backward, but rather what (to bastardize a phrase from Louis Althusser) I would call an uneven regression.[12] Modern ideologies of class survive, even in a setting that otherwise resembles the Dark Ages.

The first novella, set in the Age of Simplification (sometime in the 2500s), begins with Brother Francis of Utah discovering a fallout shelter, a remnant from before the Flame Deluge. After discovering the shelter, Brother Francis thinks about the Lord Abbot's decree: "nor shall any other excavation be initiated which does not have as its primary purpose the augmentation of the Memorabilia" (W. Miller, *A Canticle for Leibowitz*, 23). The collection of memorabilia is the prime directive of the order of St. Leibowitz, to which Brother Francis belongs. To his great surprise, the fallout shelter contains precisely what he is looking for: his "eye traveled down the list until it encountered: 'CIRCUIT DESIGN BY: *Leibowitz, I.E.*,'" and he realized that "he had uncovered relics of the Saint" (ibid., 27–28; emphasis in the original). While the design remains unintelligible to members of the order, their sacred duty remains to sequester this knowledge until such a time when it might be useful once more. Indeed, such designs will later enable the rediscovery and redevelopment of nuclear technology. The section ends when Brother Francis is ambushed on his way to New Rome, located in Denver. His mission was to deliver the sacred relics.

Set in the year 3174, the plot of the second novella hinges on conflict rather than on discovery. Largely focused on Abbot Dom Paulo, the section also introduces a secular scientist, Thon Taddeo, who yearns to discover the technological secrets in the order's archive. Miller describes this knowledge and its sequestration in the "vaulted basement" of the abbey:

> The Memorabilia, the abbey's small patrimony of knowledge out of the past, had been walled up in underground vaults to protect the priceless writings from both nomads and *soidsant* [*sic*] crusaders of the schismatic Orders. . . . Neither the nomads nor the Military Order of San Pancatz would have valued the abbey's

books, but the nomads would have destroyed them for the joy of destruction and the military knights-friars would have burned many of them as "heretical" according to the theology of Vissarion, their Antipope. (*A Canticle for Leibowitz*, 143; emphasis in the original)

This passage establishes the order's archival practices in preserving knowledge for future generations and the fact that the world has evolved in complexity from the first novella. Indeed, Brother Kornhoer develops an electrical generator using a treadmill that illuminates an arc lamp. Here the remainders of past knowledge are protected both from factions against all intellectual pursuits and from a sect opposed to the particular knowledge that has been sequestered. Meanwhile, a political plot unfolds behind the order's enclave of technological secrets: states form, alliances are made and broken, and new players emerge to vie for dominance.[13]

The third novella, set in 3781, ends after a resurgence of technology has brought on another nuclear war, signaling Miller's heavy-handed critique of the connection between technological innovation and assured destruction. A small group of monks from the order escape on a spaceship, preserving their teachings for posterity. The pronouncements of Abbot Dom Jethras Zerchi—which encapsulate the monastic enclave's mission to preserve the religious order—simultaneously describe the narrative logic of the post-apocalyptic novel:

You will be years in space. The ship will be your monastery. After the patriarchal see is established at the Centaurus Colony, you will establish there a mother house of the Visitationist Friars of the Order of Saint Leibowitz of Tycho. But the ship will remain in your hands, and the Memorabilia. If civilization, or a vestige of it, can maintain itself on Centaurus, you will send missions to the other colony worlds, and to the colonies of their colonies. Wherever Man goes, you and your successors will go. And with you, the records and remembrances of four thousand years and more. Some of you, or those to come after you, will be mendicants and wanderers, teaching the chronicles of Earth and the canticles of the Crucified to the peoples and the cultures that may grow out of the colony groups. For some may forget. Some may be lost for a time from the Faith. Teach them, and receive into the Order those among them who are called. Pass on to them the continuity. Be for Man the memory of Earth and Origin. Remember this Earth. Never forget her, but—*never come back*. (W. Miller, *A Canticle for Leibowitz*, 289; emphasis in the original)

Zerchi offers the imperatives of preserving and disseminating the tenets of a human culture as a founding principle for never forgetting catastrophe. The order, with its imperative to preserve in the bounded space of the monastery, exhibits the cataloguing device of *Earth Abides* and the communities of *The Long Tomorrow*, though here they find a new collective form in the enclave of St. Leibowitz. By remaining sequestered from the anti-intellectualism of the post-apocalyptic world, the order is able to hermetically seal technical knowledge—Leibowitz, after all, was an engineer—protecting it until it may once more be of use to them. Zerchi's address must be imagined as one of many others like it over the 1,200-year history of the order. It is part of what keeps the community together.

The order is an enclave, in the sense elaborated by Fredric Jameson. Jameson traces the development of enclaves to the utopian writings of Thomas More and William Morris. For Jameson, the enclave is an "aberrant by-product," a "pocket of stasis" within a dominant cultural milieu that "radiates baleful power," a power that "can be eclipsed without a trace precisely because it is confined to a limited space" (*Archaeologies of the Future*, 15–17). The concept operates in much the same way in Miller's novellas, but for the critical inversion of origins and ends found in the post-apocalyptic plot. The order of St. Leibowitz is a kind of historiographical thought experiment, enabled by the post-apocalypse conceit, in which the novel effectively delinks historical chronology from progress. Put differently, *A Canticle for Leibowitz* imagines conditions under which the future entails technological regress, while the past signals technological progress. Miller's novellas assume an explicitly, though not unambiguously, political character in their implicit theory of historical change. Jessica Hurley claims that "while Miller's future history does play out as a repeat of past history, opening the novel" with the discovery of the circuit design "suggests that this is not inevitable, that other paths, other developments, are possible" ("Still Writing Backwards," 66). These paths remain open and ambiguous because the wonderful device of sequestering past knowledge produces catastrophe, rather than salvation, in the storyworld. Miller's novellas combine in the order of St. Leibowitz the backward-looking glance of Stewart's novel and the idea of community in Brackett's. Although the order presents a bulwark against ignorance and anti-intellectualism, it cannot prevent the revival of nuclear power, for instance, or the use of such a technology for destructive ends. Instead, it repeats the protective enclosure of knowledge, gesturing to a future when that knowledge might prove useful once more, out among the stars.

THE LAST MAN

Matheson's *I Am Legend* welters in the atmosphere of the second red scare as much as it thinks critically about racial issues endemic in the long 1950s. It features a common trope of post-apocalyptic novels, in which the last human stands out against a number of either dead or very alive and very threatening others. This figure, across the history of the post-apocalyptic mode, tends to be a last man, and thus I use the terminology of the last man advisedly to address the gendered status of the trope itself. The opening passage of Matheson's last-man novel presents the central conflict with an air of mystery:

> On those cloudy days, Robert Neville was never sure when sunset came, and sometimes they were in the streets before he could get back. If he had been more analytical, he might have calculated the approximate time of their arrival; but he still used the lifetime habit of judging nightfall from the sky, and on cloudy days that method didn't work. That was why he chose to stay near the house on those days. (*I Am Legend*, 13)

Besides establishing the opposition of Neville and the mysterious "they," this passage reveals little about the storyworld or its characters. The narrator does relay that Neville does not easily change his habits, something that the novel will continue to reiterate as a kind of refrain. The trope of the last man is one of the longest running of the post-apocalyptic mode, dating to the dawn of the nineteenth century.[14] *I Am Legend* deploys the well-known trope to great effect, giving it new anxiety-laden meaning in the United States during the early period of the Cold War and at the birth of the civil rights era.

The novel dramatically overturns the meaning of its title, but not before allowing the reader to develop a concrete understanding of it. *I Am Legend* works through this cluster of anxieties by introducing the conceit of a world in which a strange disease has turned the population into vampire-like beings that taunt the only uninfected man, Robert Neville. The situation created by the disease, rather than the disease itself, transforms Neville into a righteous vigilante who stalks and kills the vampire-like creatures by the day and barricades himself in his house by night. The plot turns when Neville encounters a woman, Ruth, who has also survived, and welcomes her into his home. Ruth turns out to be an agent sent by a newly treated contingent of vampires. Once she has left him, Ruth's note for Neville impressively summarizes all of this plot development:

> Robert: Now you know. Know that I was spying on you, know that almost everything I told you was a lie.
> I'm writing this note, though, because I want to save you if I can.
> When I was first given the job of spying on you, I had no feelings about your life. Because I *did* have a husband, Robert. You killed him.
> But now it's different. I know now that you were just as much forced into your situation as we were forced into ours. We *are* infected. But you already knew that. What you don't understand yet is that we're going to stay alive. We've found a way to do that and we're going to set up society again slowly but surely. We're going to do away with all those wretched creatures whom death has cheated. And, even though I pray otherwise, we may decide to kill you. (Matheson, *I Am Legend*, 154; emphasis in the original)

Though the treatment has erased any violent behavior caused by the disease, this new group still resembles the nocturnal others that threaten Neville. The revelation at the end of the plot, shattering the pretense of Neville's belief in his heroic identity, is that the presumed monsters, the treated vampires, are the ones being terrorized and that the true monster is Neville, who "is a legend as vampires once were" (Žižek, *Living in the End Times*, 62).

This revelation demands a reinterpretation of the novel's title: *I Am Legend*. The philosopher Slavoj Žižek reads Neville's status as part of the realization that "one's own tradition is no better than what appears to [the observer] as the 'eccentric' traditions of others" (*Living in the End Times*, 63). Matheson puts Neville's epiphany in these words:

> Robert Neville looked out over the people of the earth. He knew he did not belong to them; he knew that, like the vampires, he was anathema and black terror to be destroyed. And, abruptly, the concept came, amusing to him even in his pain.... Full circle. A new terror born in death, a new superstition entering the unassailable fortress of forever. I am legend. (Matheson, *I Am Legend*, 170)

This shift in expectations arrives as a negotiation of plot and story, specifically through the limited narrative scope of the protagonist—who, until the plot twist, is represented as the hero. The end of the novel reveals that Neville has actually been acting as a conservative agent, constraining history from moving forward and barring the progress of humanity's transcendence of its old form: he is a force left over from a previous historical moment who is, precisely in trying to ensure his own survival, transformed into the antagonist of the emerging social collective.

In *I Am Legend*, Neville—a single white male, holed up in his house with whiskey, the works of Arnold Schönberg, and rage—signifies as completely incidental to history, manifesting the melodramatic alienation of his particular standpoint. The novel reveals a contrast in its critical and didactic lesson about the relation of the dominant (here, the white male) to diegetic historical change. The science fiction critic Robert Yeates argues that Neville "represents the insecurity of postwar masculinity" ("Gender and Ethnicity in Post-Apocalyptic Suburbia," 417). While Matheson's novel smartly engages with the changing postwar American racial and cultural milieu, it does so by introducing an ideologically volatile narrative solution: by revealing its last man protagonist as the (unwitting) champion of conservative white male values, *I Am Legend* (just as unwittingly) establishes a trope that has since been consistently mobilized to affirm the same reactionary fears it originally sought to undermine: Hugh Farnham in Robert A. Heinlein's *Farnham's Freehold* (first published in 1964), Stu Redman in Stephen King's *The Stand* (first published in 1978), Gordon Krantz in David Brin's *The Postman* (1985), and the man and the boy in Cormac McCarthy's *The Road* (2006) exemplify how the last man trope has been mobilized in non-self-critical ways. It matters less and less that *I Am Legend* ends by showing Neville's ignorance and volatility. Even readers unfamiliar with the novel will appreciate the fact that Neville is the true monster in the text—hiding by night and murdering what he sees as grotesque creatures asleep in their beds by day. The lone white male character becomes a target of critical inversion for Matheson, yet the clever reversal of political polarity in *I Am Legend* reappears in contemporary post-apocalyptic novels predominantly in failed form and is unable to affect a similarly meaningful deconstruction of whiteness. Now, Matheson's clever plot twist becomes symptomatic of nothing so much as the history of a genre too long accustomed to a reactionary conservatism. *I Am Legend* can imagine the vicious mission of one man against the world only as a consequence of the universalization of human identity.

■

Cataloguing the post-apocalypse, forming communities, building enclaves, and last man inform the tropology of post-apocalyptic novels. *Earth Abides* anticipates contemporary ecological writing that seeks to examine what impact the disappearance of modern accoutrements might have on human culture and society. It transforms the literary role of Steinbeck's interchapters into post-apocalyptic fragments, catalogues of the crumbling reminders of US modernity. Brackett's *The Long Tomorrow* maps varying responses to the post-apocalyptic setting in the form of specific communities, showing that all the while each community is divided within itself across its own narrative version of the apocalyptic end. Brackett demonstrates how post-apocalyptic plots may be incorporated in two layers: as distinct communities encountered by mobile characters and as narrative strategies for explaining those communities—as is the case with Gulliver, Ulysses, and Waverly. Miller's *A Canticle for Leibowitz*, operating as a cautionary tale, combines the first two devices to explore the vital question of whether the preservation of knowledge could actually prevent history from repeating itself, let alone work toward some better social order than the remainders of those ready to hand. Remainders signify differently to different social orders and unique traditions. Finally, *I Am Legend* plays into two unconscious fears—of being the sole survivor of a catastrophic disease or nuclear winter and of realizing that you are not the good guy—while at the same time establishing an ambivalently durable figure (the last man) of masculine longing and loneliness. Ambiguously representing remainders to critical effect presents a challenge to reader reception and generic transmission. Writers might deploy these tropes to great effect, but their own political inclinations tend to reshape and reorient these apocalypse moves.

Examining these tropes together reveals a form of wish fulfillment broadly symptomatic of a historical moment, an answer to the if-only dreams of a generation of Americans. In these postwar novels, fantasy realizes itself through the ability to explore a world devoid of humans, seek out hidden enclaves, discover how others survive amid apocalyptic ruins, retreat from the anti-intellectual world to sequester a deep knowledge, or kill one's neighbors—old and new alike. Even as *Earth Abides, The Long Tomorrow, A Canticle for Leibowitz*, and *I Am Legend* attempt to reflect critically on the stubborn reassertion of a destructive, antediluvian social telos in the wake of a radical, apocalyptic break, these postwar texts become retroactively absorbed into the post-apocalyptic mode. In this reabsorption, their tropes get stripped of their critical traction, such as when the last human survivor becomes a symbol of the white man as a tragic victim—or worse, as a savior. Over time these tropes have become delinked from their historical context and redeployed in the abstract, almost mythical time of American conservatism in the late twentieth century or used critically to dislodge readers' capacity to take such moves for granted.

These motifs are the building blocks of post-apocalyptic storytelling. The texts used here to exemplify the emergence of these tropes in the postwar period establish a framework for the operations of the post-apocalyptic mode today. Post-apocalyptic texts use these tropes to narrate the move from apocalyptic break to the restoration of the status quo. The capacity of a novel to achieve this complicated epistemological and narratological maneuver hinges on the struggle to narrate the future as difference. Books such as *Earth Abides, The Long Tomorrow, A Canticle for Leibowitz,* and *I Am Legend* put new procedures for survival in place and set the terrain for the post-apocalyptic novels that follow their path. From their forms of expression and depiction of community, post-apocalypse tropes engage historical change as much as they enable its reconstruction.

2
Reduced Futures

The post-apocalypse tropes in chapter 1 provide the post-apocalyptic mode with its tension and drama. What would the world be like after an apocalyptic event? Would the survivors remain safely sequestered? Is it possible that the enclave would be breached or compromised? How alone is the sole survivor, really? These questions conjure up dramatic scenarios in the mind—so many post-apocalyptic plots that have been played out, with each successive iteration of the post-apocalyptic story developing a deeper narrative process. In this way, the projected image of the real world has been destroyed many times over. Yet the post-apocalyptic novel sets aside many of the complexities of real-world life, leaving the nearly clean slate of the storyworld. This chapter is about what happens in a storyworld where much of the real world has withered away or become obsolete. It elaborates the processes of world destroying, binding narratology and tropology into what I describe as reduced futures: a process of focusing on the particular conflicts and the attributes that have previously gone unnoticed and become clear in the post-apocalyptic storyworld.[1]

The germ of this process can be found in early criticism about post-apocalyptic fiction. In an essay on the post-apocalyptic mode, Gary K. Wolfe suggests that the idea of a depopulated world where "humanity is reduced to a more elemental struggle with nature" presents opportunities for "heroic action," opportunities that he feels are withheld in the technocratic worlds of much science fiction ("The

Remaking of Zero," 4). From this vantage point, readers find end-of-the-world stories easier to access and understand because they do not necessitate what Wolfe describes as the cumbersome narrative apparatus found in other forms of imagining the future, such as science fiction dystopias, plots involving time travel, or space opera stories. For Wolfe, the difficulty of grasping all the details of a new technology in a science fiction story creates a stumbling block for readers. He treats the role of advanced technology as a limit to the world-building capacities of science fiction, a limit that might be overcome by the world-destroying tendency of the post-apocalyptic mode. Wolfe makes this observation in the language of removal and reduction: "Rather than introduce new machines, an author can *remove* or *reduce* the functioning of the familiar ones and still explore issues of technology and society" (ibid., 5). Despite its sometimes reactionary tilt, Wolfe's preliminary criticism about the post-apocalyptic mode uncovers a process of reduction. In this respect, his assessment of the logical underpinning of the mode is one I fundamentally agree with, though it leads him to draw different conclusions than I do.[2] Where Wolfe celebrates a clear distinction between good and evil, I outline a genre where what remains must be read against what is subtracted from the storyworld.

In this chapter, I elaborate on the genre- or mode-level features of what I call reduced futures, meaning futures in which the options have been incredibly limited by an apocalyptic event. In describing the world-shattering effects of an apocalyptic event as reduction, I necessarily abstract them from their particular fictional context. Each apocalyptic event entails a variation on reduction: the depopulating effects of contagion leave a different storyworld behind than the city-wasting force of an atomic bomb or the social insecurity of market and governmental failure. For instance, Neville Shute's *On the Beach* (1957) depicts the response of people in Melbourne, Australia, to the news of a nuclear war in the northern hemisphere. A world away from immediate threat, they wait out the arrival of radioactive devastation in relative peace. Another example can be found in *Motherlines* (1978)—the second novel in Suzy McKee Charnas's Holdfast series—which presents a world with an all-female cast. Here, the subtraction of men makes vivid the male-dominated dramatis personae of the post-apocalyptic mode. Not every scenario presents a version of Wolfe's opportunities for heroic action, yet each coheres around a similar narrative reduction to a location, in the first example, or a gender, in the second.

Harry Harrison's *Make Room! Make Room!* (1966) provides a counterexample of future reduction that serves to illustrate the concept. In Harrison's book, the world's population is on the rise, water must be rationed, and food is scarce. Harrison introduces the portmanteau "soylent" (meaning a combination of soy and lentils) as one way to feed a massive population.[3] On a representational level, *Make Room! Make Room!* cries out for a future without massive populations—that is, for future reduction. It might be considered apocalyptic if one imagines that a tipping point in population has been reached; that social structures—indeed, even city infrastructures—can no longer support the US population; and that the earth cannot sustain its population. Harrison's book projects a densely packed future, even if ideologically it imagines the reduction of future possibility.

The process that shapes the post-apocalyptic storyworld in this way is comparable to what Fredric Jameson calls "world reduction." For Jameson, this term means a particular attempt to imagine "an experimental landscape in which our being-in-the-world is simplified to the extreme" (*Archaeologies of the Future*, 269). He describes world reduction as based on "a principle of systematic exclusion, a kind of surgical excision of empirical reality" (ibid., 271). World reduction implies a process of authorial selection in which each choice the writer makes about storyworld elements eliminates other possible worlds. Jameson writes that it is "something like a process of ontological attenuation," wherein the world builder deliberately weeds out "the sheer teeming multiplicity of what exists, of what we call reality . . . through an operation of radical abstraction and simplification" (ibid.).[4] In post-apocalyptic scenarios, the process of world destroying is also a process of subtraction that allows authors to present a transformed version of reality as they remove elements from the known world, which develops the classical move of the apocalyptic mode to unveil a deeper reality.

An apocalyptic event destroys the image of the real world, subtracting real-world elements and leaving a post-apocalyptic storyworld behind. The reduced futures of post-apocalyptic storyworlds feature the remainders of an apocalyptic arithmetic.[5] The options for humanity have been limited by catastrophic events, and survivors are often presented with only a few choices for how to proceed. The logic underlying the post-apocalyptic mode works through a kind of future reduction. Moreover, the political implications of post-apocalyptic storytelling hinge on a process of world destroying that enacts such reductions.

Future reduction emerges from the shifting meaning of apocalypse after World War II. One of the clearest ways to differentiate the apocalypse story from the story told after the apocalypse is to show what kind of worlds each imagines. Both present reduced worlds, to be sure: The apocalypse story purportedly divides humanity across levels of penitence and faith as surely as those characters living in the post-apocalypse period will be divided across levels of luck and fortitude. The apocalypse story looks to a potential future that rarely arrives as expected. The real world is far too complex to say which apocalyptic tradition has it right, but in a post-apocalyptic story, the world-shattering event tends to prove at least one doomsday sect prescient. From the moment of the fictional, apocalyptic break, the reality of daily life becomes straightforward—the multiplicity of possible apocalyptic scenarios has been reduced to one post-apocalyptic future. In the following section, I turn to critics of the post-apocalyptic genre to position my own treatment of these texts as a mode.

THREE NAMES OF THE APOCALYPSE

The apocalypse as a cultural narrative has an extensive history. The literary critic John Hay traces what he calls "postapocalyptic fantasies" to antebellum American literature. Specifically, he opens his book-length study with John Van Ness Yates and Joseph White Moulton's 1824 *History of the State of New York*, writing that "at a seemingly arbitrary moment," an "imagined man, a future archaeologist, stands in reverent awe of . . . the broken remains of a massive brick edifice" left behind by a "race known as the *Americans*" (*Postapocalyptic Fantasies in Antebellum American Literature*, 1; emphasis in the original). Yates and Moulton envision the eventual demise of the United States, as Hay notes: "'It may be our turn to reign for ages masters of the ascendant,' they muse, but eventually a period will arrive 'when, by national degeneracy and criminality, we shall have become ripened for ruin'" (ibid., 2). Hay's genealogy traces the post-apocalyptic mode first to speculation using the future perfect tense to imagine the work of future historians. Even this example foreshadows Hay's conclusion: "Post-apocalyptic fantasies can thus threaten to close off the work of building and rebuilding if they are indulged too eagerly" (ibid., 227). Hay thus warns against such indulgence in postapocalyptic fantasies. However, I suggest that his words describe the ways the post-apocalyptic mode works by design.

Cultural critics of apocalyptic storytelling in the twentieth and twenty-first centuries demarcate an apocalyptic form that, by the late twentieth century, has become less oriented toward the future than it is focused on the present as a moment when it is possible to return to an idealized past. In this sense, they claim, apocalyptic forms now offer only to unveil the exhaustion of future possibility. In recent accounts of apocalyptic culture, the apocalypse as a structuring telos is replaced by the future as an unveiling of more of the same. The literary critic Teresa Heffernan connects these imaginative (in)capacities to the fallout of modernity itself. She argues that the structuring power an apocalyptic telos had for the Enlightenment loses the full force of its revelatory power in what she terms "post-apocalyptic culture." In her work, Heffernan points out the existence of a decisive shift, from apocalyptic to post-apocalyptic culture, noting that the end game of an earlier moment disappears and "the present world is portrayed as exhausted," with "no better world that replaces it" (*Post-Apocalyptic Culture*, 5).[6]

The post-apocalyptic mode preserves a certain sense of revelation and ending that is apparent in Christian apocalyptic writing.[7] Both narrative forms ground their future-oriented visions in a past event, and both produce meanings that echo across history, subject to repeated reinterpretation. The plot of the Christian apocalyptic narrative can be generalized along the following lines: after Eden comes the fall, and after that the only thing to look forward to is revelation, the rapture, and the apocalypse. Historically, this narrative logic has produced anticipation for closure in the form of the end days from millenarian cults to predictions of the return of Christ. Yet what happens when the apocalypse, correctly foretold by the right portents, does not come to pass? During a series of lectures, Frank Kermode describes one doomsday sect whose members were observed by the American sociologist Leon Festinger: they gathered for the final countdown, and for most "disconfirmation was quickly followed by the invention of new end-fictions and new calculations" (*The Sense of an Ending*, 17).[8] Sect leaders declare the presumed cataclysm false, and sycophants turn toward the future once more in trembling anticipation of the true end of days. Thus, when an anticipated moment of transformative revelation does not live up to expectations, sect leaders produce another future event to long for. Kermode's apocalyptic mode names a temporal relation whereby apocalyptic anticipation allows one to ground oneself in the present, suspended between creation and judgment. Over the course of his lectures, Kermode calls attentions to a historical shift that leaves behind one understanding of the end as imminent that is part of a new understanding of the apocalypse as immanent. The post-apocalyptic mode reverses Kermode's eschatological apocalyptic plot. In these stories, the apocalypse is not necessarily theologically determined or based on faith but instead occurs for historical reasons. War, economic collapse, and rampant disease are secular events. The post-apocalyptic mode posits that after a world-altering event, the only thing to look forward to is the possibility of a new Eden.

The post-apocalyptic plot takes the apocalypse as an origin, beginning after a diegetic, social conception of the end and proceeding toward a new origin, the beginning of a new story. Whereas the apocalyptic mode focuses on a temporal distinction, there is a spatial demarcation to post-apocalyptic storytelling: rather than an encounter with the maker that separates the finite time of mortality from the infinite time of the afterlife, the post-apocalyptic mode situates characters in a kind of perpetual present where they can explore their strange new world in the absence of what has been cleared away. Heather J. Hicks argues that ultimately post-apocalyptic fiction could be defined as "material that depicts what might be called 'globalized ruin'" (*The Post-Apocalyptic Novel in the Twenty-First Century*, 6–7). Here, Hicks alludes to the concept of combined and uneven development. Rather than depicting some future time, post-apocalyptic novels represent the immiseration of people in the periphery now coming to affect those who had previously benefited from modern social arrangements.

In the post-apocalyptic mode, the apocalyptic event rewrites what comes after it and, retroactively, what had led to it. The Christian apocalyptic mode features events that occur in terms of the judgment of the morally good life, while in the post-apocalyptic mode the world-destroying event can seem less arbitrary and more chaotic. As Connor Pitetti argues, post-apocalyptic narratives open "spaces of ambiguity in apocalypse's seamless accounts of straightforward transition from present to future" ("Uses of the End of the World," 438). The post-apocalyptic event alters social rules and often entire landscapes, yet it does not do so according to some evident code or doctrine. Along these lines, Briohny Doyle posits that rather than defining a new age, post-apocalyptic temporality "becomes abstruse, (dis)located in the ambiguous aftermath of catastrophe" ("The Post-apocalyptic Imagination," 100).

Combining these three claims, one can conclude that the post-apocalyptic mode mimetically depicts the state of the world (Hicks), creates uncertainty where the apocalyptic mode offers clarity (Pitetti), and offers further problems rather than clear solutions (Doyle). While the apocalyptic mode looks toward an impending catastrophe as a source of meaning, in the post-apocalyptic mode the end has come and gone, yet the apocalyptic revelation remains uncertain—unformed, as when Clov speaks the first lines of Samuel Beckett's *Endgame* (first published in 1958): "Finished, it's finished, nearly finished, it must be nearly finished" (6). Heffernan seems to describe Cloy's precise mood: "[post-apocalyptic] narratives seem stalled in an endless loop where disaster never gives way to a new dawn" (*Post-Apocalyptic Culture*, 95). In the face of such uncertain endings, post-apocalyptic narratives yearn for a new beginning, although that beginning is often a return to the way things were before the crash.

James Berger's *After the End* makes sense of the overlapping meanings of apocalypse with a useful rubric that contains three senses of the term. To put a spin on Berger's definitions, the three forms of the apocalypse are definite (the apocalypse), indefinite (an apocalypse), and adjectival (it's apocalyptic!). Post-apocalyptic storytelling relies on the apocalypse within the storyworld, which readers note as an apocalypse when relating one text to another or to real-world events. The third sense includes, crucially, both a clarifying function and a moment ripe for interpretation: it signifies both a revelatory effect and future reduction, positing one storyworld. "It's apocalyptic!" reaches away from eschatology (the apocalypse) and genre (an apocalypse) and toward a mode or a way of getting something done.

The eschaton provides the first sense of apocalypse that has been imagined to destroy the world from the revelation of John of Patmos and medieval millenarian movements to postwar nightmares of nuclear annihilation or ecological suicide. This version describes Kermode's sense of the ending as imminent, looming ahead in time. Rather than offering an eschatological ending, the post-apocalyptic narrows its selection from an array of possible futures. For the secular apocalypse—the apocalypse that has little to do with revelation and nothing to do with ending—some kind of future reduction must be at work, leading to a precise arrangement of what happens, who survives, and how and why.

Berger uses the second sense to name "catastrophes that *resemble* the imagined final ending," which function as "definitive historical divides, as ruptures" (*After the End*, 5). These "pivots" and "fulcrums" separate before from after: "All preceding history seems to lead up to and set the stage for such events, and all that follows emerges out of the central cataclysm" (ibid.), such as the European colonization of the Americas. This sense colludes with Kermode's sense of an ending as immanent, since an apocalypse could ostensibly be used to describe many different kinds of ending, rather than just the biblical one. In his work on the post-apocalyptic, Leif Sorenson describes a culture so obsessed with the second meaning of apocalypse that it is incapable of imagining Berger's first meaning: the use of the prefix "post" in "post-apocalyptic" projects readers "on the far side of rupture and encourages us to see any impending crisis as another transition, and not a potential conclusion" ("Against the Post-Apocalyptic," 590). Because of its very nature, the post-apocalyptic narrative tends to treat the future as a site of constant change, a deferral of longed-for resolutions. Yet post-apocalyptic stories seem consistently drawn toward resolutions that include the formation of new social worlds, even if these worlds are under constant threat.

For Berger, "apocalypse" has a third sense, which serves an "interpretive, explanatory function" (*After the End*, 5). The destructive moment of the apocalyptic event must, in Berger's words, "clarify and illuminate the true nature of what has been brought to an end" (ibid.).

It preserves the "making sense" gesture of the apocalyptic. The declaration that "it's apocalyptic!" differentiates stories set after a devastating war, such as George Orwell's *Nineteen Eighty-Four* (first published in 1949) or William Gibson's *Neuromancer* (1984), from those that fit within the post-apocalyptic mode. To counterpose this sense of what might not be considered part of the post-apocalyptic mode, let me clarify what might be included. A way of delimiting the archive, as in the above examples, is to ask "what is this work trying to get done?" In the examples from chapter 1, I detect a kind of exploratory function: each example represents people coming together after a massively world-altering event.

Another clear negative example of this is *Planet of the Apes*, directed by Franklin J. Schaffner. The film may be set on a post-apocalyptic Earth, but based on what I have been describing here, it does not necessarily follow that the film is in the post-apocalyptic mode. *Planet of the Apes* is not about building a community against the odds. Instead, it is about misrecognition and what happens when one's position of assumed authority evaporates: humans are now caged creatures, and the previous test subjects have all the power. The revelation at the end is one of setting, not of narrative mode. When Taylor (played by Charlton Heston) discovers the Statue of Liberty at the end of the film, the audience realizes that he did not crash on an alien planet but on earth in the future. Yet, this understanding has not affected the events of the story in the same way that the evolution of the apes and the enslavement of the humans has.[9] Though I would not consider *Planet of the Apes* a post-apocalyptic text, its central conceit does make something crucial apparent about such texts.

Post-apocalyptic fiction tends to be set almost exclusively on Earth. The shock of seeing recognizable locations in ruins seems to necessitate the earth-bound setting.[10] The distinction between post-apocalyptic setting and post-apocalyptic mode hinges on the status of the remainder: its setting alone does not a post-apocalyptic novel make.[11] To fit within the mode, other components must be present—such as world destroying, a post-apocalyptic plot, and some form of future reduction. Post-apocalyptic works adhere to fairly strict demarcations of good and evil or, to soften this claim, possible friends and potential threats. Whatever the source of destruction, future reduction focuses on particular events, people, and places at the expense of others, limiting the storyworld and its inhabitants to their perceived lowest common denominator. Conflict enters here. In the storyworld, the conflict may be over safe spaces or scarce resources. Yet the positions taken within texts also resonate in the real world. As writing in the post-apocalyptic mode proliferates, there is a widening of the range of authorial and readerly conjectures on what kind of a storyworld should be built in the ashes of the world that was destroyed.

WORLD DESTROYING

The world in which Rick Grimes (played by Andrew Lincoln) wakes is not the one he was expecting (*The Walking Dead*). The pilot episode of AMC's *The Walking Dead* (and the first issue of the 2003 comic on which it was based) arguably share one of the best introductions to a post-apocalyptic storyworld. Grimes's exploration of the hospital in the opening scenes may remind some viewers of *28 Days Later* (directed by Danny Boyle), when Jim (Cillian Murphy) wakes up to wander into a deserted London. This trope of having a character wake up, both safe and unaware of outside events, originates in mid-twentieth-century post-apocalyptic novels such as John Wyndham's *The Day of the Triffids* (1951) and George R. Stewart's *Earth Abides* (first published in 1949). Though Stewart's protagonist, Isherwood Williams, is not in a hospital, he survives an endemic disease that ravages North America because he is held up in the Sierra Nevada by a snake bite. Wyndham's protagonist, Bill Masen, is saved from a blinding meteor shower because of the eye treatment he happens to be receiving in a hospital. Thus, he is unaware of the rise of the sentient, mobile, and predatory plants known as Triffids. As with Grimes and Jim, Masen must make sense of the world as he encounters the strange changes since his sequestration in the hospital. This trope introduces the reader (or viewer or listener) and the character to the post-apocalyptic setting at one and the same time. Something has changed to make the storyworld different from the real world, but what precisely that change is does not become clear until, for instance, Grimes encounters a zombic torso in a park. Clawing its way toward him and gnashing its teeth, it shows that the storyworld has been dramatically altered. As viewers, we expect to see zombies in a show titled *The Walking Dead*, yet we also know that Grimes does not expect the dead to walk (or crawl). This low-threat encounter serves to prepare Grimes and satisfy our expectations at once.

What gives the post-apocalyptic mode some coherence is the way that it builds storyworlds through sheer quantitative reduction—clearing the space of populations, infrastructure, and government. The post-apocalyptic mode is primarily subtractive. Even if it adds elements—zombies, toxic wastelands, new diseases, and so on—these are often effects of a more fundamental subtraction from the world as we know it. Yet while post-apocalyptic works tend to be subtractive, they range from those that flirt with fantastic elements, as in Claire Vaye Watkins's *Gold Fame Citrus* (2015), to those that embrace them, as when alien-human hybrids and the manifestation of superhuman abilities becomes the norm in Octavia E. Butler's Xenogenesis trilogy. In the case of the latter, such additions tend to drive the narrative and create a distinctly different world in the wake of the subtraction of elements from the primary (that is, previous) world. Even when such effects are futuristic—as in post-apocalyptic stories set in the distant future such as *After Earth* (directed by M. Knight Shyamalan), where technological advances such as pistols and spaceships exist—they are secondary in importance to the fundamental subtractive reduction of the reader's real experience of the world. It is that reduction that defines the post-apocalyptic storyworld and around which the drama also typically revolves.

The nature of the post-apocalyptic storyworld rests uneasily between that of a primary and that of a secondary world: it is neither a world that emulates our own nor one defined by its foreignness (Ekman and Taylor, "Notes toward a Critical Approach to Worlds and World-Building," 9). Throughout this book, I will use "real world" to distinguish the empirical environment from storyworlds, whether primary or secondary. The novelistic reshaping of what the science fiction critic Darko Suvin would call the author's "empirical environment" creates a strong connection between the problems of the real world and the apocalyptic destruction of its storyworld image ("On the Poetics of the Science Fiction Genre," 372). Jameson reformulates this link: "The concept of *extrapolation* in SF means nothing if it does not designate . . . details . . . in which heterogeneous or contradictory elements of the empirical real world are juxtaposed and recombined in piquant montages" (*Archaeologies of the Future*, 276; emphasis in the original). Being able to compare storyworld and empirical reality is a crucial critical gesture because within the post-apocalyptic story, pre-apocalyptic time in the primary storyworld and present time in the real world are taken to be the same. By beginning with a storyworld in the image of the end of the historical time of the reader, the post-apocalyptic story simultaneously extends and breaks with the imagined telos of the real-world present: the post-apocalyptic storyworld exists in an imaginary interregnum after the end (of the reader's historical present) but also before the beginning (of a definitely new imagined historical world).[12] In the post-apocalyptic story, the origin of historical time in the storyworld is identical with the end of the real-world historical time of the reader.[13]

In post-apocalyptic novels, readers do not confront the destruction of the real world; instead, they encounter a storyworld shaped by apocalyptic forces. In the post-apocalyptic mode, world building is also, effectively, world destroying. Wolfe writes that "the 'end of the world' means the end of a way of life, a configuration of attitudes, perhaps a system of beliefs—but not the actual destruction of the planet or its population (though this population may be severely reduced)" ("The Remaking of Zero," 1). He adds that "it is perhaps most enlightening to regard such stories as tales of cosmological displacement: the old *concept* of 'world' is destroyed and a new one must be put in its place" (ibid.; emphasis in the original). Given Wolfe's parenthetical nonchalance—most people will die in the imagined apocalypse, but accepted systems of belief will persist—I must further specify the nature of this creative destruction, especially considering the way "world," "setting," and "situation" work dialectically across the post-apocalyptic mode and the American century. World destroying occurs through a reduction of the complexities of the storyworld: large populations on Earth are wiped out; elaborate systems of production and government are rendered redundant or irrelevant; and cities collapse, along with the infrastructure that holds them together. Such processes are highly selective, whether purposively or unconsciously so. Just as the world-building practices of science fiction offer information about the sort of future that creators imagine, what gets destroyed in the transition to a secondary, post-apocalyptic world provides insights into a text's politics.

In this sense, what gets destroyed and what survives can be read in terms of the inverted narrative strategies of defamiliarization and familiarization. The former denotes the process of revealing the normal as strange, whereas the latter aims to present the strange as normal. Either process can be said to be political, and one could argue that the same text can contain both. On the whole, one effect of the prevalence of the post-apocalyptic mode of storytelling is a growing cultural familiarity with reduced futures. Rhys Williams explains that defamiliarization (or estrangement, in science-fictional parlance) allows the science-fictional text "to reveal the historical specificity of contemporaneous human relations . . . and allow the cognition of a certain pattern of affairs that is otherwise obscured" ("Recognizing Cognition," 623). Rather than making something strange familiar and thus apprehensible, defamiliarization presents an opportunity for one to recognize a pattern or structure that is otherwise unintelligible. The science fiction critic Carl Freedman writes, "The science-fictional world is not only one different in time or place from our own, but one whose chief interest is precisely the difference that such difference makes" (*Critical Theory and Science Fiction*, 43). The key here is not just the defamiliarization that a text can produce, but also the sense of that effect on the storyworld itself. In science fiction such effects might create storyworlds full of wonder or horror, yet in the post-apocalyptic mode defamiliarization most often arrives with the destruction of the recognizable world.

The literary critic Phillip Fisher identifies familiarization as the core cultural work of popular fiction. Examining tendencies in the nineteenth-century US historical novel, Fisher addresses the "hard facts" of the eradication of Native Americans in the work of James Fenimore Cooper, the emancipatory representational practice of Harriet Beecher Stowe's *Uncle Tom's Cabin* (1852), and the emergence of the individual and the economic in the city of Thomas Dreiser's naturalism. For Fisher, familiarization describes a "making familiar or making ordinary [that] is the radical 'work' done by popular forms" (*Hard Facts*, 19).[14] Fisher calls this process "a psychological rehearsal that creates an ordered resignation that lets a group 'face' . . . a future that they have already chosen and set in motion, but have not yet morally or psychologically passed through" (ibid., 18). To even provisionally accept this characterization of the fundamental function or desire of popular fiction is to also suggest a model for thinking about the historicity of such forms. If popular fiction fundamentally works toward familiarizing, then whole sets of generic conventions that appear in retrospect to be reactionary could be understood as doing crucial cultural work, such as making a changing world intelligible. Like the nineteenth-century US historical novel, the post-apocalyptic novel provides a way for readers to imagine how historical change takes place.[15] Yet the post-apocalyptic novel does not prepare the reader for actual circumstance, imagining instead future scenarios. What makes the post-apocalyptic mode difficult to situate generically is that it is caught between the science fiction described by Freedman and the historical novel described by Fisher: it offers a grounded explanation of how the characters find themselves in their current situation and such events to a wrecked future. Like massive stellar bodies, familiarization and defamiliarization distort the post-apocalyptic mode through their sheer gravitational force. The symbolic logic of the post-apocalyptic mode gains force as more stories, referents, and interpretations are added to it. In this way, the mode is formed through the virtuality of potential future disasters.

In what follows I turn to two instances of future reduction: Sherri S. Tepper's defamiliarization of feudal eugenics in *The Gate to Women's Country* (first published in 1988) and Stephen King's familiarization of partisan political deadlock in *The Stand* (first published in 1978; the unabridged version was published in 1990). Jameson identifies a mid-1970s crisis in New Wave science fiction, which "leaves the field divided into feminist SF on the one hand and a regressive resurgence of 'fantasy' on the other" ("Towards a New Awareness of Genre," 323). This rift shook post-apocalyptic writing as well. My argument will not be that feminist post-apocalyptic writing presents rich futures, while post-apocalyptic writing based on regressive fantasy offers reduced ones. Rather, I compare the reduced futures of *The Gate to Women's Country* as a feminist *détournement* within the post-apocalyptic mode and *The Stand* as an intensification of the mode's reactionary swing. Both present reduced futures, though they each subtracts different storyworld elements to get there.

A RIFT BETWEEN FUTURES

Following more than two decades of feminist utopian writing, Tepper sets *The Gate to Women's Country* after a nuclear war once city-states have been formed.[16] Neofeudal and secretly matriarchal in orientation, the novel separates the male population into castes: the warriors, who live outside the cities, and the servitors, who live with the women in the city. A number of festivals mark the passage of the year, including a ritual of sexual encounter between the women of the town and the warriors. In this way, the mode of production seems to have regressed to feudalism. The complexity of the storyworld matches the scope of a fantasy novel that keeps its characters close to town (why would they need to go elsewhere?). This regression also subtracts the weapons of modern warfare, transport vehicles, agricultural practices, and city living, replacing them with swords and shields, horses, farmland worked by human muscles, and the small village centered on the market square. Art too has changed. The protagonist, Stavia, participates in a staging of Euripides's *The Trojan Women* (415 BC), as forms of drama and theater become ascendant once more (though notably the novel turns to Greek tragedy, rather than some imagined future dramatic form). The future in *The Gate to Women's Country* has been reduced to a tempered and hyperlocalized medieval setting.

While the novel starts by presenting a feudal world, it reveals that some technologies remain in secret. The festivals, initially presented as a mating ritual, are later revealed to be a complex ruse: through a complicated birth-control mechanism, the enclave of women who secretly rule the women's country have been selectively breeding to genetically eliminate masculine aggression.[17] They are not really procreating with the warriors. Instead, the women use birth control to prevent insemination during festival times. They then use advanced techniques of artificial insemination to reproduce the more placid (read: evolved) sperm-donor servitors and propagate a nonviolent masculinity. In effect, they are breeding the warrior gene out of the population. In *The Gate to Women's Country*, the complexities of modern life are filtered through quasi-feudal city-states that rely on a eugenics program disguised as ritual. The potential for human evolutionary development is literally being reduced to curb masculine aggression.

In Tepper's novel, the rising action of the plot takes places as the protagonist and one of the aggressively masculine warriors are captured in an irradiated wilderness by the patriarchal fundamentalist group known as the holylanders. The novel does more than simply portray this group as a threat to the main characters: it shifts its focus to present the world from the holylanders' point of view as characters facing the same irradiated world as the pair from Women's Country. This revelatory sequence makes Tepper's novel apocalyptic in Berger's third sense of the word. By offering a sense of the thoughts of this community, the novel makes the case that patriarchy has its own built-in form of eugenics. For instance, Elder Resolution Brome spends several pages thinking through his family relations. Here, the women have names such as Plentitude, Restitution, and Chastity. Brome also thinks to himself, "Damn Sushannah anyhow. . . . Any other wife a man could do his duty on for most of a year if he was minded to without her getting pregnant. It was like she did it to vex him" (Tepper, *The Gate to Women's Country*, 205). Note Brome's twisted logic. Duty connotes the propagation of the species, yet in a metaphorical slippage Brome uses "duty" as an aphorism for sexual activity, indicating that he would not impregnate his partner.[18] Here, the novel's shift in narrative focus from Stavia to Brome presents a point of comparison that connects the top-down policing of gender by Women's Country with that of the holylanders and justifies the compassionate, future-oriented form of reproductive policy in Women's Country. Moreover, in Women's Country, duty and pleasure are separated: festivals are for fornicating, and insemination happens artificially. The women and the warriors are divided, yet united, internally—threatened by outsiders with a vastly different post-apocalyptic worldview.

The Gate to Women's Country's orientation to particular ideas of feminism, futurity, and utopia is clear. Not all feminist post-apocalyptic storytelling relies on misconstrued genetic assumptions, but the fact the Tepper's novel does provides a clear instance of the contested politics of the post-apocalyptic mode. It is not just about Wolfe's "natural aristocracy." That version of its politics can be resisted—and is, by writers such as Tepper. Tepper's book exemplifies a reduced future in two crucial ways. First, it shows how a future might be selectively pruned, at the level of the story. Second, it questions which futures are properly post-apocalyptic, at the level of the mode. The conflict at the level of the plot resonates with the conflict at the level of cultural production: the men who dominate the field of science fiction publishing do not want to get out of the way. I return to this argument at the end of the chapter and develop it further in chapter 3.

Let us turn now from feminist science fiction to epic fantasy. In King's *The Stand*, a top-secret military-grade of the influenza virus is released from storage and kills more than 90 percent of the US population. The disease, a first step of apocalyptic reduction, merely sets the stage for what is to come. *The Stand* offers salvation to a complex set of characters, all of whom survive due to some form of destiny that simultaneously acts to divide them based on morality. Unlike Tepper, whose secret rulers of Women's Country make genetic decisions, King uses a supernatural device to explain characters' survival that comes down to the forces of two extrahistorical characters. These characters, Abigail Freemantle and Randal Flagg, inhabit different temporalities and may they even inhabit different planes of existence from the other characters. They exist in a larger spiritual world. Moreover, whether eventually siding with Flagg in Las Vegas or being drawn to Freemantle's cabin in a cornfield during their dreams and ending up in Boulder, Colorado, characters in *The Stand* make choices that develop with cosmic significance.

The Stand proceeds through the catastrophe of the disease, which prepares the United States to be the site of a battle between the forces of good and of evil. *The Stand* has only two sides.[19] The two camps ready themselves in contrasting ways for a second apocalyptic event as the political territory of the post-apocalyptic storyworld solidifies and the possibilities for the future are reduced. The open and empty landscape left by the disease is transformed into a terrain of conflict, full of epic significance. Each side of this conflict presents its own affective payoff for the reader. "Trashcan Man" starts massive fires across the United States, finding satisfaction in destroying the infrastructure of modernity. Other characters, such as Stu Redman and Glen Bateman, rebuild the American nation. In each instance, these characters seem to be building on the symbolic overtones of their remaindered collectives: the fixation with explosions and self-determination of the Las Vegas bad guys and the liberal democratic self-righteousness of the Boulder good guys. King does not frame his conflict along the gender (or even genetic) lines of Tepper's novel; instead, he draws a line between criminal pyromancers and political intellectuals, implying that after the end one can either have fun with no rules, or have fun trying to make the rules apply once more.

In *The Stand*, the apocalypse happens twice: first through the strain of the influenza virus developed by the US military and then through the final showdown between the opposing camps assembled around Freemantle and Flagg. The virus signifies as an apocalypse in Berger's sense, because it marks a historical transition from the new origin of the apocalyptic end to a middle temporality between the past and future. The agent of that transition is the disease, which also enables the exposition of the fictional storyworld: the narration follows the spread of the disease, describing the transformed storyworld it leaves in its wake. King employs the image of characters coughing as he weeds out the inconsequential. The first section of the book, "Captain Trips," has a revelatory function: peeling away most of the population of the United States leaves only handfuls of survivors in a form that is world building and world destroying all at once. The characters that remain are as complex as the descriptions of the gory massacre in the first third of the book. In contrast, the final section, "The Stand," closes the apocalyptic rupture and offers the revelation of a new beginning. In this way, *The Stand* structurally restores order by balancing its apocalyptic disorientation with a second apocalyptic revelation.

Compare the future reduction in Tepper's novel to that in King's. Characters in King's novel discuss disaster scenarios from other apocalyptic stories and, crucially, act on their knowledge of them. The world-destroying virus in *The Stand* transforms an image of the world, meaning that elements from the primary world, such as post-apocalyptic fiction, appear to be common knowledge. This kind of metacommentary also appears in other genres, as when characters in a horror flick insist that they stay together, saying, "haven't you seen a horror movie before?" In this manner, King too figures his characters as people of the world with particular knowledge applicable to the story they are living within. At one point, the widower Glen Bateman, while speaking with the former factory worker and gas station attendant Redman, even speculates about how they might expect society to be reformed:

> "There are two possibilities," Bateman said. "At least two that I see now. The first is that the babies may not be immune . . . [the second is] that we may finish the job of destroying our species ourselves. . . . Not right away, because we're all too scattered. But man is a gregarious, social animal, and eventually we'll get back

together, if only so we can tell each other stories about how we survived the great plague of 1990. Most of the societies that form are essentially primitive dictatorships run by little Caesars unless we're very lucky. A few may be enlightened, democratic communities, and I'll tell you exactly what the necessary requirement for that kind of society in the 1990s and early 2000s is going to be: a community with enough technical people in it to get the lights back on. . . . This isn't the aftermath of a nuclear war, with everything laid to waste. All the machinery is there, waiting for someone to come along . . . and start it up again."
(*The Stand*, 323)

Bateman's speculative musings set aside the first possibility that everyone will die, encapsulating what will animate the rest of the novel: two communities in the post-disease United States struggling for dominance. In a metafictional move, King's characters hypothesize about the version of the end of the world that they inhabit. Bateman points out that they are not in a postnuclear United States and that much of the nation's infrastructure is still intact, ready for the use of the survivors, although by the novel's end they will be postnuclear. Unlike Tepper's novel, King's presents itself neutrally—it does not seem to stand for any particular cause, despite its title. A closer look at its world-building strategies finds a carefully developed politics. Both novels subtract elements from the real world to produce a story-world, but they have different goals: Tepper raises ethical questions about eugenics for feminists, while King unfolds a conflict of epic proportions without a clear political message beyond some vague comparison between anarchy and bureaucracy, each of which has its own malfunctions and destructive tendencies.

This rift within King's novel can be situated historically in the wake of the actual radical movements of the 1960s and the economic crises of the 1970s—movements to which Tepper and other science fiction authors respond. In *Danse Macabre*, King describes the period in the United States during which he wrote *The Stand*:

> Its writing came during a particularly troubled period for the world in general and America in particular; we were suffering from our first gas pains in history, we just witnessed the sorry end

of the Nixon administration and the first presidential resignation in history, we had been resoundingly defeated in Southeast Asia, and we were grappling with a host of domestic problems, from the troubling question of abortion-on-demand to an inflation rate that was beginning to spiral upward in a positively scary way. (*Danse Macbre*, 372)

While extratextual, these comments isolate a desire deep in the heart of the post-apocalyptic mode: to reproduce the pre-apocalyptic present both in the real world and in the storyworld. A number of traces from the social and historical context of its composition mark *The Stand*, seeming to shape the aims of the novel. The epic-fantasy tropes that King's novel takes on are no mistake. King writes, "For a long time—ten years, at least—I had wanted to write a fantasy epic like *The Lord of the Rings*, only with an American setting" ("Stand"). Where Tepper opted to follow the path of the feminist utopias of Ursula K. Le Guin, Marge Piercy, and Joanna Russ, *The Stand* draws on a genre with clear delineations of good and evil and forces most of its characters to fall in line with one or the other. Its bricolage of a *60 Minutes* segment on biological warfare, the movie *Rage* (directed by George C. Scott), J.R.R. Tolkien's *The Lord of the Rings* (1954–55), and post-apocalyptic tropes and settings is synchronized with the Cold War competition of two dominant ideologies.[20]

The Stand reveals that what appears in the text and what remains conspicuously absent are central to future reduction in the post-apocalyptic novel. In the novel, the two opposed factions intentionally congregate along either side of the divide, meeting along the way to either Flagg or Freemantle. The novel relies on these two factions' moving toward collectivity and mutual aid—in the effort to either restore order or seek out weapons stockpiles and cause havoc. The world-building process in the novel is one of subtraction and concentration: those susceptible to "Captain Trips" are killed off, and then the remainders are divided into two camps. Harold Lauder and Nadine Cross are exceptions to this rule. They betray Freemantle's coalition in Boulder just as it attempts to restore democracy to the United States. Such a betrayal marks the absence of any neutral ground on which the two groups could resolve the opposition of their aims. The storyworld is built on a foundation of conflict, not cooperation. In a sense, King's novel forecasts the uncertain future of a liberal state threatened by the forces of destruction. When Lauder and Cross plant a bomb to kill some of Boulder's leaders, they appear to be a force beyond the residual process of democracy. Instead, they should be treated as constitutive of the fictional re-formation of the United States. Unlike Tepper's use of future reduction to portray a unified, if eugenic, feminist struggle, King's produces characters who do not have anything to stand for besides some vague ideas about politics. What the novel reveals is that the two factions are deeply related and even rely on the existence of the other to function, despite appearances to the contrary. Though it was reissued in 1990, *The Stand* suffers from being a loose Cold War allegory through and through. Written in the mid-1970s, King's novel is legible as a formal resolution of Cold War anxieties, where two forces at loggerheads can finally duke it out (with just one nuclear bomb). The novel simultaneously clings to a way of imagining the future from the postwar period. While this makes it a good indicator of its history, its imagined future also indexes the reactionary character of the post-apocalyptic mode as one that reduces future possibility.

The Gate to Women's Country treats a different historical understanding through its reduced future. In Tepper's novel, unlike in King's, multiple outposts exist: the story told in the novel is of Marthastown, but other towns exist on the horizon. Each has its own garrison of men, and each is playing its own long game for a future beyond aggression and violence. Where King's world destruction acts as a filter that eliminates more than 90 percent of the US population, Tepper's world destruction presents the opportunity to establish and test a political hypothesis: it reduces its future to a matter of eugenic politics. This comparison reveals what Wolfe described as an opportunity for heroic action. Each novel projects the image of a reduced future, yet the ways they do so are crucially distinct. Where King imagines a face-off between the forces of democracy and anarchy recoded in the cadence of the epic mode as good and evil, Tepper presents a compelling image of post-apocalyptic conflict. *The Gate to Women's Country* symbolizes the field of post-apocalyptic writing—indeed, of science fiction writing—in the mid-1980s: the women and servitors represent feminist authors and their allies, and the warriors outside the gates are the authors of so-called hard science fiction such as space operas and romantic adventures. The component of the comparison that makes it work is Tepper's inclusion of the religious community—a remainder of the apocalyptic tradition, yet also a viable threat within the storyworld and beyond. This reconsideration of Tepper's novel offers a glimpse at the potential of the post-apocalyptic mode to clarify, even as it reduces, future possibility. In this way, what *The Gate to Women's Country* leaves out on a representational level, it reclaims on a symbolic one: the cultural dominance of one version of the end of the world, or of what the future might look like, is politically contested. Just as any apocalyptic vision must compete for believers, post-apocalyptic writing must compete for readers.

So far, I have approached the archive of post-apocalyptic texts from a literary standpoint, outlining the core moves of the post-apocalyptic mode. In this chapter, I built on that foundation to posit world destroying and future reduction as the core logics emerging from the use of post-apocalyptic tropes. In chapter 3, I take another conceptual step back from the archive to consider these texts as material commodities produced in the shifting conditions of twentieth-century publishing. With these shifts in abstraction in mind, I move from narrative and storyworld remainders to consider post-apocalyptic mode in terms of remaindered books.

3
Remaindered Books

> *Laboriously, he scooped up a handful of books; first one and then another was tossed into Allen's lap. "A bunch more of them. Novels of the twentieth century. All gone, now. Banned. Burned. Destroyed."*
> —PHILIP K. DICK, *The Man Who Japed*

As Allen Purcell stepped out of his transport, "The ash sank under his feet; it was like standing on mush. The ash was complicated, a mixture of organic compounds. A fusion of people and their possessions into a gray-black blur." (Dick, *The Man Who Japed*, 62). In scenes such as this one, Philip K. Dick's *The Man Who Japed* (first published in 1956) establishes the residual character of life in the wake of a world-destroying event. This scene is framed by Purcell's visceral encounter with postnuclear remainders: a "fusion" of objects and people. The narrator adds that "during the postwar years the ash had made good mortar" (ibid.). Here the remainders of nuclear holocaust have been put to work in rebuilding destroyed buildings. The destructive event took place in the distant past, but signs of its occurrence still surround the characters. The novel is set in 2114, nearly 150 years after the war. The reigning government is known as Moral Reclamation (Morec, for short).[1] In the scene described above, Purcell illegally visits some old friends in Hokkaido, Japan.[2] Dick adds to his framing of remainders with the bricks made of postnuclear ash, writing about "a litter of books, furniture, paintings, cans and boxes and jars of food, carpets and bric-a-brac and just plain junk" (ibid., 63).

Purcell tries to buy a vase. Tom Gates, a trader in rubbish and bric-a-brac, says, "Three bucks.... We've got to move this stuff. Fast turn-over, assure profit.... What do you want? Bottle of Berringer's Chablis? One thousand dollars. Copy of *The Decameron*? Two thousand dollars" (ibid.). The title fetching one of the highest prices is none other than James Joyce's *Ulysses*, a book Gates describes as "not bad" by an author he describes as "excellent" (ibid., 65). It seems that such books from the fictional setting of the novel have retained their literary reputation and merit exorbitant prices.[3] Here, *The Man Who Japed* imagines the fate of cultural forms that no longer signify in the way they once did: for such forms, there is either a last-minute sale or the rubbish heap.

The vision of books in post-apocalyptic writing—items that have become useless, sodden, and illegible—has carried on into the twenty-first century. Cormac McCarthy vividly describes such an encounter with the ruins of codices: "Years later he'd stood in the charred ruins of a library where blackened books lay in pools of water. Shelves tipped over" (*The Road*, 187).[4] These books have been rendered doubly useless: in the aftermath of the event, the elements have left the books rotten beyond reading, and the reshaping of the world has turned any text that survives into a false account of the present. In a metafictional gesture, such post-apocalyptic novels imagine their own unexpected fates. They look to a world where the circulation of knowledge could become restricted, people may not be able to read or may not want to, or books may be destroyed.[5] Unlike other post-apocalyptic libraries—such as the fantastic project in M. K. Wren's *A Gift on the Shore* (1990), when after a catastrophe two women seek to build a massive collection of surviving books—the immolated library found in *The Road* hints at the sheer futility of any kind of knowledge preservation.

In 1956, Dick imagines *The Decameron* and *Ulysses* to be the re-mainders of the long arch of modernity in a humorless world, yet by 2006, they have come to represent actual remaindered books (publishers mark remaining copies of books that have sold poorly to be liquidated at greatly reduced prices and eventually destroyed). Today, remaindered books do not fetch what Gates's *Ulysses* or *The Decameron* might—a title's longevity will certainly prove its worth to its publisher. A crucial difference separates Dick's novel from McCarthy's. Yes, both imagine the destruction of books and the reduction of people's capacity to read them, but *The Man Who Japed* and *The Road* have had very different fates as books. First published in the Ace Doubles series in 1956, *The Man Who Japed* was rereleased by Ace in 1975, published in London by Eyre Methuen (now owned by Penguin) in 1978, and reprinted in 2002 by Vintage Books and 2012 by Mariner Books. Because of Dick's status as a science fiction author, *The Man Who Japed* has almost become a literary classic. *The Road*, first published by Vintage Books in 2006, has remained in print, with many new editions released in the past decade.[6] Unlike Dick, McCarthy has been able to witness the success of his book.[7]

What happened between these two moments? The literary critic Dan Sinykin traces McCarthy's success to his hybridization of literary and genre fiction that aims to "marry literary fiction's symbolic capital with genre fiction's financial capital," adding that such titles "want to be prizewinners *and* best sellers" ("The Conglomerate Era," 478).[8] Dick and McCarthy both wrote genre fiction as a livelihood, but the conditions in which they operated differ dramatically. The cultural studies scholar Frederick Buell described this development in the post-apocalyptic mode as a shift from the "margins" to the "mainstream," arguing that in the early twenty-first century, post-apocalypse has become "an eminently saleable and easily-packaged setting for action-adventure, soap-opera serials, romances, even young adult and children's fiction" ("Post-Apocalypse," 9 and 10). Buell adds that the "scenarios of post-apocalyptic fictions are designed to interest, not awaken" (ibid., 10). In this light, remainders might be thought of emerging from the tricky negotiation between authors, agents, presses, bookstores, and readers as those tropes, characters, plots, and settings that get taken up in highly successful titles (remainders) and as those titles are doomed to the fate of Dick's junk sellers or McCarthy's sodden library (remaindered books).

Since the early twenty-first century, post-apocalyptic works have flooded the market. In 2017 alone, at least seventy titles were published with the Book Industry Study Group's subject heading "Fiction / Science Fiction / Apocalyptic & Post-Apocalyptic."[9] Some of these were reissues of previously published works, including Octavia E. Butler's Earthseed books and Ward Moore's *Lot and Lot's Daughter*. Some others were self-published. The remaining fifty titles were published by a variety of presses, largely in the United States. While certain titles stand out, such as Anne Corlett's *The Space between the Stars*, Omar El Akkad's *American War*, N. K. Jemisin's *The Stone Sky*, and Jeff VanderMeer's *Borne*, many will reach only a niche audience. The media scholar Stephen Joyce ties the twenty-first-century "surge of post-apocalyptic novels" to "transformations in publishing" ("Convergence Publishing and Prestige Niches," 123). On Joyce's account, the publishing industry is currently undergoing "turmoil as its business model crumbles," accompanied by "a boom in genre fiction at the expense of literary fiction." Sinykin tracks another important transformation into the twenty-first century: the conglomeration of publishers into the big five.[10] Joyce corroborates Sinykin's and my suspicions: "publishers have become more risk averse," which has had two consequences—"a pursuit of blockbuster hits and investment in reliable genres" (ibid., 125). According to Joyce, such conditions establish a solid audience for the post-apocalyptic novel, a form whose popularity has attracted the likes of Colson Whitehead and Emily St. John Mandel to the mode.[11] Yet as big-name literary writers work the post-apocalyptic mode to produce salable titles, many other titles are published and then ignored by most readers. At the other end of the spectrum, the rise of digital- and self-publishing has opened the door for many aspiring post-apocalyptic authors. Either way, post-apocalyptic enthusiasts today face piles of books remaindered by a publishing industry that is adapting to a growing market.

As I have argued above, the tropes that became the foundation for the post-apocalyptic mode emerged in the 1950s. The rift between Sheri Tepper's and Stephen King's post-apocalyptic futures in the previous chapter tells only part of the story. In what follows, I track the shifts in genre publishing from Dick's moment to McCarthy's: in the 1960s, a new wave of midlist science fiction authors crests; in the 1970s, publishers and publishing change along with the urban geography; in the 1980s, a legal case produces a remaindered books crisis, and publishers reduce the number of their midlist authors; in the 1990s, mass markets emerge, and publishers seek best-selling authors; and in the 2000s, self-publishing authors and literary writers both turn to writing in the post-apocalyptic mode. Each step highlights the cultural process of the remainder, serving to display the post-apocalyptic material transactions that subtend narrative ones. Remainders and remaindered books are formed in worlds of mismanaged plenty and become clearly legible in retrospect.

MIDLIST PUBLISHING

Over a decade, Dick published five novels that involve nuclear catastrophe: *The Man Who Japed* (1956), *The World Jones Made* (1956), *Vulcan's Hammer* (1960), *The Penultimate Truth* (1964), and *Dr. Bloodmoney, or How We Got Along after the Bomb* (1965).[12] Four of them were published by Ace Books, while *The Penultimate Truth* was published by Belmont.[13] Founded in 1952, Ace Books started publishing Dick's work in 1955. Ace supported emerging science fiction authors whose reliable sales and chance to build name recognition might ensure the publisher steady revenue, even if its books could not compare with best sellers and more widely popular texts. Midlist authors were to become a reliably steady source of income for presses.[14] Though they would not produce enormous profits for their publishers or themselves, their books would sell consistently. They might also achieve name recognition, and in that case, one of their books might do fairly well in the course of its lifetime, as long as the press was able to keep it in print. Because of the niche interests of the science fiction readership, several of the authors writing books for Ace in 1950s became its midlist authors. Repeat customers wanted similar experiences.

Several of Dick's post–nuclear holocaust titles were released in the Ace Doubles series, which paired in one volume two short novels by different authors. *The Man Who Japed*, for instance, was published with E. C. Tubb's *The Space-Born*.[15] Putting two titles together meant that readers got more value for their money, and in this way, Ace could hedge its bets on a single title. Furthermore, "selling two titles together dimin[i]shed the risk associated with publishing new authors or genres whose success with Ace's audience had not yet been proven" (Fulton, "Donald A. Wollheim's Authoritative Universe," 367). In this way, Ace Doubles introduced readers familiar with one author to the work of another. This ploy was designed to increase the number of recognized authors in the Ace catalogue.

In 1968 Ace introduced the Ace Science Fiction Specials series, which also sought to introduce science fiction readers to new authors.[16] Terry Carr, the editor of the series, included in it new novels or reissues of particularly good older works. The idea was to give exposure to the works of authors who were not unknown, but whose books had not yet become best sellers. The series bolstered sales and gave emerging authors a chance at reaching a larger audience. The Ace Double series included titles such as the first edition of Ursula K. Le Guin's *The Left Hand of Darkness* (1969), which won both the Hugo and the Nebula Awards; a reissue of Alexei Panshin's *Rite of Passage* (1969), which had also won the Nebula Award; Joanna Russ's *And Chaos Died* (1970); a reissue of Le Guin's *A Wizard of Earthsea* (1970); and John Brunner's *The Traveler in Black* (1971).[17] Some of these works, such as Le Guin's titles, are still in print today. Whereas the Ace Double series sold two novels bound together for 35 or 40 cents, the Ace Science Fiction Specials series sold titles (each of which had an introduction from Carr) for 60–95 cents.[18]

In 1962, Dick published *The Man in the High Castle* with G. P. Putnam's Sons, which would acquire Ace Books in 1982.[19] In 1964, Ace published Dick's *Dr. Bloodmoney*. From this point on, Dick rarely returned to the post-nuclear holocaust setting. After *Dr. Bloodmoney*, he published several other titles with Ace, including *The Simulacra* (1964), *The Crack in Space* (1966), *The Ganymede Takeover* (1967), *The Preserving Machine* (1969, in the Ace Science Fiction Specials series), and *Our Friends from Frolix 8* (1970). Aside from a few other small presses, Dick published much of his work from the mid-1960s on with Doubleday, including the critically acclaimed and widely taught and adapted *Do Androids Dream of Electric Sheep?* in 1968.[20] In 1977, Dick published *A Scanner Darkly* with Doubleday.[21] By that time, the publishing industry had begun an apparent metamorphosis.

The appearance of new US publishers in the postwar years meant many more options for science fiction writers, such as Dick, who earned their living by selling their works. Dick was a prolific author in the 1960s and 1970s, publishing around two novels a year (Internet Speculative Fiction Database, "Summary Bibliography: Philip K. Dick"). Dick's work moved from items in the Ace Doubles series to stand-alone novels and from Ace to Doubleday, which might be read as indicating his or his works' growing success. However related to Dick's capacity or challenges, these shifts also signal the diversifying and maturing tastes of the publishing market. I do not mean to imagine the market in the abstract, but rather to see it as a concrete entity formed by relationships among authors, presses, booksellers, and readers.[22] Midlist authors emerged from the specific postwar market conditions. After the war, more people were seeking an education, which meant that more people were reading and, crucially, writing.[23] As R. E. Fulton claims, "Historians understand their subjects through categories—highbrow and lowbrow, literature and pulp—but no historical actor reads according to such categories. They read what appeals to them, and in the mid-twentieth century, paperbacks appealed to everyone" ("Donald A. Wollheim's Authoritative Universe," 350). In this context, writers who had previously struggled to be published found success bound up in the form of the paperback.

Along with science fiction, post-apocalyptic writing was an ideal niche for the midlist author in the decades following World War II.[24] However, in the 1970s, midlist genre authors faced new challenges. For example, in 1974 Suzy McKee Charnas published *Walk to the End of the World* with Ballantine Books.[25] Ballantine had been founded in 1952 by Ian and Betty Ballantine and was acquired by Random House in 1973. Though *Walk to the End of the World* was a finalist for the John W. Campbell Award for best first science fiction paperback of 1974 and such notoriety made it a valuable addition to the Random House imprint, Charnas had great difficulty getting her second book published. *Motherlines* was the next installment in the Holdfast Cycle—a title that ought to attract readers' attention. However, concerned with the book's marketability because it had only female characters, Ballantine refused to publish *Motherlines*.[26] It took Charnas a year to find a publisher—Berkley/Putnam—for the book, which was slow for the 1970s when the market was quite hot and most books were initially published as paperbacks.[27] The challenges Charnas faced in placing *Motherlines* can be traced to Ballantine's fate as an imprint of Random House. Larger publishing houses were often more conservative and thus hesitant to publish titles that were radical departures from narrative norms and, according to the publishers, less likely to do well in the market. The reasons for this conservative carefulness might include the changes at that time in the way readers were discovering and purchasing books in the United States. Following the boom of suburbanization and the automobile's becoming the principal mode of transportation for middle-class American families in the

1960s, booksellers began opening stores in US malls. Such stores appealed to a different clientele than bookshops in urban centers did. The mall stores offered easy access to best sellers and sought to draw shoppers in to browse and buy. Charnas's work emerged as the 1970s wave of feminist science fiction was cresting; *Motherlines* might not have faced such difficulties if it had been proposed a year or two earlier.

In the 1980s and 1990s, retailers brought about a vicious cutback in the sales of midlist novels that fell under the headings of science fiction and fantasy. In 1989, Charles Platt published a piece in the science fiction magazine *Interzone* titled "The Vanishing Midlist." He lamented the gulf that separated emerging authors from big names—which deepened the divide between struggling and established career authors. In the 1960s, according to Platt, American midlist science fiction novels typically sold in the range of 20,000–40,000 paperback copies. Yet in the late 1980s, though publishers did not release their figures to Platt, he guessed that "they typically print around 30,000 copies of which perhaps 15,000 are actually sold" ("The Vanishing Midlist," 49). Though much of Platt's piece is anecdotal and speculative, this guess of his is not far off from how publishers and retailers were and are handling books that would not sell.

In an article on the rise of corporate publishing, the cultural materialist Sarah Brouillette explains the decline in midlist offerings (which largely consisted of feminist science fiction, such as Charnas's) by offering the example of the Return to Nevèrÿon series by the science fiction writer and critic Samuel R. Delany: "Major bookstore chains were thought to have played an important role in suppressing the third and fourth books in the series, on the basis of their homoerotic content" ("Corporate Publishing and Canonization," 191).[28] Here, the relationship between bookstores and publishers overshadows the one between readers and books, as readers' imagined reactions affected which manuscripts a press would publish.

In 1979, Bantam had published the *Tales of Nevèrijon* as a paperback, which sold a quarter of a million copies.[29] Bantam was acquired by Bertelsmann in 1980. The 1983 sequel, *Neveryóna or: The Tale of Signs and Cities*, also sold very well. Yet in 1985 Bantam reduced the print run for the third volume in the series, *Flight from Nevèrijon*, to seventy-thousand copies. In light of the content, Barnes and Noble—a major distributor—opted to order only five thousand copies of *Flight* and to carry it only in a handful of East Coast stores. Given that, Bantam could not justify a larger print run. And it refused to publish Delany's subsequent book, *The Bridge of Lost Desire*. Brouillette writes, "When Delany then took the book to Tor Books, their interest in the novel was also undermined by bookstore intervention," adding that "B. Dalton and Waldenbooks [both mall chain stores], then the two largest bookstore chains in America, are said to have refused to carry any novel Delany had written" ("Corporate Publishing and Canonization," 192). Delany published the book with Arbor House in 1987 and then with St. Martin's Press in 1988 and Grafton in the United Kingdom in 1989 as *Return to Nevèrÿon*.[30] The fate of the work of Delany, a midlist author, was substantially affected by retailers' assessments about what might sell and what might not. Though speculative, this bias increased retailer pushback against the perceived risk of particular titles. As midlist authors such as Delany faced retailers' disapprobation, the market sought to replace their works with fare that appeared to be more acceptable (read: salable). The 1980s saw a resurgence of post-apocalyptic titles, notably published by emerging science fiction presses, and this development entrenched the regulation of content, as in the case of Delany, and promoted the return of niche publishing strategies. In this instance, the attack had not been on the midlist but on black, feminist, and queer authors and content that, once purged from the larger presses and booksellers, meant a new set of largely white, male midlist authors could be encouraged.

In the early 1980s, during the time of retailer pushback against midlist science fiction authors, Carr decided to revive his series as the New Ace Science Fiction Specials, which had run from 1968 to 1971 and again in the mid-1970s. The revived series began publication in 1984 with five novels, including William Gibson's cyberpunk novel *Neuromancer* (which won the Nebula and Hugo Awards) and Kim Stanley Robinson's *The Wild Shore*—a post-apocalyptic tale about an irradiated Orange County, California. In his introduction to *Neuromancer*, Carr explicitly looks back to the heyday of New Wave science fiction:

> In the early seventies science fiction was an exciting field: quality science fiction novels appeared from many publishers, they sold

very well, and science fiction moved toward the front of literary achievement. It was reviewed in the *New York Times* and analyzed by academic critics; major universities offered courses studying science fiction. It seemed science fiction had become respectable. (Carr, "Introduction to *Neuromancer*," vii)

Looking to the buzz of activity around science fiction in the 1970s for inspiration, Carr's New Ace Science Fiction Specials series attempted to reinvigorate science fiction publishing in the face of the vanishing midlist and the ongoing conglomeration of book retail markets. He wrote introductions for seven of the twelve titles in the new series.[31] Despite this attempt, Platt describes the end of the New Ace Science Fiction Specials series, suggesting that Ace Books "let the 'specials' lapse" because the series was not "cost effective" ("The Vanishing Midlist," 72). Once a champion of novelists such as Le Guin and Russ, this series participated in filling the midlist range of the book market with emerging cyberpunk and post-apocalyptic titles and introduced two new authors who would become highly regarded and widely read.

The field of publishing in the 1980s contains the kernel of the field's characteristics today: conglomerated, competitive, and hybrid. Two novels featuring an Earth ever changed by a passing comet were published: Larry Niven and Jerry Pournelle's *Lucifer's Hammer* (Del Rey, 1977) and Fredrik Pohl and Jack Williamson's *Land's End* (Tor, 1988).[32] Doubleday published Butler's continuation of the patternist series *Wild Seed* in 1980, but the next installment, *Clay's Arc*, was published by St. Martin's Press in 1984 (St. Martin's also reprinted Delany's *The Bridge of Lost Desire*). Doubleday also published *The Gate to Women's Country* in 1988. Science fiction imprints tended to publish more than one post-apocalyptic title in the 1980s: Ace published two post-apocalyptic titles, Steven R. Boyett's *Ariel* (1983) and Robinson's *The Wild Shore* (1984). Ballantine published Paul O. Williams's *The Fall of the Shell* (1982); a rerelease of Sterling E. Lanier's *Hiero's Journey* (1983; first published by Chilton in 1973); Lanier's prequel, *The Unforsaken Hiero* (1983); and Mitch Berman's *Time Capsule* (1988). Bantam published David R. Palmer's *Emergence* (1984) and David Brin's *The Postman* (1985) and rereleased Tepper's *The Gate to Women's Country* (1989; first published by Doubleday in 1988).

Arbor House, an independent press, published the science fiction author Greg Bear's 1985 *Blood Music* and would go on to publish Delany's *The Bridge of Lost Desire*. Warner Books published Butler's Xenogenesis trilogy.[33] Warner also published Robert Silverberg's *At Winter's End* in 1988. Silverberg's *The Queen of Springtime* was published by Victor Gollancz in 1989. Putnam, released Frank Herbert's *The White Plague* in 1982 and William Prochnau's *Trinity's Child* in 1983. Meanwhile, some presses published only one post-apocalyptic title in the 1980s.[34] Finally, some now well-known authors released post-apocalyptic titles during the decade: Paul Auster, Le Guin, and Kurt Vonnegut Jr.[35] That is thirty-four titles (and I certainly could have missed some) published by presses that specialized in everything from literary to science fiction and operated either as an imprint for a larger house or as independent publishers. When we look at this list of post-apocalyptic titles, two strains emerge: those that became midlist titles or even best sellers and those that did not sell—those that would be remaindered.

BEST SELLERS AND MASS PUBLISHING

As midlist titles recede, sales are consolidated among fewer authors, with some selling millions of books. The publishing market leads retailers and presses to look for authors who will pen salable books, and at the same time the number of post-apocalyptic titles being published increases annually. Best-selling titles are most often associated with regular lists of fiction and nonfiction that show which titles (some new, some old) have sold the most in a given period. A best-selling author's book might consistently sell better than a midlist title does. The requirements for certain lists may be strict or lax, and such varied practices mean that publishers tend to use the phrase "best seller" as they see fit. The shift in expectations here—from a qualifying fixed number to a relative assessment of a book's performance—indicates an intensifying of publishers' and booksellers' reliance on the market. As Fredric Jameson writes, "Everyone is now willing to mumble, as though it were an inconsequential concession . . . to public opinion[,] . . . that no society can function efficiently without the market and that planning is obviously impossible ("Postmodernism and the Market," 263). As with Jameson's indictment of belief in the necessity of the market as a paucity of the collective imagination, the phrase "best seller" comes to mean to consumers that a book is worth reading and to publishers that they should minimize risk and reject difficult books.[36]

Best-seller lists reveal much about the content of cultural production. Sinykin points out that "before 1980, the best seller lists included a mix of prestigious and popular fiction: William Faulkner beside Leon Uris; Saul Bellow beside Herman Wouk; Mary McCarthy beside Harold Robbins" ("The Conglomerate Era," 473). He pinpoints a change in the early 1980s, when "the best seller list suddenly becomes dominated by a small group of brand-name authors: Tom Clancy, Michael Crichton, John Grisham, Stephen King, Danielle Steel, and the like." King is the only author on this list to pen a post-apocalyptic novel. He earned his place as a best-selling author with his first novel *Carrie* (1973). In September 1979, Carol Lawson reported that *Carrie* had sold 4,000,000 copies, which she credited in part to the 1976 film based on the book. In comparison, she notes that King's fourth novel, *The Stand*, "had a short run on the hardcover bestseller list and sold 65,000 clothbound copies" ("Behind the Best Sellers"). In the 1980s, the best-seller lists included the same set of names over and over, which speaks to the shrinking midlist, the ongoing corporatization of publishing houses, and the increased use of fiction to sell books.

Doubleday published *The Stand* in 1978. In 1979 the book won the Locus award for best science fiction novel and was nominated for the Balrog and World Fantasy awards for best novel and the Gandalf prize for best book-length fantasy. It was nominated again for a Balrog award in 1980. It won Locus awards in 1987 (placing twenty-third on a list of all-time best fantasy novels), 1991 (second on a list of best horror or dark fantasy novels), and 1998 (twentieth on a list of all-time best fantasy novels published before 1990). In 1990, Doubleday released *The Stand: The Complete and Uncut Edition*, restoring some four hundred pages that had been cut from the original edition. In 1990, *The Stand* was a *Publisher's Weekly* best-selling novel, placing seventh on a list for the year.[37] The success of this novel continues: ABC produced an eight-part miniseries directed by Mike Garris in 1994, and CBS auspiciously completed filming a ten-part miniseries in March 2020 amid calls for lockdown, shelter in place, and quarantine due to the COVID-19 pandemic. According to *Vanity Fair*, "there will be no reference to the actual coronavirus" in the series (Breznican, "Exclusive"). As discussed in chapter 2, King's novel represents the tendency to tell politically limited stories in the post-apocalyptic mode, and its initial publication, accolades, and second release speak to the conservative tastes of post-apocalyptic fiction's readers. The showrunners wanted more of the same in both senses: repetition and expansion of the same story.

Alongside King's post-apocalyptic story emerge post-apocalyptic series that offer a related kind of more of the same: the post-apocalyptic mode has its share of series, publishing imprints, and even whole publishing houses dedicated to producing post-apocalyptic texts. For instance, James Axler authored the post-apocalyptic action-adventure Deathlands series, which began with *Pilgrimage to Hell* in 1986 and contained 125 books.[38] In the same year, Barnes and Noble purchased B. Dalton, a chain of mall bookstores, signaling a turning point in book selling. Mall stores were on the way out. With their big-box bookstores, Barnes and Noble introduced a new way to be a reader. In addition, the owners of big-box bookstores considered their establishments as entertainment destinations. With their large parking lots, big-box stores ensured ease of access for suburban shoppers, their extended hours catered to weeknight or weekend shoppers, and economies of scale enabled them to provide a breadth of selection and discounted best sellers that enabled them to undercut traditional booksellers and mall stores alike. These conditions were ripe for post-apocalyptic series, such as Axler's Deathlands series, to take off.

Axler's publisher was Gold Eagle Books, an imprint of Harlequin, which also holds the copyright on the name James Axler: in fact, the novels in this series were written by at least a dozen men (as may be clear by this point in the book, the post-apocalyptic genre has been dominated by men)—including Rik Hoskin and Laurence James, who have each written over thirty titles. Founded in 1949, Harlequin was purchased by Torstar Corporation in 1981. Traditionally a publisher of romance, Harlequin branched out in the late 1980s, creating the Gold Eagle Books imprint to publish action-adventure fiction. The *Los Angeles Times* reported that in 1987 Gold Eagle Books had shipped "500 million copies of titles in its five leading men's adventure series alone," and that as of July 29, 1988, there were sixteen publishers and sixty-six series of action-adventure romances, a classification that "represented 4.3 percent of sales for the U.S. paperback market" (Mehren, "Some Dare Call It Romance"). Gold Eagle's editorial director, Randall Toy, suggested that one common thread for readers was military service (ibid.). The fortunes of both the action-adventure and the post-apocalyptic genres waxed in early 2000s. However, in August 2014, Harper Collins purchased Harlequin and decided to discontinue Gold Eagle Books. The imprint published its final titles in 2015.[39]

Such a shift could be tied to the changing tastes of readers. One need only refer to the catalogue of novels published by Permuted Press, a publisher that had come relatively recently to the scene, to see the quantity of titles published by enthusiasts for a certain kind of apocalypse.[40] At the time of this writing, Permuted Press has published over 500 titles, with 290 in the apocalyptic, post-apocalyptic, and survival or horror-fiction categories. Specializing in post-apocalyptic and zombie fiction—its slogan is "Enjoy the Apocalypse"—its titles include Neil A. Cohen's *Welcome to Nuke Jersey* (2017) and Craig Martelle's End Times Alaska series. The press offers more than just fiction about the end of the world: it also published Deborah D. Moore's Journals series (2014–17) and *A Prepper's Cookbook: Twenty Years of Cooking in the Woods* (2016).[41] Roughly twenty-five Permuted Press titles have appeared on the *New York Times* best-seller list, according to the publisher's website (Permuted Press, "About"). Incidentally, Moore also has a blog on *survivalweekly.com* called "The Self-Reliant Woman" and reportedly runs a woman's group on Yahoo.com where she teaches preparedness. The complex relationships among niche authors, publishers, booksellers, and readers are part of the publishing market.

The post-apocalyptic mode, then, is part of what Rachel Malik describes as "relatively predictable networks" of "specialized popular fiction genres" ("Horizons of the Publishable," 729), yet with a crucial difference. The Permuted Press's website includes a curious comment along these lines: "In the ever changing literary world, particularly that of 'genre fiction' where Permuted Press has found much of its success, it is important to keep your finger on the pulse of the business. We feel that our constant analysis of industry trends, and our ability to act quickly on the data we gather, has been—and remains—a key component to our company's ongoing success" (Permuted Press, "About"). Overall, the post-apocalyptic mode uses niche books to entice readers, and it has done so in ways that have creatively adapted to changing conditions in the publishing market. For instance, members of the niche audience may be ready to support their ideological position by buying particular authors' books, such as titles in the best-selling Christian Left Behind series by Tim LaHaye and Jerry B. Jenkins. The series had four novels on the *Publisher's Weekly* best-seller list between 1999 and 2001, with several titles also on the *New York Times* best-seller list.[42] As of 2016, the series website claims that eighty million copies of books in the series have been sold ("Tim LaHaye"). Aside from *The Stand*, books in the series are the only post-apocalyptic titles to appear on the *Publisher's Weekly* best-seller list.

I have been discussing successful titles. Yet as the midlist vanished, another facet of contemporary publishing increased: remaindered books. Platt, who raised concerns about the science fiction midlist, also addressed this part of the publishing industry: unsold titles "are 'stripped'—that is, the retailer strips the cover off the unsold book, throws books away, and returns the cover to the publisher for credit" ("The Vanishing Midlist," 49). The next section opens with a discussion of a legal case that had a significant impact on independent and midlist publishers. The outcome of this case began to transform the ecology of book sales in the United States, making way for a start-up company to transform book sales using new forms of distribution and logistics.[43]

REMAINDERED BOOKS THEN

The fallout from the landmark case *Thor Power Tool Company v. Commissioner of Internal Revenue* had a major impact on book publishing and retail sales. In 1979 the US Supreme Court upheld the Internal Revenue Service (IRS) regulations that limited how taxpayers could record inventory. The story goes like this: Using multiple parts produced in house, Thor manufactured power tools. The company's accounting practice was to take a loss on the unused parts kept in inventory and to record them for accounting purposes. Thor effectively claimed the cost of the unused parts. But IRS regulations stipulated that this method could be used for tax purposes only if the taxpayer could demonstrate that the market price had been reduced or that the parts were somehow defective. The crucial question was whether companies could write down the cost of excess goods in inventory for the reason that they were not selling the goods. The Supreme Court ruled that they could not. The issue affected most of the retail industry at the time, which had benefited from the previous tax policy that allowed retailers to reduce the carrying cost of bulk orders and remain responsive to fluctuations in consumer demand. This context of publishing produced the condition that started to make something like Amazon's business model sensible for selling books.

The Supreme Court's ruling against Thor reduced the capacity of companies to maintain large inventories. The impact of the ruling on the publishing industry was as pervasive as it was uneven. The science fiction author Kevin O'Donnell Jr. did not miss the implication for small presses. In 1993, he describes how the Thor ruling deeply affected publishing: it "eliminated a tax dodge" and made it much more costly to carry inventory from year to year, which in turn led to reduced print runs; smaller inventories; and, far worse, an increased readiness to "dispose of inventory—i.e., pulp it—before the end of the fiscal year" ("How Thor Power Hammered Publishing"). O'Donnell notes that a decision to remove a book from a publisher's catalogue put even greater pressure on the publisher to replace the "steady (if small) income stream that book would have generated." He explains:

> The publisher must release not only the new title it would have published anyway, but a second new one, to make up for its lack of a backlist. This results in title proliferation, which itself promotes both lower advance orders on the part of major buyers and a higher return rate. That means writers must write more, and sell more often, in order to survive. (ibid.)

O'Donnell clearly singles out some serious consequences for publishing, particularly for small presses and midlist authors: Each subsequent book published has a shorter run, and more titles are published overall. The changes increase demand for titles, despite the fact that presses cannot afford to carry the stock necessary for a new book to build a reputation and sell over time. O'Donnell's choice of the metaphor of survival here is worth thinking through. Though authors' lives certainly did not depend on this ruling, their livelihood did. One way to understand the shift in publishing and retail that O'Donnell describes is to realize that US tax law now prohibits the publishing industry from holding stocks in reserve.

The aftermath of these changes had further consequences for publishing. The pressure on publishers to cut back on stock in their warehouses led to the growth of third-party companies that work with publishers under exclusive contracts to look after the transport, warehousing, and resale of "'hurt books' [books physically damaged in some way] and books that will not sell" (Mantell, "My One and Only," 16). These books are remaindered. Moreover, it has long been a practice in the publishing industry to buy stock that did not sell back from retailers—stock that would be remaindered. John B. Thompson's reports that "books are supplied to booksellers, retailers, and wholesalers on a sale-or-return basis, so that unsold stock can be returned to the publisher for full credit" (*Merchants of Culture*, 17–18).[44] Thompson also notes that this practice "marks it [publishing] out as somewhat unusual among retail sectors" (ibid., 18, fn. 13). Part and parcel of this dynamic is the rise of the bargain bookstore, which sells remaindered books at pennies on the dollar (Dahlin, "Plenty of Product," 42) and where people stand "shoulder to shoulder" to look over the "tables piled high with bargain, remainder and hurt books" (Nawotka, "Down Economy Pushes University Press Remainders," 8).[45] Success with a particular title at this level of the industry can be difficult for players with little capital on hand. According to Thompson, even when a book has good sales, presses are likely to receive large returns of unsold stock.[46] Even though the press still has to pay the printer, these returns are "credited to the retailer and deducted from their receivables by their distributor" (*Merchants of Culture*, 171). Small publishers may not have the cash flow to fund the publication of unproven titles after their midlist titles and bestsellers. Putting out new titles is a risky endeavor. Small presses are particularly challenged by the fact that book publishing is now only marginally profitable.

Starkly different from the works of midlist authors that emerged in the 1970s and 1980s, the mass-marketed, mass-produced titles from Gold Eagle and Permuted Press—not to mention the Left Behind series—evidence one response to the Thor decision: rely on genre and house names, just-in-time production, and readers' convictions to drive sales, avoid tax pitfalls, and keep from producing remaindered books. However well Axler's and LaHaye and Jenkins's books may have sold between the mid-1980s and early 2000s, anecdotally, each title I have picked up or seen has been at friends of the library book sales or in a used bookstore. No title is beyond the threat of becoming remaindered.

The economic and legal shortfall of the Thor decision would be solved by the rise of online retailers such as Amazon. With massive warehouses, purchasing power, and an interest in books, Amazon would transform the problem of remaindered books into a source of revenue. Amazon.com got its start in the 1990s, yet it was not until the 2000s that it began to turn steady profits. If retail chains seemed to provide the ultimate in breadth of selection and ease of shopping, Amazon.com took this development a step further by allowing shoppers to browse from home, boasting the widest selection of titles of any bookseller. Amazon.com's success pioneered now-ubiquitous approaches to the interface of online retail and the logistics of stock management and distribution, as well as a method for successful expansion into new markets.[47] "Books," because of "their relative physical uniformity, durability, and differentiated numerousness," were "the ideal commodity with which to venture into the new world of online commerce" (McGurl, "Everything and Less," 455). The rise of Amazon.com has been a boon for title availability, because it can afford to stock titles that other retailers cannot. Yet Amazon's rise to dominance does not mean the end of other ways of selling books.[48] Independent booksellers did not simply vanish, though the mall and big-box bookstores did make it more difficult for them to operate. However, as this brief account of the tumultuous world of book selling makes clear, such shifts in how people sell books are often followed by further upheavals.[49] Indeed, in many cases specialty bookstores have responded to the arrival of big-box stores and online venders by specializing, catering to readers looking for more obscure titles and particularly those that fall in the category of fantasy or science fiction. The next set of post-apocalyptic titles to achieve best-seller status would be those written not by genre writers or Christian authors but by recognized literary writers.

LITERARY WRITERS AND SELF-PUBLISHED AUTHORS

According to a bibliography of titles I produced, the number of US post-apocalyptic titles more than doubled between 2001 and 2014, which signals that genre publishing has contributed to the growth of markets for the book industry, even if those measures of growth

(1–2 percent of revenues) do not match the standards in other industries (Bellamy, "A Working Bibliography").[50] As Thompson points out, the market for publishing is essentially static (*Merchants of Culture*, 189). The literary critic Mark McGurl puts this claim in perspective by framing Amazon's current book sales: Amazon's sales from books shrunk dramatically from the mid-1990s to 2014, when book sales amounted to only 7 percent of its estimated $75 billion in yearly revenue. Yet, as McGurl suggests, "if books are now only a fraction of the business of Amazon, that fraction is no small part of the book business, accounting for roughly half of all US book purchases" ("Everything and Less," 448).

Though the post-apocalyptic mode was long the purview of genre authors alone, by the early 2000s authors of literary renown began publishing in it. Writing about Cormac McCarthy's *The Road*, Michael Chabon argues that the post-apocalyptic is one of the easiest modes of science fiction for mainstream authors to deploy because of its "hard-edged naturalism" ("Dark Adventure," 96). And literary critic Andrew Hoberek argues that *The Road* partakes of a "transition in parenthesis" ("Cormac McCarthy and the Aesthetics of Exhaustion," 486) as part of the undoing of a long disregard of genre by literary writers. Hoberek reads *The Road*'s position in the field of literary cultural production as being both a genre text (it is post-apocalyptic) and a literary one (it is a Pulitzer-prize-winning novel by a leading American literary author). According to Sinykin's account of the rise of publishing conglomerates, the adoption of a generic mode of storytelling is one of the ways literary writers respond to the book market's shift from fantasy and the western to the post-apocalyptic novel.[51] McGurl puts these arguments into context by turning to the way books circulate most ubiquitously today: paying attention to "the recent mass migration of otherwise 'literary' writers into the space of genre, one might go as far as to say that fiction in the Age of Amazon is genre fiction" ("Everything and Less," 460).

In each of these respects, McCarthy's *The Road* is a breakthrough novel. Though certainly not the first literary writer to adapt the post-apocalyptic mode, McCarthy was a forerunner of this tendency. One earlier example might be Margaret Atwood, whose first title in the MaddAddam trilogy was published by Doubleday in 2003. According to *Publishers Weekly*, *Oryx and Crake* and its sequel, *The Year of the Flood* (2009), "together sold close to 400,000 copies" ("This Week's Bestsellers").[52] After *The Road*, Doubleday (by then an imprint of Random House) published Colson Whitehead's *Zone One* in 2011, and Alfred A. Knopf (another imprint of Random House) published Peter Heller's *The Dog Stars* in 2012. Riverhead Books, a division of Penguin, published Chang-Rae Lee's *On Such a Full Sea* in 2014 and Claire Vaye Watkins's *Gold Fame Citrus* in 2015. These titles are easily classifiable as post-apocalyptic fiction. Atwood, Whitehead, Heller, Lee, and Watkins are not, strictly speaking, science-fiction authors, nor are they put off by the label of "genre." McGurl posits that genre fiction is crucial because it "implies an audience ready to be pleased again and again within the terms of an implicit contract," with the trope-savvy author able to achieve success as the result of the employment of durable genres ("Everything and Less," 460).

I will offer two examples of such genre acumen. First, in the same year that McCarthy published *The Road*, Max Brooks published *World War Z*. Second, five years later, Hugh Howey self-published his short story "Wool" (first published in 2011). Both imagine life in the wake of an apocalyptic event: a zombie war for Brooks and toxic blight for Howey. *World War Z* delivers serious, well-researched, zombie kitsch in the form of interview transcripts. It is a literary treatment of what is emphatically a genre fiction conceit: the dead have come back to life, and they are threatening the survival of humans. Brooks's novel is sensitive to political economy, but in an older mode. In telling the story of the global spread of a zombie threat, *World War Z* maps commodity circulation through the shadow economy of organ transplants.[53] To imagine how a zombie virus might spread, Brooks must come to terms with the way capital moves commodities around the planet. As it turns out, both virus and commodities flow freely. The author uses the post-apocalyptic mode to present the end of humanity's becoming coterminous with, if not an effect of, the end of capitalism. The spread of the apocalyptic disease cannot be imagined except as capital's circulation. The book's backward-looking narrative frame establishes that even a zombie-related economic crash cannot devastate the world market or wipe out the human species. Conversely, "Wool" follows a character as he prepares to venture outside the hundred-story subterranean silo where the remnant of Earth's human population has taken refuge. His mission: to clean the camera lenses through which humanity looks out on a world wasted by nuclear apocalypse. Both works rely on post-apocalyptic tropes, yet what distinguishes them is that *World War Z* tells a horizontal while "Wool" provides a vertical tale.[54] These two story shapes—flow and quarantine, network and isolation—do not exist separately in the real world, but they can be presented this way in fiction.

The publication history of these stories also distinguishes them. Brooks published *World War Z* with Three Rivers Press, an imprint of Crown Publishing Group, which is a subsidiary of Random House; Howey self-published "Wool." In 2013 *World War Z* would be released as a major motion picture directed by Marc Foster, and Hugh Howey would make a print-only distribution deal for his omnibus novel based on "Wool," subsequently selling the film rights in 2014. Brooks is a known entity: he is the son of the comedy director Mel Brooks. His decision to write a book about a zombie apocalypse and then sell the film rights positions him for success in the corner of the field of cultural production where the end-of-the-world story reigns. As a former bookstore clerk, Howey starts with no visibility in that same field, but he put his work out into the world, and it has met with resounding success.

Howey represents an interesting case of post-apocalyptic self-publishing. He first published *Wool* through Amazon's Kindle Direct Publishing system.[55] In 2014, he published an article on the website authorearnings.com titled "The 7k Report," wherein he showed that though Amazon had only published 4 percent of genre ebooks (in the categories of mystery or thriller, science fiction, fantasy, and romance), these titles account for an amazing 15 percent of the sales.[56] According to Thompson, 21,560 self-publishers had a registered ISBN in the United States in 2004, and self-publishers made up roughly 35 percent of the estimated active publishers in that year (*Merchants of Culture*, 153–54). Meanwhile, companies making $50,000,000 or more make up an estimated 0.8 percent of active publishers.[57] It may appear that self-publishing is the future, but that is the case only when we look at publishing in the aggregate, rather than from the perspective of a single publisher or author. These changes mean a great deal of revenue for Amazon and Kindle, but little for most self-published authors.

Amazon Publishing launched its seventh imprint, 47 North, in 2011 to publish works of speculative fiction. According to its website, the publisher does not accept unsolicited manuscripts (Amazon Publishing, "Work with Us"). Picked up by 47 North and reprinted in 2016, Meg Elison's *The Book of the Unnamed Midwife* was originally published in 2014 by Sybaritic Press and won the Philp K. Dick Award. The subsequent books in The Road to Nowhere series—*The Book of Etta* (2017) and *The Book of Flora* (2019)—were both published by 47 North.[58] In 2018 it published David Sosnowski's post-apocalyptic *Happy Doomsday*. Sosnowski is not a completely unknown entity, but this selection does seem curious.[59] *Happy Doomsday* does not seem to be doing well, which raises an interesting contrast to McGurl's assessment of Amazon's literary sway.[60] It seems that self-publishing authors, literary authors, best-selling authors, and science fiction writers have figured out how to put the post-apocalyptic mode to work, but why publish Sosnowski's book instead of any others?[61] Of course, one must remember that Amazon doesn't need to succeed with a single title, because it succeeds with all titles: it sells new, self-published, and remaindered books, and it is now working on publishing post-apocalyptic books.

At both ends of the publishing spectrum—literary titles and self-published titles—authors rely on the post-apocalyptic mode as a way of marketing and selling their work. Rather than constituting a post-apocalyptic future reduction or last-man trope, these authors participate in and build upon the tropes of the catalogue, community, and enclave. While the field of publishing post-apocalyptic works is overcrowded, these tropes begin to make sense of it by creatively dividing the field by genre, amount of recognition, and publishing platform. If anything, this approach encourages allegorical readings, such as Nick Levey's reading of Andy Weir's *The Martian* (2011) ("Post-Press Literature) or Jeremy Rosen's of Lee's *On Such a Full Sea* ("Introduction to Ecologies of Neoliberal Publishing"). For example, Rosen quotes an apt point made by Sarah Brouillette and David Thomas:

> if you leave the mediating factor of the nature of the production of culture out of your analysis, you risk leaving out some crucial dimensions of your object; that is, some crucial dimensions of the world-literary itself perhaps cannot be understood in the absence of analysis of the global production of literary works targeted at

selected readerships. ("First Responses," 511, quoted in Rosen, "Penguin Random House, Co-Opted Values, and Contemporary Cli-Fi")

There is much to unpack here. I want to focus on one point that Rosen makes in passing about Atwood's MaddAddam trilogy and Butler's Parables books. Both series "depict the disastrous consequences of neoliberal deregulation, privatization, and monopoly to the point where private contractors have replaced all functions that were once reserved for government entities," and "in these novels, few people read anymore, making the poems of the God's Gardeners and Lauren Olamina's Earthseed psalms another set of texts that are legible to us but impossible to circulate meaningfully within the novels' diegetic worlds" (Rosen, "Penguin Random House, Co-Opted Values, and Contemporary Cli-Fi"). Capable of cataloguing the degradation of the social good, such works show how, at both ends of the publishing spectrum, post-apocalyptic writing grasps its own theatrical role as that of the chorus: able to diagnose and critique, but seldom to intervene.

REMAINDERED BOOKS NOW

Book retailing changed dramatically between 1960 and 2000. During this time, science fiction publishing boomed and then faced unique cultural and legal threats. The way retailers and authors imagined what genre means also changed, as more literary authors started writing science fiction—with a few of them even calling it that. The emergence of big names in publishing (authors and presses alike) has recently been challenged and complemented by a growing number of self-publishing authors. The driving fantasy of post-apocalyptic scenarios (with off-the-grid living and do-it-yourself labor) is apparent in some authors' shift from press- and retailer-oriented publishing to self-publishing. Moreover, the fact that the history of self-publishing is in some ways merely part of a battle between giant publishing corporations, retailers, and distributers reveals the growing contradictions of post-apocalyptic fantasy: starting over with a clean slate involves the clearing away of what, or who, was there to begin with and always leaves behind some form of remainder, accountable or otherwise.

As described here, the field of publishing has become increasingly uneven, with massive publishing conglomerates on the one hand and small presses alongside self-publishing authors on the other hand. Publishers can profitably chase both best-seller and niche marketing in search of profits, acquiring recognizable authors at the same time as they diversify their catalogues and reduce costs through shorter print runs (or no print runs at all). Authors and presses alike face the pressures of the market, and self-publishing authors take the cost of doing business on themselves. Authors succeed based on the reach of their platform and size of their readership, rather than on the recognizability of their publisher's imprint—with the exception of Gold Eagle Books and Permuted Press, and despite the fact that Doubleday, for instance, publishes quite a number of post-apocalyptic titles. McGurl reads the late-twentieth-century shift in publishing as part of the "result of a large-scale transformation of industrial relations of production into postindustrial relations of service" ("Everything and Less," 453).[62] I wholeheartedly agree and would add that the relations of production might also be described in the terms laid out by Giovanni Arrighi (*The Long Twentieth Century* and *Adam Smith in Beijing*) and others as tremors of US hegemony, which is buckling under the strain of waves of deindustrialization and financialization. Books that have been returned (or not) to the publisher by stores that could not sell them sometimes find their way onto the Amazon Marketplace. As in the case of the copy of *Ulysses* in *The Man Who Japed*, authors do not profit from such books, and meanwhile new books on Amazon became less likely to sell because of the increased availability and lower cost of used books, especially in the case of the same title. Who would pass up the opportunity to buy a book for one or two dollars when it typically costs over twenty? Morris Rosenthal laments this situation:

> Remainders can be publisher overstock books that are sold directly to liquidators, but often they are books that were purchased on a nonreturnable basis by a retailer who decides to dump them. The worst case is when they are really being credited as returns by a publisher who doesn't actually process returns, counting on the distributor or retailer to put on a remainder mark and dispose of them. If such a book is counted as a return, the author gets no royalty, and the book goes on to

cannibalize a new sale. (Rosenthal, "Sale of Remainders, Review Copies and Deep Discount Books on Amazon")

Rosenthal's cannibal metaphor is apt. The surviving best sellers of the book industry have to fend off the remainders of the publishing world, a feat that increasingly fewer books are capable of these days. The shifts from small retailer to mall store to big-box store to Amazon.com; the power retailers have over presses; the strategies of aiming big and selling niche; and the constraints on small presses still interested in publishing physical books all work together to determine the publishing field for fiction in general and for post-apocalyptic fiction in particular.

Though authors and presses associated with other generic niches face the same difficulties, the post-apocalyptic genre in particular re-presents this situation in its very storyworlds. By the early twenty-first century when literary authors started writing books in this vein, the situation was already weirdly post-apocalyptic, masquerading as business as usual. In this light, the plight of contemporary publishers and authors eerily resonates with the fictional worlds of post-apocalyptic novels. More particularly, in the case of post-apocalyptic fiction, what this means is that each fictional version of the apocalypse always already has an element of planned obsolesce. Each imagined and printed story of the end must sell only enough copies so that the press can afford to print the next title in the line. Put otherwise, the immanence of the post-apocalyptic mode to publishing guarantees the failure of every apocalypse. The pretense of the industry is that presses publish an author's work that is sold in stores, and everyone gets a piece of the profit. However, in fact the industry has experienced a catastrophic event that renders it a remainder of itself—things keep happening in the way that they do, despite all of the constraints on sheer force of habit and despite the fact that, in the case of remaindered books, the publishers are being undercut by their own product, which they have effectively decided is actually valueless.

In the long run, the problem, as expressed in publishing, is that the contest over a small piece of the market seems not only unwinnable but also insignificant, particularly from the vantage point of those living in the wake of real-world, yet unimagined, upheavals. What the success of literary authors writing in the post-apocalyptic mode goes to show is the sheer number of titles that do not reach the same level of success. Contemporary retail and legal structures create a demand for more products at a steady rate, guaranteeing a market for new apocalypses at regular intervals. As one version of apocalypse grows stale and fails to produce the end it promised, new ones rise up to take its place. Each new apocalyptic scenario faces the fact of history's own unfinishableness. This bad infinity of historical progress has come to be replaced by a notion of apocalypse that privileges that concept's fungibility. If you do not want to buy this end of the world, just wait for the next one.

Part Two
The Contested Politics of US Decline

4
Old and New Americas

Here, at the start of part 2, this book shifts focus from an overview of the post-apocalyptic mode to distinct sets of post-apocalyptic texts. I do not leave behind the narrative moves of the post-apocalyptic story, nor the concept of reduced futures and remaindered books; each appears in the analyses that follow. Enclaves are central to most post-apocalyptic texts, as is the act of cataloguing what has transpired. The trope of the last man and the ways communities are represented also feature prominently through the examples I develop. The rift between futures that I described in chapter 2 continues in two ways: for instance, in this chapter the titles under consideration take the respective places of Stephen King and Sheri S. Tepper, and in subsequent chapters other titles are discussed in the context of their own contests over the capacities and meanings of the post-apocalyptic mode. However, the world of publishing and the role of genre in the world are largely set aside. In the following specific examples, I elaborate on the remainders of the American century, beginning with the frontier and the nation and turning to community, family, and energy in subsequent chapters.

This chapter focuses on two texts from the 1980s that maintain a romantic attachment to the frontier and the nation. The old and new Americas of its title indicate the way that national ideology gets redeployed in US culture during the 1980s as both an echo and a new development—as a remainder. This chapter charts the remainders known as the frontier and the nation in two stories set in what the science fiction critic William H. Katerberg describes as "imagined histories of the future" (*Future West*, 4).¹ The narrative conceit of the post-apocalyptic mode bears a striking similarity to the way the frontier has functioned as an imaginary space. Both represent a locale in which social desires and fears are free of the messiness of intransigent social complexity. "When sociality collapses," the science fiction critic Carl Abbot remarks regarding the post-apocalyptic frontier, "head *west* to reconstruct it" (*Frontiers Past and Future*, 217 n. 11; emphasis in the original). The world-destroying gesture of post-apocalyptic storytelling works toward the same end as the frontier. The difference is that the space-clearing process of the post-apocalyptic frontier is less spatial (taking the reader to a new open horizon) than it is temporal (taking the reader to a different time—indeed a different, reduced future). The new depiction of the old frontier aims to relive those heady days of settlement, and more than that, the frontier-focused post-apocalyptic novel of the 1980s draws attention to the ways the United States reenacts frontier history. These novels premise their spatial imaginary on a subtraction of the complexities of the global situation from their diegetic worlds. They locate a limit within the post-apocalyptic narrative form, especially its capacity to depict the global reality of a period that is after the Vietnam War and the Organization of Petroleum Exporting Countries crisis, yet still during the Cold War.

A spirit of self-reliant settler know-how predominates in David Brin's *The Postman* (1985) and Kim Stanley Robinson's *The Wild Shore* (first published in 1984). As these novels tell new stories set in old spaces, they return to the old problematic of the American frontier, which resurfaces with the spatial imaginary of the 1980s in a complex relation to a Reaganite program of economic development and transformation carried out by the United States at home and abroad. Set against this much wider history of a political and economic process, the imaginary space of 1980s post-apocalyptic novels presumes the frontier as a central fact or precondition for the restoration of the national imagined community, to use Benedict Anderson's terminology (*Imagined Communities*). In this sense, the post-apocalyptic conceit puts into relief the historical, or historiographical, valence latent in narrative genres such as the western that are typically associated with the use of the frontier as setting and sustained metaphor. The post-apocalyptic frontier story differs because it seeks to repeat what was once actual history. It turns back to the frontier as a narrative solution to the historical problems of late capitalism: deindustrialization, offshoring, and economic crisis. The frontier, in these novels, is both a remainder and the setting of a reduced future, one that features the imagined rebuilding of the American nation.

The Postman and *The Wild Shore*, each in its own way, spatially reconfigure and temporally invert a preoccupation with the American mythology of the frontier, as Sam Peckinpah's *The Wild Bunch* did for the western cowboy flick. *The Postman* and *The Wild Shore* do not approach the frontier—or post-apocalyptic storytelling, for that matter—in the same way. In *The Postman*, frontier logic remains in the background, allowing Brin to focus on a restored American nation housed in the state of Oregon. Though Brin's post-apocalyptic novel includes a dynamic of old and new, it is preoccupied with the reconstitution of the liberal subject and the rebirth of the US nation. Rather than looking back to the mid-nineteenth century American southwest, it posits an imaginary future from which to look back at and grapple with the present. While the frontier marks in "letters of blood and fire" (Marx, *Capital*, 875) the origin story of US industries and imaginaries, for Brin the apocalyptic destruction of those industries becomes an origin story, a place to reform civilization with an American face.[2] The novel is interested in an imagined frontier setting, and it relies on a physical remainder, a postal service worker's uniform, to inaugurate the plot. The titular figure of the postman waves nationalism's banner, transforming a frontier tale into a story of nation building.

The Wild Shore—the first novel in Robinson's Three Californias triptych—supports my argument with a case that seems to mirror the spatial structure of Brin's novel. Yet in Robinson's novel, the United Nations, under Russian control, has aggressively cut the United States off from modernity. Like Brin's novel, Robinson's expands the known territory of the protagonist through exploration, but it then takes a different path by critically reflecting on how it describes the frontier setting. Rather than narrowing the scale of *The Wild Shore*, Robinson has the protagonist expand his awareness of the global through a novel within a novel—a travelogue that explains and exposes the reasons why the United States was banished from modernity. In this way, the spatial dialectic of *The Wild Shore* accounts for bloody frontier history and the question of US reformation in ways *The Postman* does not. In *The Wild Shore*, the stakes of each possible future are weighed carefully against each other, and by the novel's close none has achieved complete dominance over the others.

In these two cases, the remainder of the frontier is deployed as a horizon for the characters. Yet as we shall see, Brin and Robinson take up the space of the American west in markedly different fashion. Each reading that follows cleaves to the plot as a way of tracing the trope of community in *The Postman* and *The Wild Shore*. The frontier informs the narrative structure of each book, both of which are organized into sections that expand the geographic bounds and social world. In the analysis that follows, these similarities make for a sharper contrast to use in describing the conceptual location of the frontier as a remainder of the American century.

THE POSTMAN, THE LIBERAL SUBJECT, AND THE RESTORED UNITED STATES

Brin's *The Postman* begins with an acknowledgment that sets the stage for the fantasy about space and identity that follows: "It hardly mattered anymore what had done it—a giant meteorite, a huge volcano, or a nuclear war. Temperatures and pressures swung out of balance, and great winds blew. . . . The Earth turned. Men still struggled, here and there" (n.p.). From the start, the novel marks the cause of the apocalyptic event as irrelevant, despite the vastly different effects produced by the extraterrestrial, geothermal, and atomic catastrophes envisioned in the brief "Prelude: The Thirteen-Year Thaw" that opens the novel. To adopt the outlook of the narrator, the cause of the depopulation of North America and the reasons why "men still struggled" are hardly worth pondering. However, the effects are more definite: a newly cleared space—a frontier sandbox—ripe for narrative conflict.

The "Prelude" may render the cause of the apocalyptic events in *The Postman* irrelevant, yet the novel treats various imagined responses to the events as a central concern. The conflict of the novel is not related to surviving a host of apocalyptic threats to the present, as witnessed from a godlike or top-down view.[3] Instead, the characters fight to reboot modernity along democratic, if also nationalistic, lines.⁴ While my own reading is broadly aligned with the consensus of commentators on the novel that it imagines a civilizational reboot as a horizon of possibility, the fight to resurrect modernity requires further specification.⁵ It is not simply a renewal of modernity that Brin's novel stages, but the reconstitution of the liberal political subject and the social contract that has traditionally been imagined as its political precondition.⁶ Fundamental to this story of renewal and reconstitution in *The Postman* is the category of work and shared labor. Insofar as the novel narrates the renewal of the American nation, it is important to reiterate that it does so by having its characters cling to the remainders of an imagined community that has long been dormant in the storyworld.

Contrary to the nearly global frame established in the prelude, the story is set within the bounded space of what was once Oregon. The novel progressively expands its spatial scale, gradually replacing a set of old problems with a new one in each of its four sections ("The Cascades," "Cyclops," "Cincinnatus," and "Neither Chaos"). Along the way, some conflicts are left unresolved while others are simply forgotten. In "The Cascades," the main character faces the challenge of overcoming the harsh postcatastrophic landscape as he travels between small towns in search of food and shelter. In "Cyclops," these smaller social groups are brought together by the titular postman to face smaller threats such as raiders. In "Cincinnatus," these smaller groups band together under the banner of the "Restored United States" to face the mounting threat of a vast army. Finally, in "Neither Chaos," the postman dreams of heading west in search of other communities to bring into the fold of the Restored United States.

This sketch of *The Postman*'s plot begins to suggest some basic analogies with the early-twentieth-century American historian Fredrick Jackson Turner's sequence of frontier exploration and development. Compare, for example, the people Carl Abbott identifies as populating Turner's history—"miners, engineers, farmers, community builders, city dwellers" (*Frontiers Past and Future*, 32)—with the villagers, mail carriers, city dwellers, and nation builders found in Brin's novel. Turner's frontier thesis remains deeply embedded, and continues to resonate with meaning, in the US cultural imaginary of the 1980s.⁷ Though Turner elides the displacement of Indigenous peoples and the violence wrought on them as their lands were bartered away or stolen from them, the deeply spatial process that he theorizes around the beginning of the twentieth century emerges once more in the work of scholars who study the way capital accumulates at the turn of the twenty-first century. Placed within the long historical context of the reproduction of capital, the relevance of Turner's frontier thesis reasserts itself in a new way.[8] The frontier returns here as a concern that fuses the American national mythology with capitalism's increasingly anxious relationship to the dwindling spatial horizon upon which both have long depended.

This sense of a post-apocalyptic return to the social and technological order of nineteenth-century frontier is rendered clear in summary. However, in the act of reading *The Postman*, matters are less obvious, obscured by a bulky narrative apparatus and the narrow immediacy of the protagonist's point of view. The novel focalizes the reconstitutions of liberal sociality through the split vision of an unidentified narrator and the novel's central character, Gordon Krantz. For instance, the novel begins as a group of bandits rob Krantz and leave him to die. Rather than focusing on his predicament, in the midst of this incident the narrator ruminates on a US tradition of survival:

> Post-Chaos America had no tradition but survival. In his travels, Gordon had found that some isolated communities welcomed him in the same way minstrels had been kindly received far and wide in medieval days. In others, wild varieties of paranoia reigned. Even in those rare cases where he had found friendliness, where decent people seemed willing to welcome a stranger, Gordon had always, before long, moved on. Always, he found himself beginning to dream again of wheels turning and things flying in the sky. (Brin, *The Postman*, 33)

This passage illustrates that way that *The Postman* operates on two narrative registers at once: Krantz faces the trials of the post-apocalyptic setting and its denizens, and the narrator offers long-winded reflections on the post-apocalyptic world and the possible return of civilization. In the narrator's musings, the temporalities of old and new Americas coexist, as each appears in the same rhetorical gesture:

America is both new (that is, "post-Chaos") and old, possessing "no tradition but survival." The narrator's characterization and point of view are utterly clichéd, mimicking the figure of the rambling minstrel—easily substituted for the railroading bluesman, cowboy, or sailor—who travels "far and wide," always returning to the road and leaving his troubles behind. Krantz's movements seem to indicate listlessness, or at least an unsettled desire to keep moving as described in the passage above. The way Krantz begins to "dream again of wheels turning and things flying" underlines the tension at the heart of the combination of old and new within the post-apocalyptic novel. The "again," after all, marks his return to a personal dream—to return to the pre-Chaos America that is now twenty years in the past. He longs for the return of modernity and to make this remaindered world whole once more.

The Postman is riddled with examples such as this one of the narrator's nostalgia for civilization. Typically portrayed as a longing for the nation, the narrator's desires are rarely aligned with Krantz's own: Krantz seems to want just food and shelter, while the narrator has grander designs for him. It is precisely in this gap that I locate a political opportunism on the novel's part. The novel performs its belief in the inevitability of the liberal nation-state. The narrator speaks from the point of view of historical necessity, while Krantz remains embroiled within the limited ambit of an actor wholly unaware of what he is really doing. As Krantz fumbles on, the novel generates nationalistic meaning through the narrator's asides. It identifies the right-minded way of proceeding to restore the republic.

To continue with the example of the book's beginning, the narrator's musings subside, and Krantz—wounded and robbed of his possessions—faces the necessity of retrieving his stolen gear from a group of bandits, despite the likelihood that doing so will require that he kill one or more of them. Rather than have Krantz resolve this moral dilemma, the novel provides a deus ex machina in the form of a material remainder, an "abandoned, rusted jeep with ancient US government markings, and the skeleton of a poor, dead, civil servant within, skull pressed against the passenger-side window" (Brin, *The Postman*, 22). The jeep provides shelter and a natural pause in the plot development, which allows the narrator to further reflect on

Krantz's situation. The patch on the mailman's jacket triggers a nostalgic reflection on the part of the narrator, who experiences

> a sad poignancy—something like homesickness. The jeep, the symbolic, faithful letter carrier, the flag patch . . . they recalled comfort, innocence, cooperation, an easy life that allowed millions of men and women to relax, to smile, or argue as they chose, to be tolerant with one another—and to hope to be better people with the passage of time. (ibid., 24)

Once again, the narrator overdetermines Krantz's experience, describing him as a character with longings for liberal modernity in the harsh reality of the present. It is not Krantz but the narrator who understands symbolic meaning in the uniform. Krantz is much more pragmatic, treating the encounter as an opportunity to obtain shelter.

When Krantz takes the dead postman's belongings, a transformation occurs. In acting the part of the postman, he inherits the outfit's symbolic power, which in turn transforms the economic problematic of the novel from bare survival to trade. The outfit offers Krantz a way into the tightly guarded small communities, such as Oakridge (which is where he travels next). He no longer has to worry about finding food and shelter, and he assumes some authority over the problems of the town, as evidenced in an exemplary salvo that he launches at Oakridge's mayor: "Mr. Mayor . . . [d]on't force me to exercise my authority in ways both of us would find unpleasant. You're on the verge of losing your privilege of communication with the rest of the nation" (Brin, *The Postman*, 76). Krantz assumes the power vested in the uniform and becomes a civil servant to a now-dead state, which he insists is alive and well. The body politic leveraged by Krantz no longer exists—the United States is nothing more than a memory in this storyworld. Indeed, the social contract of Krantz's appeal is little more than a spectral force, a remainder. As Krantz bluffs his way into Oakridge, he inadvertently steps into a state-sanctioned role as a mail carrier. The people he speaks with do not let go of the fiction: he must use his prop mail bag for its intended purpose and actually deliver the mail.

Without meaning to, Krantz secures an entry point into the social contract and begins to fulfill the narrator's set of objectives. His strength and cunning become the means to better others. His use of the postal uniform starts the process of forming a social whole, whether or not he intends this to happen. He sets in motion events that, the novel suggests, will leave its characters stronger together than they would be on their own. Krantz's performance raises old questions about the nature of the state and the provenance of its sovereignty that begins—as I hope to acknowledge with the invocation of the social contract—with Rousseau, Locke, and Hobbes: specifically, from whence does the power of the state flow? *The Postman*'s implied answer seems to be that by speaking the right way, wearing the right clothes, and above all having these signs recognized by others, anyone can become an agent of the state, even if that state itself does not exist.

Brin's selection of the US Postal Service resonates in a symbolic register as well. Another kind of civil servant—fire fighter, librarian, schoolteacher, or tax collector—would be treated differently and would not represent regional connectivity in the way the postal worker does. By claiming to be from the Restored United States, Krantz restores the idea of simultaneity to the post-apocalyptic storyworld. People living in Oakridge can now begin to imagine how others (not only the people in the next town, but even more distant others) are living their lives within a national consciousness, albeit one still limited by the extreme locality of the novel's scale. In the way that Anderson describes the "imagined communities" that print capitalism enabled, *The Postman* imagines how its titular character might similarly re-form a national imaginary of countless unknowable others. Anderson writes that "an American will never meet more than a handful of ... fellow Americans," "has no idea what they are up to at any one time," and "has complete confidence in their steady, anonymous, simultaneous activity" (*Imagined Communities*, 26). The idea that one might communicate with people from the next town leads to the idea that people one does not know may be doing the same thing—think of all those other letters with recognized destinations yet inscrutable addressees or, more scandalously, imagine that the recipient and sender are familiar and wonder what they might be saying to one another!

As Krantz's talk of the Restored United States spreads, towns start to assign their own postmasters and letter carriers. Though Krantz sought only to ensure his own survival, he inadvertently generates the bonds of community. His lies cease to be lies at this critical point and become reality in the manner of J. L. Austin's description of performative utterances (*How to Do Things with Words*): as Krantz circulates the mail, his tales about a Restored United States start to enfranchise the people of Oregon. This storytelling serves the individual end of seeing that he has food and shelter as he travels, but for the narrator, at the moment when Krantz begins carrying letters, a collectivity is forged. As others take on the recently revitalized occupation of postman, they are investing themselves in a collective life, reforming old structures of communication, and participating in a technology that (though outmoded even by the telegraph) becomes pertinent once more. As in Anderson's claim about the role of print capitalism in forging the common feeling of early European nationalism, here too the nation is rebuilt by a shared language and a common narrative.

As the towns begin to Americanize, to adapt Turner's term "Americanization" (*The Significance of the Frontier in American History*, 4), and work together to establish mail routes, they start to shed what the narrator notes are signs of feudalism (Brin, *The Postman*, 72), turning toward more sophisticated social relations that include democratic elections; declarative, juridical acts; and new patterns of exchange. Section two of the novel, "Cyclops," opens with the text of the recently ratified National Recovery Act, which signifies the strides toward a re-formed nation that Krantz made in the first section. The act states that the "people and fundamental institutions of the nation survive" (ibid., 87) and contains four main principles and one amendment: first, men and women are granted freedoms under the Bill of Rights and the right to a trial for all serious crimes conducted by an impartial jury; second, slavery is forbidden; third, there will be regular elections using secret ballots; fourth, citizens shall keep safe the resources of the United States, including books and pre-Chaos machinery; and finally, citizens are required to cooperate with mail carriers, and any interference with a carrier is a capital crime (ibid., 87–88). The act is signed "by order of the Provisional Congress Restored United States of America May 2009" (ibid., 88). This document signifies the effects produced by Krantz's articulation of a national imaginary in a space where no such governing body exists. Like the preamble to the US Constitution, the National Recovery Act brings a body into being in the same breath that it makes a declaration: "We the people . . ." for the *Constitution*, and "Let it be known by all now living within the boundaries of the United States of America that the people and fundamental institutions of the Nation survive" (ibid., 87) for *The Postman*. Until "the people" are declared into being, they did not exist; until the people and institutions of the nation are declared into being, they had not survived.[9] The letter of the law is always already a social contract, a performance bound by convention and commitment.[10]

The antagonist in "Cyclops," like the Willamette Valley communities in "Cascades," eventually joins Krantz in his mission of pulling Oregon back together again. The titular Cyclops—a military-grade supercomputer—has been defunct for years, and this secret is carefully guarded. With a smoke-and-mirrors show reminiscent of *The Wizard of Oz*, the people are fooled into thinking that the machine is still running, still calculating the soundest course of action for them. Krantz recognizes it as like his own farce. Here, the novel provides yet another figure of virtual power and authority as if to insist on both the capacities of the people to work toward collective aims and the necessity of an externalized container of knowledge and power. In this way, though Cyclops is a presence in the midst of the community, it operates in much the same way as Krantz's description of a Restored United States in the East. Both generate cohesion and direction through an externalized entity, which in truth represents the capacities of the people. Once Krantz uncovers the secret of Cyclops, the Servants of Cyclops, who secretly operate behind the actually defunct supercomputer, agree to join him and the resurgent nation.

The tensions of the climactic, penultimate section, "Cincinnatus," mount under the pressure of additional communities, spaces, and ideologies that pulled together to face a threat from the Holnists—the raiders who serve the warlord Nathan Holn. The narrator describes the coalition as "counties tied together by their reverence of Cyclops, more recently by a growing postal network, and now by a common foe" (Brin, *The Postman*, 197). The townsfolk realize that their combined forces are not enough to triumph, so Krantz travels south in search of other allies who are rumored to have repelled the Holnists. The pace of the plot accelerates as Krantz attempts once more to draw on the power of the national imaginary to pull the people of Sugarloaf Mountain—with their ex-military leader, George Powhatan—into the fold of the Restored United States. Whether Brin named him for the Indigenous tribe or for its leader, Wahunsenacawh, whom the English colonizers sometimes called Powahatan, the inclusion of a leader with this name weaves into the novel the history of settlement that drove the historical frontier in the first place.[11] Even an inadvertent inclusion of an Indigenous character brings with it the violent history of settler colonialism. The history of dispossession and displacement follows Brin's George Powhatan across the post-apocalyptic United States: the ancestral lands of the Powhatan are located in what is now known as Virginia, and he leads a group of people in what was once known as Oregon. Like Wahunsenacawh, George Powhatan is not easily swayed when the settlers come looking for help, and Krantz is sent home with a clear refusal to provide aid. The people need to decide how to respond to the Holnist threat without Powhatan's backing. The novel resists the problems posed by the return of the frontier through democratic assembly and the armed protection of the rights and freedoms of those participating in that assembly.

En route back to Corvallis, Krantz and his small band are captured by the Holnists. The novel makes clear how the capture and conflict must be resolved from the narrator's standpoint: Powhatan and his followers need to join with the Restored United States to face the survivalist threat. Powhatan arrives just in time to battle the leader of the Holnists, saving Krantz from a confrontation he could not hope to win. As the political theorist Claire P. Curtis argues, "The typical post-apocalyptic novel uses the threat to the safety of the small collective of survivors to cement their ties and to push those survivors into a more self-consciously organized system. A community is formed, one that can actually fight back" (*Postapocalyptic Fiction and the Social Contract*, 8). The final conflict reveals that Powhatan, like Holn, is a military-enhanced cyborg warrior. Powhatan was designed and rebuilt by the US military, meaning that he is simultaneously the only one who can intercede on behalf of the Restored United States and the only one with good reason not to. This unexpected development stretches the novel's genre by introducing military science fiction components. Powhatan eventually acts as a deus ex machina in the response to Holn, but his social position in the novel is not fully mapped out. Instead, Brin positions Krantz and his resuscitation of the social against the Holnists.

The Holnists present a threat because of their lawless, anarchic behavior: theirs is a different form of social organization. Where Krantz relies on images of a restored American nation, Holn pens his own ideological documents. His great work within the novel is *Lost Empire*, which forms the ideological basis for the horde of raiders who use his name. *Lost Empire* rejects political binaries, instead advocating a return to feudalism. A fragment of the text is included in the novel, so readers are able to read what Krantz does:

> Feudalism has always been our way, as a species, ever since we foraged in wild bands and screamed defiance at each other from opposing hilltops. . . . Think back to how things were when the Nineteenth Century was just dawning in America. Back then the opportunity stood stark and clear to reverse the sick trends of the so-called "Enlightenment." The victorious Revolutionary War soldiers had expelled English decadence from most of the continent. The frontier lay open, and a rough spirit of individualism reigned supreme throughout the newborn nation. (Brin, *The Postman*, 252–53)

Holn's lament for a lost empire and his understanding of US history, which casts Benjamin Franklin as an evil genius, is not surprising, and neither is Krantz's reaction to the text as he slams it down, unable to read any more. But the logic at the heart of Holn's text is the same as that underlying Krantz's Restored United States: what is needed to address the problems of the post-Chaos present is a return to old techniques of power, reaching out and taking what is needed for survival. Holn's favoring lawless violence grounded in a feudal economy and Krantz's valuing the enfranchisement and empowerment of the people differ in means only. Both seek the return of national power and authority. What infuriates Krantz is Holn's libertarian program of domination that founds itself on brute force; Holn's aspirations form a regressive mirror image of Krantz's.

Krantz and Holn present two proposed solutions to the post-apocalyptic return to the frontier. David Harvey uses the term "accumulation by dispossession" for what he credits Hannah Arendt with calling "the original sin of simple robbery," a process that enabled the accumulation of capital in the first place and "had eventually to be repeated lest the motor of accumulation suddenly die down" (*The New Imperialism*, 180–81). Arendt's words offer a strangely resonant account of the fictional situation—the post-apocalypse period—as imagined in *The Postman*: the motor of accumulation has indeed suddenly died down. Holn's raiders enact a process of simple robbery. In political-economic terms, they aim to subsist by stealing from the subsistence farmers in communities such as those in the Willamette Valley. The Marxist feminist Silvia Federici extends Harvey's thesis to name primitive accumulation as a process that "has accompanied every phase of capitalist globalization, including the present one, demonstrating that the continuous expulsion of farmers from land, war and plunder on a world scale . . . are necessary conditions for the existence of capitalism at all times" (*Caliban and the Witch*, 13). The thought experiment of mapping this process onto the post-apocalyptic novel of the 1980s is not solely meant to echo the insistence by Arendt, Harvey, and Federici that so-called primitive accumulation subtends capital accumulation as a constant, rather than existing only as its precondition. Rather, it is to properly position the horizon of the democratic liberal economics underlying Krantz's mission. Krantz actually comes to stand in for the way in which the state produces economic conditions. Krantz is morally opposed to conflict, yet it makes a better situation for free trade. He connects the communities he meets, expanding their trade networks. And he deputizes the postal workers—indeed, forms a militia—to protect property. He symbolizes the necessity of circulation and investment. While Krantz presents an opportunity for communities to bring their goods to their neighbors, establish new partnerships, and develop more robust markets, the endgame of the Holnist project is regressively feudal in its aims.

Insofar as the novel follows the structure of the bildungsroman, with Krantz gradually becoming a better subject, he comes to understand only the narrator's nationalistic aims, not their underlying economic implications. When Krantz, the agent of civilization's return, is captured, he experiences a revelation of the future that anticipates the outcome of the novel: he begins to see the narrator's vision of a Restored United States and he sheds his doubts. Strung upside down in a rundown shack, Krantz's commitment to the promise of civilization keeps him from submitting to the Holnists:

Only there, in the blackness, he encountered the one ghost that remained. The one he had used the most shamelessly, and which had used him.

It was a nation. A world.

Faces, fading in and out with the entropic speckles behind his eyelids . . . millions of faces, betrayed and ruined but surviving still . . .

—for a Restored United States.

—for a *Restored World.*

—for a fantasy . . . but one which refused obstinately to die—that *could not* die—not while he lived. . . .

In the darkness within himself the dream glowed—even if it existed nowhere else in the Universe—flickering like a diatom, like a bright mote hovering in a murky sea.

Amidst the otherwise total blackness, it was as if he stood in front of it. He seemed to take it in his hand, astonished by the light. The jewel grew. And in its facets he saw more than people, more than generations.

A *future* took shape around him, enveloping him, penetrating his heart. (Brin, *The Postman*, 290; emphasis in the original)

What takes shape around Krantz—"more than people, more than generations"—heralds itself as the remaking of the old, that "one ghost that remained," through the redemption of a liberal narrative of subjectivity. The passage strongly equates a Restored United States with a restored world. In this instant, the drive of the post-apocalyptic character to make whole again the destroyed storyworld merges with the national aspirations of *The Postman*. Re-forming the nation and rebuilding the world are one and the same. For this novel, the restoration of the American nation is a foregone conclusion. The remainders of this reduced future only add to a Restored United States and are described in the novel only in the language of freedom. The nationalistic response to the return of the frontier sounds like a form of liberalism but behaves like neoliberalism *avant la lettre*.

The importance of neoliberalism to my argument here hinges on its absolute faith in the market to manage production, circulation, and consumption, which results in the rationalization and economization of every aspect of life. Despite its long incubation period, neoliberalism did not reach dominance until the mid-1980s.[12] According to Perry Anderson,

> The keynotes of the Carter Administration were tight money and deregulation, to weaken labour and strengthen business. In Congress, the Democrats lowered the capital-gains tax and raised the payroll levy, while—in one vote after another—rejecting reform of health care, indexation of the minimum wage, consumer protection and improvement of electoral registration. At the Fed, Volcker was entrusted with a hard deflation. Neo-liberalism was now in the saddle. ("Homeland," 10)

Anderson flags the moment when neoliberalism achieves dominance with a telling cowboy metaphor. It is perhaps no accident that President Ronald Reagan, who becomes even more than President Jimmy Carter the ruggedly charismatic hero of 1980s neoliberal reform, first achieved recognition playing Hollywood cowboys in westerns of the 1950s and 1960s. Out of these associations, a hybrid figure glimmers into being: a composite of the gunslinger and *homo economicus*. With the dissolution of the Keynesian public good and its corresponding social networks of support, the individual subject once again finds itself at the mercy of the elements, so to speak. Neoliberalism is thus characterized by an international drawing inward (from the periphery to the center) and a national drawing upward (in seizures of public wealth by corporate interests). At each moment wealth is transferred to the capitalist class, in a redistribution from the margins and the marginalized to those who are in control of the means of production and the state itself, including municipal and regional police budgets. These processes are also hyperviolent dispossessions that tend to criminalize the homeless (often black and Indigenous people), echoing the European conquest of the Americas. *The Postman* presents this strange combination of nineteenth- and twenty-first-century imaginings of the frontier, in which post-apocalyptic survivors appear on the new plains of the Americas—liberated, as it were, to pursue happiness through the harnessing of human capital in an embrace of the entrepreneurial spirit.

Although the novel is firmly centered on Krantz throughout, the gradually expanding scale of the narrative—from individual to town and then to state—reaches still further at the close of the book, which opens onto the frontier described by Holn: Krantz dreams of California and what survivors it may hold. This narrative turn reveals the symptomatic absence of the global. *The Postman*'s fantasy is premised on the effacing of the supranational scale of the social. However, Krantz's desire at the end of the novel intimates his desire for another frontier, another set of relations to enfranchise under the aegis of the Restored United States. *The Postman* stages a series of events in the development of the liberal state, working through the frontier state of nature, the idea of the social contract, the formation of alliances against common enemies, and the expansion of territory. The novel depends on an unstated theory of history in which reason and progress follow from the development of the always already rational subject— who must realize this potential for reason in their work and world. It retells American myths about the social contract through the separation of the narrator, as the voice of reason, and Krantz, as the subject who must come to see himself as a creature of reason.

A mode of production develops subtly at the same time: here the development of liberal political philosophy is followed by political economy stage by stage as the collective moves from subsistence survival to the reproduction of daily life, and then to the possibility of full-scale production within the storyworld. *The Postman* takes the categories of the rational individual and the democratic state as the determining factors of social life, rather than centering post-apocalyptic political economy. One of the key impasses of the post-apocalyptic mode reasserts itself: *The Postman* fantasizes about returning to a liberal democratic social order and replays the imaginary stages of historical development that led to the present, crystallizing old and new Americas within Krantz's final vision of hope for the future.

In the face of what I have been describing as a return to the frontier, both narrative and historical, *The Postman* stages the development of liberal subjectivity. The novel presents an opportunity for a political reading that imagines a Restored United States as an opportunity to right the wrongs of a United States that, in the 1980s, has become increasingly neoliberal and globally aggressive. The novel simultaneously rewrites the history of the frontier, details a process of accumulation in the American west, and generates the desire for a return to collective life. The return to the concerns of the frontier in the 1980s is a layered one: the frontier is an imaginary space where people might find a living for themselves. Through perseverance and hard work, according to the cliché, they might build a stable form of subsistence. This desire permeates the post-apocalyptic frontier—the difference between the historical and post-apocalyptic frontier being the picked-over remainders of US colonization and settlement otherwise described as modernity. Yet the frontier also represents a figuration of the US spatial domination of other countries, a desire to tear down the public investments of the mid-twentieth century, and an attempt to rewrite US history. The relation between old and new Americas is at once connected to the history of the systematic genocide of Indigenous peoples, the murders of Mexicans and settlers, and the naked opportunism of whichever gang laid claim to whichever territory. To figure the appearance of the frontier in post-apocalyptic fiction of the 1980s as a "return," then, belies the continuity of accumulation by dispossession shown by Harvey and Federici. In this sense, the story of the frontier of the American southwest in the mid-nineteenth century is as active as ever in the story of the offshoring of manufacturing and the neoliberal deregulation of corporate power.

The question of how the novel rewrites the nineteenth-century American frontier appears rather straightforward in retrospect: the frontier remains so persistent in the mid-1980s because the ideological oppositions between terrain and property remain unsolved, and because the driving force of capitalist expansion is recasting itself anew in the neoliberalization of the state and the market. The frontier persists as a key category for American imaginaries because it still captures the motor of capitalist expansion, which always seeks new zones to make productive for capital. One way to think about the anxieties expressed in 1980s post-apocalyptic novels is that they are a sort of hand-wringing over the economic contingencies of deindustrialization, especially in the wake of mid-century Keynesian investment in public works, building projects, and other infrastructures. The consequences of economic downturn had a dire impact on the US working class, whose members had slowly become affluent through the mid-century by working in steel and automobile manufacturing.[13] As much as it engages in an imagined the history of US political development, *The Postman* can be read as an attempt to think the present historically. It attempts to think beyond the end of the story by representing a form of future reduction. Past modes of production overshadow the desire for collectivity in Brin's novel, which remains haunted by the feudalism of its survivalist gang and the accumulation by dispossession of the American frontier. What if old and new America were projected differently, not in a theoretical account of the frontier or a symbolic future reduction, but in a radical neutralization of US domination?

TARGETED APOCALYPSE IN *THE WILD SHORE*

The novels of Robinson's Three Californias triptych—*The Wild Shore*, *The Gold Coast* (first published in 1988), and *Pacific Edge* (first published in 1990)—are each set in Orange County in the late twenty-first century and respectively stage post-apocalyptic, dystopian, and utopian futures.[14] Unlike Robinson's Mars Trilogy, which could be read as one long novel, his Three Californias novels operate along parallel trajectories—one could read them in any order without becoming confused about plot or narrator, for instance. *The Wild Shore* depicts a post-apocalyptic United States through the subsistence of one small community, which already marks its difference from other post-apocalyptic fictions, in which the stakes are so often set at the level of a sole survivor. *The Gold Coast* pictures a hypercapitalist future for Orange County, in which designer drugs rule the people and the endless highways are navigated by fully automated cars—recalling the cyberpunk corporate megacities envisaged by William Gibson and later by Misha Nogha and Neal Stephenson. Finally, *Pacific Edge* imagines an ecologically sound future along utopian lines, in which the local is privileged over the global, and the corporations that held such remarkable sway in *The Gold Coast* have been removed from their seat of power. This future is still one based on economic relations and production, but it is one that is motivated by fantasies other than those of limitless expansion and growth that lie at the heart of the other two novels, in which capitalism is either full realized or haunts the present in its absence.

Of these three parallel accounts, it is the specific critique articulated in *The Wild Shore*—the post-apocalyptic novel in the triptych—that principally interests me. The imaginary of old and new Americas maintains a role in structuring meaning across the whole triptych, but it takes on a rich explanatory force when considered within an individual text. *The Wild Shore* imagines an overgrown Orange County after the United States has been destroyed in a 2047 nuclear strike by a Russian-led United Nations. The novel opens sixty years after the United States was banished from modernity. The Russians, Japanese, and their allies still monitor the United States to ensure it does not begin to rebuild. These concerns are not introduced until much later in the novel. Instead, relying on the same conceit of redevelopment that Brin deploys in *The Postman*, Robinson paints the picture of a small community, San Onofre, struggling to survive while caught between the scavengers who occupy the ruins to the north and the forces of remodernization in San Diego to the south. Unlike in *The Postman*, the apocalyptic novum here is nameable, and its form matters. The 50–60 residents of San Onofre divide the labor of subsistence farming and fishing among them. They participate in municipal rituals, such as bathing in the bathhouse, celebrating bounty, and mourning loss. After sequestering the United States, the outside world continued to progresses. Later in the novel, the protagonist, Henry Fletcher, encounters Japanese ships that patrol the coast—intent, along with the rest of the world, on preventing the United States from re-forming and rebuilding technologically. *The Wild Shore* inverts real history by transforming what Giovanni Arrighi has described as the US global "protection racket" into the negative: the United States is not the policeman of the world but policed by the world.[15] The novel imagines what Orange County, as a microcosm of the United States, would be like in the absence of global concerns. It ponders how the United States would change if its interests became circumscribed, echoing a protectionist desire in US political culture. Furthermore, the novel plays out a fantasy of starting over without the immense political and economic weight of global hegemony. In this sense, it sidesteps narratives of decline and rebuilding altogether to work through alternative modes of governance and decision making.

    Structurally similar to Brin's novel, *The Wild Shore* has four sections that successively increase its scale. With this widening, conflicts that begin as internal to the community telescope outward, revealing the sources of antagonism within and outside San Onofre. Each section is narrated by Fletcher, a teenager who explores the nearby ruins and is the beloved student of Tom Barnard, one of the few survivors from before the attack on the United States. Only at the end of the novel is it revealed that the text is Fletcher's own account of events, recorded in an empty codex that Barnard supplied. The expansion of each section mirrors the frontier promise of bounty and the political conflicts in *The Postman*, but it does so critically. The widening of the narrative frame does not introduce new and open fantasy spaces but instead extends the narrative conflict, moving from the local to the national and then to the global. The crucial difference between these two post-apocalyptic novels is that the shift in narrative scale in *The Wild Shore* from a small settlement and scavenger swap meets to city politics and global relations does not obliterate the social problems of the prior setting. In fact, the plot is driven by the encounters between the varied spaces and relations: the more readers grow into the world with Fletcher, the better positioned they are to understand its complexities. It is this movement in *The Wild Shore* between plot and story, narrative sections and storyworld scales, that signifies Robinson's specific contribution to the treatment of old and new Americas in the post-apocalyptic novel.

The first section of *The Wild Shore* describes daily life in San Onofre: the tutelage of Fletcher and Steve by Old Barnard, familial relations and conflicts, the community's reliance on the sea, its relationship with local scavengers, and the regular swap meets. In this section, tension is tuned to the scale of the community. For example, Fletcher, Steve, and a group of their friends go into the ruins of San Clemente to dig up graves in search of treasure—an outing that Fletcher describes as "the start of it" and what "gave us a taste for . . . more than fishing, and hoeing weeds, and checking snares" (Robinson, *The Wild Shore*, 6). This excursion brings them into conflict with the scavengers, another group of survivors who would prefer to live off the remains of the urban, rather than farm and fish in a community such as San Onofre. The scavengers do not present a great threat and tend to stick to their territory; the community of San Onofre maintains a regular relationship with scavengers and other small subsistence groups through swap meets. Fletcher recounts San Onofre's popularity at such meets: "We were the only seaside town at this meet, so we were popular. 'Onofre's here,' I heard someone calling. 'Look at this abalone,' someone else said, 'I'm going to eat mine right now!' Rafael sang out his call: 'Pes*c*ados. Pes*c*ados.' Even the scavengers from Laguna came over to trade with us; they couldn't do their own fishing even with the ocean slapping them in the face" (ibid., 34). Fletcher beams with pride at his community's ingenuity and knowledge of the sea, marking the novel's difference from *The Postman* and other post-apocalyptic novels. Here, even on the local scale, the storyworld is a functioning one with plausible communities and economies. Moreover, unlike in *The Postman*, the discovery of a larger world beyond San Onofre—much as it may shift the center of conflict and accelerate the plot—does not replace or disrupt the relations that have already been established.

The second section of the novel, "San Diego," introduces the mayor of San Diego, a figure who subscribes to the variant of the nationalism and restorative patriotism in Brin's novel. After meeting with a group of San Diegans at the swap meet, Fletcher and Barnard learn of the mayor's project to lay new railway lines and conceal them from United Nations satellites. One of the San Diegans muses, "no question they've got cameras that can image a man . . . the question is, how much will they notice?" (Robinson, *The Wild Shore*, 89). So Fletcher and Barnard travel by train to the south to, in the words of a representative of the mayor, "talk about trade agreements and such" (ibid., 60). Once they arrive, they discover that San Diego and its mayor represent a fixation on technology as a means of reclaiming US world dominance—this fixation is also what drives the mayor to reconstruct the railways. The two novels focus on different technologies of nationalism in a manner that is powerfully suggestive of their divergent standpoints: Brin's presents the postal worker, with his communicative enterprise, as a respectable figurehead of the state, while Robinson's focuses on the infrastructure of the community and the possibilities of emancipatory transportation. The construction of united national railways goes back to the mid-nineteenth century: "the iron pouring in millions of tonnes all over the world, snaking in ribbons of railway across the continents" (Hobsbawm, *The Age of Capital*, 16)—a moment that Eric Hobsbawm identifies as a turning point, the beginning of what he calls "the quiet but expansionist 1850s" (*The Age of Revolution*, 4).[16] The historical fantasies of the frontier myth were undergirded by the expansion of the rail system across the United States, and these fantasies are certainly at play in the novel as well, especially in the mayor of San Diego's designs "to rebuild America" for its reemergence on the world stage (Robinson, *The Wild Shore*, 103).

Indeed, rail is not the only technology being rediscovered. The mayor has a minor print operation, which allows Robinson to comment on cultural production and the cognitive work of literature. The principle text in production, *An American around the World: Being an Account of a Circumnavigation of the Globe in the Years 2030 to 2039*, by Glen Baum, recounts in travelogue fashion the adventures of an American boy who slips past the sentries on the island of Catalina and journeys around the world. Once back in San Onofre, Fletcher and his friends take great pleasure in reading the book aloud. It stimulates their imaginations and expands their sense of the world beyond their little valley, over the next hill, and across the ocean.

Again, unlike *The Postman*, *The Wild Shore* does not dislocate the global in the interests of simplifying relations in the United States and avoiding the messy world of global politics. Instead, the larger conflict in the latter novel comes from the united world's intention to keep a watchful eye on the United States. On the way back to their village by boat, Barnard and Fletcher encounter a Japanese patrol ship and Fletcher is captured, which substantiates San Diegan claims about Japanese surveillance of the coast. In a dramatic sequence, Fletcher escapes his captors and plunges into the Pacific. He manages to make it back to shore, where Barnard and others rescue him. Barnard and Fletcher are now in a position to return to San Onofre with news from outside the small community and its area. This expansion of scale, from the local to the global, is reflected in the title of the third section: "The World." It does not take long for the pressures from outside the community to appear within it, as the community becomes divided between those who wish to mind their own business, living as they have been, and those who wish to join the San Diegans in their nationalistic revitalization project. Fletcher and Steve dream of being a part of the "American resistance," but others oppose them (Robinson, *The Wild Shore*, 165).

The residents of San Onofre gather in the bathhouse to hear about Barnard and Fletcher's journey, which provides a sense that Robinson has been offering the other side of *The Postman*'s narrative all along.[17] In contrast to Krantz's role as a self-determining liberal subject, it is the collective that is given agency in Robinson's novel. *The Wild Shore* highlights deliberation in collective decision making, emphasizing the use of language as a medium for the will of the people who form the community. In this way, the novel works through what Jürgen Habermas would call communicative action, a deliberative process in which at least two people work together based on their shared assessment of a situation or event.[18] Rather than externalizing the decision maker or ultimate goal onto an outsider—as with Krantz's Restored United States or the idea of the supercomputer Cyclops—each actor trusts that the others have the capacity to make decisions and that they aim to reach such decisions through persuasive argument and shared understanding. However different this manner of decision making is from the scenario projected in Brin's novel, the American resistance of *The Wild Shore* is plainly similar to the Restored United States. Yet Brin's novel does not imagine geography in the same way that Robinson's does. In *The Postman*, the world outside of the United States—even the world outside of Oregon—may as well not exist. In *The Wild Shore*, in contrast, the tensions of a globe are figured as a totality of complex and indirect relationships that reverberate in the local, ongoing conflict between old and new Americas. The question of joining the American resistance is presented as a real question. Unlike the way events seem to unfold of their own accord in *The Postman*, the expansion of the scale of action in *The Wild Shore* has tangible consequences from the start, especially the survival and safety of San Onofre.

The fourth section of Robinson's novel, "Orange County," concludes the San Diegan plot. Against the wishes of the community, Robinson's adolescent protagonists, led by a bloodthirsty Steve and a reluctant Fletcher, decide to help the San Diegans attack a group of Japanese tourists who have come to see post-apocalyptic California. The attack results in the death of the protagonists' companion, Mando. Afterward, word comes from San Diego that the mayor has been ousted by a more reliable leader. Finally, Fletcher sits to write *The Wild Shore*. He thinks: "The old man [Barnard] told me that when I was done writing I would understand what happened, but he was wrong again, the old liar. Here I've taken the trouble to write it all down, and now I'm done and I don't have a dog's idea what it meant" (Robinson, *The Wild Shore*, 377). Robinson does not employ a split between a liberal omniscient narrator and an inadvertent political actor (as Brin does in *The Postman*), instead presenting Fletcher as narrator, character, and author of the events that happen around him in all of their messiness.

But Fletcher writes the final sentences: "my hand is getting cold—it's getting so stiff I can't make the letters, these words are all big and scrawling, taking up the last of the space, thank God. Oh be done with it. There's an owl, flitting over the river. I'll stay right here and fill another book" (Robinson, *The Wild Shore*, 378).[19] The book Fletcher refers to here is actually Robinson's to write—that is, *The Gold Coast*, the second novel in the Three Californias triptych, which presents a different series of events staged in the same space and underpinned by a similar imaginary of US progress. The impetus of the series to project and compare variant futures should be read back into each of its component novels. Indeed, as Brackett mapped in *The Long Tomorrow*, a number of variant futures exist within *The Wild Shore*: the subsistence farming of San Onofre; the scavenger lifestyle based on ruins; the autocracy of the mayor of San Diego; the border town on the island of Catalina; and the geopolitical, globalized society of the United Nations (though this latter way of life is beyond the comprehension of the regressed post-Americans). The variant possibilities for social organization presented in *The Wild Shore* speak to the broader contest over the potential of the future in the post-apocalyptic mode writ large. *The Wild Shore* pushes back against the kind of future reduction on display in Brin's *The Postman* by refusing to imagine there are only a few responses to apocalyptic catastrophe.

In both *The Postman* and *The Wild Shore,* the new Americas of the mid-1980s post-apocalyptic novel recapitulate the old Americas of the frontier. Both novels imagine the space left behind by apocalyptic world destruction as an opportunity to describe subsistence communities, their national and technological aspirations, and how they might manage threats to their existence. Moreover, this recapitulation allows both novels to suggest a path from the remainders of a destroyed United States to a reinvigorated form of social democracy. Robinson's post-apocalyptic novel, rather than siding with a nationalistic future, turns toward a narrative solution of extrapolation: *The Wild Shore* presents a reduced future, yet it gets there by critically inverting US hegemony. It allows the contradictions between variant forms of survival and community to exist within the novel and to become the plot.

Though the two authors describe similar groups emerging, the obstacles those groups face are quite different. Both novels are interested in deploying the idea of the frontier as a sandbox for experimenting with nation building, but where Brin makes the subtraction of the supranational a precondition of the narrative, a subtraction that is given without explanation and by authorial fiat, Robinson locates this subtraction from the world within the novel. Robinson's is a move characteristic of science fiction: for Robinson the apocalypse does not "hardly matter," and in fact its origin could not matter more. In *The Postman*, Brin neutralizes the globe as problem, asking what if the world disappeared and the problem of the United States was worked out on the social scale of neighboring tribes? In contrast, Robinson takes aim at the current configuration of US power and dominance, asking how would things be different in Orange County if the United States was stripped of its influence on the globe and, thus, of modernity? As *The Wild Shore* suggests, the image of a truly united world offers both a resolution and an impossible task in the interregnum of the 1980s: in the novel, the fictive conceit of a world government banishing the United States to technological backwardness and political obscurity becomes important to the discursive contest of the post-apocalyptic as a genre. The novel meditates on what life might look like in the wake of a targeted apocalypse on US soil. I wish to distinguish here between apocalypse and post-apocalypse as narrative modes and real-world targeted attacks on US soil. These are not the same thing, and I am not suggesting that Robinson is conflating them. Instead, I endeavor to read *The Wild Shore* as producing a narrative resolution to real social problems.

In light of the desire for reconstitution apparent in Brin's novel, old and new Americas seem to collapse their temporal dimension into an imagined space that stands ready for populating, building, and modernizing. In other words, the fantasy of a restored United States is the fantasy of starting over again, with a clear enemy and a clear telos. The trope of old and new Americas cleanly maps the narrative logic of the post-apocalyptic novel: unlike the historical frontier that was perceived as a new place to explore and inhabit, these novels look back to the old as a way of restarting the American social experiment anew. The trope also reconfigures the catalogue and community tropes from earlier post-apocalyptic novels. In this way, these old and new

Americas novels rely on parentheses in their world building. They develop the storyworld community by community. Yet Krantz and his narrator take the old America for a new one, turning the residual US nation into an emerging social order. *The Wild Shore* imagines a future after the elimination of US hegemony. Robinson overlays the possible futures of Orange County in the hope that mapping the space of the future could reconstitute, at least to some small degree, a collective path toward another possibility.

The mid-1980s post-apocalyptic novel is riddled with inherited contradictions. It temporally displaces imagined frontiers onto the future, suggesting that its mythic promise could be fulfilled again as it is remembered as happening once before. Old and new Americas can thus be conceived of as a space caught between the time of the frontier and the time of the dispossessed future: a desperate imagination in the present that seems to insist that this cannot be happening now, even as the remainders of the Keynesian welfare state were deregulated and privatized in new enclosures at home and as wars were being funded and armies supplied abroad. Turner's frontier never fully receded. It expanded from the terrain of resources and land to that of investments and markets no longer limited by any national boundary.

One of the frontier's own legacies is that of the partitioned post-apocalyptic imaginary. To put this observation more clearly, I mean that the spatial configuration of post-apocalyptic storytelling nestles comfortably together with the remainder of the frontier myth. Such remainders operate with a kind of epic-fantasy convergence theory—a holdover, perhaps, from King's *The Stand*. The rising action of both frontier narratives seems to belie the supposed openness of such spaces by pitting characters against one another in climactic confrontations. Such conflicts might be read, on any register of the post-apocalyptic frontier, as a contest over the collective determination of the future. What will the new America be like, how will its people be connected, and who will have a say in shaping its social arrangements?

5
Segregated Futures

Implicitly or explicitly, race shapes the way post-apocalyptic novels draw the lines of community.[1] It is understood that this relationship between race and community changes over time, which requires me to turn back, if only briefly, to the earliest novel of the post-1945 period. Returning to this period, and specifically to a novel discussed in chapter 1, underlines the manner in which the impact of race on these narratives is made secondary to the post-apocalyptic scenario itself. In *Earth Abides*, Isherwood Williams happens upon a family living just off the highway. The way George R. Stewart describes this group sets them apart. Indeed, unlike the other characters that Williams encounters, he passes these by nearly in silence. Williams meets these survivors just outside of North Little Rock, Arkansas, on his way toward Memphis, Tennessee. The Arkansas location would come to have much more significance in the decade following the novel's publication, as a site of contest over equal access to education for black students.[2] Williams's reaction to seeing the house and garden and meeting three other survivors helps situate the context of struggles against segregation:

> An hour on the road the next morning, at the edge of a small town, he started, as his eyes fell upon the unaccustomed sight of a well weeded and tended garden. He stopped, went to investigate, and found for the first time what might, by generous interpretation, be called a social group. They were Negroes—a

man, a middle-aged woman, a young boy. By the obvious look of the woman, there would soon be a fourth member. (Stewart, *Earth Abides*, 54)

The first way that the novel marginalizes these three characters is with the use of the term "Negroes"; the second is that the narrator will describe Williams as "white." In this manner, the narrator and Williams are aligned. Williams thinks that the group suffers "not only from the shock of the catastrophe" but also from what he characterizes as "the taboos carried over from before it," noting that "they talked with diffidence in the presence of *a strange white man*, dropping their eyes" (Stewart, *Earth Abides*, 55). This indicator also associates the narrator with whiteness, a fact made all the more obvious by the description of Williams's reaction to this group.

The encounter does not end there, nor does its import for understanding race in the novel and the post-apocalyptic mode. After trading what he thinks of as a now-worthless dollar for some eggs, Williams mulls over the idea of staying in this town:

"Here," he reflected, "I might be king in a little way, if I remained. They would not like it, but from long habit they would, I think, accept the situation—they would raise vegetables and chickens and pigs for me, and I could soon have a cow or two. They would do all the work that I need to have done. I could be king, at least, in a little way."

But the idea was only fleeting, and as he drove on, he began to think the Negroes had really solved the situation far better than he. He was living as a scavenger upon what was left of civilization; they, at least, were still living creatively, close to the land and in a stable situation, still raising most of what they needed. (Stewart, *Earth Abides*, 55–56)

Despite his role as record keeper of the post-apocalypse period, Williams cannot seem to assess the situation clearly. Here the novel projects a classic trope: it is white man's restraint and his distance from nature that dooms him to fail where the natural potency of the black body succeeds. The narrator's tone and Williams's fantasy work together in a subtle and contradictory fashion.

The book explicitly disavows the racism of pre-apocalyptic society as "taboo," yet at the same time it snidely reproduces such racism. The attitude of the narrator frames the encounter—specifically, his "generous" use of the designation "social group." Moreover, Williams simultaneously longs for a past that never was, thinking "I might be king." This one small moment, where the narrator and Williams share a discrepant mix of disgust and nostalgic longing, shows the latent white anxiety that permeates *Earth Abides*. This observation raises a question: is this novel about Earth abiding or the continuation of a particular white version of the world?

One more element of this scene stands out: the characterization of the woman as both "middle-aged" and pregnant. Here *Earth Abides* represents the black woman as supernaturally fecund in such a way as to contain both a moral condemnation of unrestrained or even irresponsible reproduction and the perversely acquisitive calculation of the American slave owner for whom the reproductive system of the black woman is a principal means of production. The man's age is not marked in the same way—the narrator does not seem to notice him in the same way as the woman—which suggests an unconscious assessment of her sexual value to Williams and the narrator in terms of both her attractiveness and her fertility. Here Williams and the narrator play out a compact series of racializing tropes, remainders filtered through the apocalyptic transformation of the storyworld, that are merely incidental to Williams's cataloguing of the post-apocalyptic United States and his prospects for survival.

This encounter along the road in *Earth Abides* can be all too easily overlooked. Similar returns could be made to Leigh Brackett's *The Long Tomorrow*, Richard Matheson's *I Am Legend*, Walter Miller Jr.'s *A Canticle for Leibowitz*, and many of the other texts discussed in previous chapters. Criticism of the post-apocalyptic mode could, in this way, always begin with the dominance of whiteness in the genre, the racially conflicted definition of apocalypse, and the varied responses to the end of the world. But such a start might miss a critical intervention made even earlier into the entangled thinking about apocalypse and race.

Originally published in *Darkwater: Voices from within the Veil* (1920), W.E.B. Du Bois's "The Comet" brilliantly depicts a post-apocalyptic New York City to eliminate or suspend the social relations that reproduce racialization. As the literary critic Mark Jerng memorably puts it, "historical possibility begins with the end of the world" (*Racial Worldmaking*, 211). Jim Davis, a black man, and Julia, an upper-class white woman, survive the gas burst of the comet. They explore the decimated city, finding no one else alive until the final climactic moments, when a kind of second apocalyptic event occurs and they realize that only New York City has been affected by the passing celestial traveler. The reality of pre-apocalyptic white supremacy crashes down upon them as money is thrust in Davis's hands, enforcing his role as racialized worker, and a disembodied voice threatens to lynch him, identifying his life as one lived under the constant threat of death. Yet Du Bois does not produce a tragedy: instead, the final moment implies a reunion of Davis with his "somebody," who is alive after all (Du Bois's "The Comet," 57). Both in terms of plot and setting, "The Comet" is a brilliant example of how the post-apocalyptic mode was forged in a crucible of critical analysis as a conceit capable of critiquing the status quo, rather than as a genre entrenched in simply reproducing the everyday world. Moreover, here we have an instance of a black writer producing a text that critiques post-apocalyptic visions, such as Stewart's, in advance. The positions of the protagonist and the narrator in *Earth Abides* have already been described from the critical standpoint of race in "The Comet," and in this way, we might connect Williams's daydream of enslaving the people by the road with the gestures of payment and threat at the end of "The Comet." Even when seemingly held in suspension during an apocalyptic interregnum, white supremacy and antiblack racism have baleful power. The key to challenging such power lies in remembering Du Bois's description of the return to racializing social relations. There is power in naming and describing such systems, in making them legible. Similarly, Du Bois's story enables the realization that Williams in fact does not act on his fantasy, which is itself a remainder. Jerng further clarifies the historical possibility he alludes to by describing it as the "task of an antiracist racial worldmaking," which finds its ultimate project in leaving "our racist worlds incoherent" (*Racial Worldmaking*, 217).

In this chapter, I track the development of race in the post-apocalyptic mode to show its move from a concern with a narrowly white future toward the possibility of more diverse futures. Yet even with a greater diversity of authors and characters, the post-apocalyptic storyworld presents a difficult context for antiracism. Old features of US politics and culture tend to resurface here. Historically, race is often coded simultaneously with gender and reproduction—an observation evident in racist fears such as those related to miscegenation—or it is simply washed out by white supremacy's claims to whiteness as a neutral or dominant category. A survey of post-apocalyptic novels reveals a conspicuous tendency to imagine survivors of the apocalypse as white. Though a number of novels stand as exceptions to this tendency, white people overwhelmingly dominate the post-apocalyptic worlds of American fiction. Indeed, such is the extent of the racial homogeneity of American post-apocalyptic worlds that whiteness is usually assumed. The marginalization and erasure of racialized characters—almost a constant today in theories of race in American literature and culture—in no way diminishes the force of race in these stories. As critics from Toni Morrison to Richard Dyer have repeatedly observed, to attend to the shadows of American fiction is to uncover a world of anxious fantasy, repressed longing, and unbearable suffering.[3] Moreover, it is a world that once exposed reconfigures the meaning of these narratives in dramatic and often unexpected ways. In the case of the post-apocalyptic novel, this system of racial disguise and disavowal assumes a form and consequence that are subtly distinct within American fiction.

It is in this light that I argue post-apocalyptic novels have their own unique criteria for determining who survives and what persists. As I explored in previous chapters, the criteria for survival have included cosmic selection (*The Stand*), the contingency of disease (*I Am Legend*), and the selection of military targets for nuclear strikes (*Alas, Babylon*). This process of selective world destroying is never a neutral one. For instance, real-world patterns of urban habitation and development have profound impacts on 1950s postnuclear apocalyptic stories, which resonate at a different cultural frequency for suburban white Americans than they would for black Americans left behind in the inner cities after white flight. To continue with this example, in Laura Finch and Jessica Hurley explain that "White flight, aided by federal and municipal investments in highway construction, suburban housing stock, and mortgage guarantees, recreated the inner city as predominantly African American at the same time that the inner city was being written off as the inevitable ground zero of a future nuclear war" ("Philadelphia"). The overlap of real-world ghettoized city cores and the imagined space of nuclear destruction shows the racialization implied in post-apocalyptic world building.

In the late 2000s, Mark Bould reminded readers of *Science Fiction Studies* that one of the core lessons of black science fiction produced by "Samuel Delany and Octavia Butler, as well as Sun Ra, Public Enemy, John Coltrane, Anthony Braxton, Miles Davis, Wayne Shorter, Jimi Hendrix, Afrika Bambaataa, Ishmael Reed, and Earth Wind and Fire" is a recognition that "'Apocalypse already happened,' that, in Public Enemy's words, 'Armageddon been in effect'" ("The Ships Landed Long Ago," 180). This realization presents the apocalypse as an unevenly distributed real-world descriptor that also provides narrative fodder for most white authors and readers at the same time as being all too real for certain black authors and readers. This statement may be historically inflected, referring to the long-term disorienting catastrophe of the black Atlantic and the middle passage that brought Africans to the Americas as slaves.[4] Alternatively, "Armageddon been in effect" could refer to the nature of living as a racialized subject within a world of the Ku Klux Klan, police brutality, and mass incarceration. It could refer to the urban development and city planning of the second half of the twentieth century as outlined by George Lipsitz, which saw the development of white suburbs and the gutting of black inner cities through highway projects and so on,[5] or to the current inversion of that tendency as inner-city life reflects gentrification's coffee-shop empires, artists' lofts turned into start-up offices, and boutique clothing stores for pets, while suburbs become affordable places to live for people displaced from urban cores. Each point of departure for examining the history of racial oppression and what has been characterized as antiblackness in the United States can be sutured into one long history of abuse, dispossession, and incarceration.[6] These starting points, and the countless others left unnamed, reveal that thinking about the apocalypse in the United States could always begin with an account of racial trauma and memory and specifically with a critique of the domination of whiteness. To put it bluntly, the dominance of whiteness in the US post-apocalyptic novel, in light of racial history, hinges on the conceit that the white characters are experiencing the apocalypse for the first time. In what follows,

I adjust my focus from the unconscious and incidental to the decided and explicit, if not thoughtful, ways that race is expressed in two US post-apocalyptic novels—Robert A. Heinlein's *Farnham's Freehold* (first published in 1964) and LeVar Burton's *Aftermath* (1997). Heinlein's novel has been much discussed in terms of its own merits, but it can be used to show how Matheson's last man trope can be put to different work than it is in *I Am Legend*. And Burton's text uses the post-apocalyptic mode in a way that demonstrates the paucity of criticality in Heinlein's assessment of racial domination in the post-apocalyptic United States.

CRITICAL INVERSION IN *FARNHAM'S FREEHOLD*

Published at the height of the US civil rights movement, in the very year that the Civil Rights Act became law, Heinlein's *Farnham's Freehold* attempts a critical inversion of race. Set in the years following World War II, the novel opens on the eve of an attack on US soil. Rather than narrating the events that immediately follow the catastrophe, the novel uses the conceit of a precise atomic bomb strike that transports the characters through time. The novel is both post-apocalyptic and a story of time travel. The future it envisions is one in which black people have created a technologically advanced social order and white people have become slaves.[7] Greatly shaken during the nuclear attack, the Farnhams emerge into a green, sunlit landscape, but they do not at first realize that they have skipped forward in time. In this manner, the novel unfolds in stages: first, a nuclear attack followed by the start of subsistence survival; then, capture and enslavement; and finally, an escape and the return to the time of the nuclear attack. The novel initially suggests that the freehold of the book's title is the bunker turned homestead à la Swiss family Robinson in which the family stays during the first phase. It is not until the end of the novel, when Hugh Farnham; his new love, Barbara; and their twin boys travel back in time to the night of the attack, that the titular freehold is revealed: a sheltered cave that they convert into a safe haven to weather the nuclear aftermath and prepare for the irradiated future to come. This ultimate haven is not the Farnhams' freehold, the novel's title implies, but that of Farnham, one man. Indeed, the title represents not a pastoral homestead but, ultimately, a holdout against a future dominated by a new (white) slavery. Heinlein's novel takes a critical stance on race through its inversion of racial domination, but it takes this tactic too far. Rather than offering a critique of the way race works in the United States, *Farnham's Freehold* clings to the possibility of a specifically white future.

To understand the impetus behind Heinlein's novel, it is crucial to have a sense of the author's political ideology, which comes out of a particular moment in science fiction writing. Brian W. Aldiss and David Wingrove found Heinlein "verbose and pedantic"; H. Bruce Franklin thought he was "optimistic," "expansionary," and filled with "missionary zeal"; and George Edgar Slusser described him as "a dogmatic optimist, a soapbox preacher who peddles his pet theories in the guise of fiction" (Aldiss and Wingrove, *Trillion Year Spree*, 268; Franklin, *Robert A. Heinlein*, 73; Slusser, *Robert A. Heinlein*, i; all quoted in McGiveron, "Heinlein's Inhabited Solar System," 246). Rafeeq O. McGiveron determines that "Heinlein thus is chastised not only for his particular views but simply for daring to express them" (ibid.). Samuel R. Delany makes a crucial observation about the science fiction community that contextualizes the kind of "daring" opinions that McGiveron seems ready to defend, whether or not they are soapbox-y and zealous:

> Understand that, since the late '30s, that community, that world had been largely Jewish, highly liberal, and with notable exceptions leaned well to the left. Even its right-wing mavens, Robert Heinlein or Poul Anderson (or, indeed, [John W.] Campbell), would have far preferred to go to a leftist party and have a friendly argument with some smart socialists than actually to hang out with the right-wing and libertarian organizations which they may well have supported in principal [*sic*] and, in Heinlein's case, with donations. ("Racism and Science Fiction")

The community that nurtured Heinlein's early work was fueled by dissenting views and loud disagreements. Later observers, such as Aldiss, Franklin, and Slusser, were not wrong to identify what they saw as bad behavior.

Much more recently, Jeet Heer provides a broad overview of Heinlein's move from the political left toward the political right. *Farnham's Freehold* has a central position in Heer's analysis, and he provocatively summarizes its aim: "Heinlein wanted to use *inversion* to show the evils of ethnic oppression" ("A Famous Science Fiction Writer's Descent into Libertarian Madness"). But Heinlein's inversion racializes blackness through stereotypes: his future black masters threaten white men with castration, take white women as companions, and eat white children.[8] At the same time, Heinlein's novel glorifies Farnham's patriarchal whiteness. Heer concludes that "*Farnham's Freehold* is an anti-racist novel only a Klansman could love" (ibid.) It is this inability to carry out the task of critical inversion that makes Heinlein's novel a challenge to interperet. While Stewart's novel features traces of a racist worldview, Heinlein's aims more surely at a racial problematic, but its execution reproduces the racist and sexist vitriol that is supposedly its target. Heinlein cannot seem to turn what Isaiah Lavender III has described as the "blackground" of science fiction writing into any sort of critical foreground (*Race in American Science Fiction*, 6; see also 7). Despite its inversion of the relations of historical US slavery, Heinlein produces a novel that results in the characters' desire for a whitewashed future.

The book follows the fate of the Farnhams and their company. The group consists of Hugh and Grace Farnham; their adult children, Karen and Duke; a black man named Joe, who is referred to on the first page as the "houseboy" (Heinlein, *Farnham's Freehold*, 5); and Karen's divorced friend Barbara, who serves as the focal point for the narration in the first chapters. The casualness of its racial and sexual overtones makes this a difficult book to read today. For instance, in the first chapter when Barbara whips up crêpes suzette, Hugh offers her a job as cook, suggesting that in that case Joe could stay on as housekeeper. Another example is when Duke, put off by the fact that Barbara had spurned his advances, objects to this too easy arrangement, saying "Don't you *know*? Barbara[,] . . . Dad is a notorious sex criminal" (ibid., 13; emphasis in the original). The group makes light of this interaction, with Hugh joking that it's the reason he studied law (to avoid having to pay lawyers' fees), and the evening goes on. Narrated from Barbara's perspective, the initial scene shows her working through her attraction to Hugh and her spiteful judgment of Grace—"Did women *have* to become so fretful and useless?" (ibid., 10 emphasis in the original)—with all of this serving to build Hugh's character at the expense of everyone else's. Heinlein's flippant style in these instances and many others like them betrays a form of braggart masculinity.

The first half of the novel features Hugh as a capable, determined, self-assured character, as it documents his domination of the rest of the group. In this way it prepares the reader for the moment of inversion. Heinlein's treatment of Hugh, his main character, has not aged well, and to a reader today, Heinlein's protagonist quickly comes to function as a point of ironic tension. Hugh reacts with speed and determination when he gets news of an airstrike over the radio, efficiently hustling his family into his well-stocked bunker. While Heinlein seems to be at pains to cast Hugh's self-possession and preparedness in a heroic light, readers today might see the same attributes as being those of a detestable character. In his recent review of the audiobook, Dale Darlage describes Hugh Farnham as the figurehead of one of the most dysfunctional families in science fiction:

> Hugh advocates eugenics, seriously threatens to kill his son several times, orders everyone to take sleeping pills and alcohol or other drugs on a regular basis, openly leers at his daughter's naked body, insists that everyone walk around naked in multiple scenes and conceives children with his daughter's best friend during the nuclear attack while his wife sleeps in the next room after he has drugged her. (*"Farnham's Freehold"*)

Hugh's actions are not neutral, nor are they justifiable in the face of catastrophe. As Darlage's summary above demonstrates, Hugh's actions in the novel produce solid ground for a critical approach to his character.

The novel creates oppositions between its characters, placing Hugh at the center as the injured party. Son turns against father as surely as wife turns against husband. Once they find themselves transplanted to an Edenic future United States, Hugh guides the group through the tasks of survival: farming, hunting, and recreation. Despite his confidence, Hugh deals poorly with his wife's alcoholism and his son's challenges to his authority. His greatest failing is in his inability to preserve his daughter's life—Karen dies during childbirth because of Hugh's attempt to save her child. Hugh's power is finally usurped with the arrival of the new rulers of the future: the African Protectorate.

The novel describes the first encounter with the future humans as though describing the sighting of alien spacecraft:

> A shape had appeared over the eastern rise. It slanted through the air on a course that would have missed them, but, as it neared the point of closest approach, it stopped dead, turned and headed for them.
>
> It passed majestically overhead. Hugh was unable to guess its size at first; there was nothing to which to relate it—a dark shape proportioned like a domino tile. But as it passed about five hundred feet up, it seemed to him that it was around a hundred feet wide and three times that in length. He could make out no features. It moved swiftly but made no noise. (Heinlein, *Farnham's Freehold*, 153)

Before revealing themselves or communicating with Hugh's group, the beings destroy the garden, freeze Duke in place, and produce a big red pavilion out of thin air. Here, the book uses the science-fictional conceit of alien life to introduce the protectorate—a narrative ploy often read as a strategy for the defamiliarizing of otherness. The fact that aliens could stand in for racialized others speaks to what Bould has described as a "color-blind future" ("The Ships Landed Long Ago," 177) imagined by most science fiction from 1950 on. While the encounter with alien life has provided a famously generative narrative conceit through which to explore alterity, it can also function to foreclose the exploration of concrete experiences of social difference among the human characters. When readers are faced with extraterrestrial aliens, more earthly forms of alienation and difference are squeezed out or relegated to the past, allowing authors to project a unified humanity. André Carrington provocatively describes the uneasy relationship between reality and figurative estrangement in science fiction with cutting accuracy: "when the metaphor eclipses its subtext, it mystifies rather than demystifying" ("The Unbearable Whiteness of Science Fiction"). Science fiction that seeks to emphasize or even criticize racial inequality walks a fine line that separates an insight-producing estrangement from an obfuscation of the complexities of racialization. In much this way, *Farnham's Freehold* presents future human culture through the science-fictional techniques of describing an alien encounter.

The alien encounter trope complicates Heinlein's critical inversion of racial ascription. Hugh's description of Ponse, the lord protector, replays space adventure descriptions of the encounter with an unknown, unplaceable, yet eminently describable other:

> Out of the pavilion strode a man. He seemed seven feet tall but some of this was helmet, plumed and burnished. He wore a flowing skirt of red embroidered in gold and was bare to the waist save that an end of the skirt thrown across one shoulder covered part of his broad chest. He was shod in black boots.
>
> . . . He had an air of good-natured arrogance and his eyes were bright and merry. His forehead was high, his skull massive; he looked intelligent and alert. Hugh could not place his race. His skin was dark brown and shiny. But his mouth was only slightly Negroid; his nose, though broad, was arched, and his black hair was wavy.
>
> He carried a small crop. (Heinlein, *Farnham's Freehold*, 155)

The narrator's description moves from fashion to phenotype. Hugh "could not place" the man's race yet racializes him nonetheless. With all the analysis that goes into situating this figure, his character, and his position, Heinlein offers one crucial detail with little comment: the small crop. What could a small crop mean for a person who travels in floating ships and calls forth buildings as though out of nothing?

So far, I have been using the concept of inversion as a structural one to explain the kind of world building that follows the apocalyptic time travel conceit of Heinlein's novel. Yet the inversion happens for the characters at a precise—indeed, even a personal—moment. As soon as Ponse strides out of the tent, this inversion happens. This point in the story leaves behind the possibility that Heinlein's inversion could become a critical one. Though the novel has revealed little of these future humans, it is at this moment that the Farnhams realize they are indeed in the distant future. Now, Ponse will speak only with Joe, who discovers that he must use what French he knows as a lingua franca. The *longue durée* of colonial domination and education rears its ugly head: not only does Joe know French, but Ponse does as well. The Farnhams are separated and taken away. As the setting changes from the pastoral to the slave pens, the novel takes on the dystopian inflections of a constrained situation, governed from the top down.

Family members receive advanced medical and dental attention, are well fed with delicious food, and live under the threat of being whipped or restrained by powerful force field technology. Barbara has her twins without the complications faced by Karen. Everyone is forced to undergo reeducation, learning details about how to properly address the Chosen and how to determine who to address in a given social situation. They are punished for failure and rewarded for success: "Good. But drop your eyes when you say it" (Heinlein, *Farnham's Freehold*, 168). If time travel has presented a problem situation for the Farnhams, then it also presents an awkward situation for the lord protector and his estate. One instructor tells Hugh:

> "Now about your status—" The teacher looked pained. "You haven't any. . . . I've tried to find out. Nobody knows but our Lord Uncle and they have not yet ruled. You're not a child, you're not a stud, you're not tempered [castrated], you don't belong anywhere. You're a savage and you don't fit." (ibid.)

Here the limits of inversion begin to reveal themselves. The impetus seems to be to put a white father in a situation (slavery) and see how it might make the way slavery works understandable and renounceable. Part of the basic assumption here suggests a deep mistrust of the knowledge already produced about slavery, from the slave narratives of Fredrick Douglass and Harriet Ann Jacobs on, and a commitment to the production of knowledge from a distinctly white vantage. Indeed, bell hooks describes the issues facing this kind of inversion for a racialized subject:

> Yet, blacks who imitate whites (adopting their values, speech, habits of being, etc.) continue to regard whiteness with suspicion, fear, and even hatred. This contradictory longing to possess the reality of the Other, even though that reality is one that wounds and negates, is expressive of the desire to understand the mystery,

to know intimately through imitation, as though such knowing worn like an amulet, a mask, will ward away the evil, the terror. (*Black Looks*, 166)

She pinpoints the limits of the kind of inversion of racial hierarchy that Heinlein attempts and describes the world of white supremacy as a world of "mystery," "evil," and "terror." Crucially, it is also one of representation, signification, and symbolism, which can be assessed, named, and interpreted.

Following this line of thinking, if the inversion of racial social relations from white supremacy to the new black ascendency in Heinlein's novel reveals anything, it does so through Joe's character. This occurs not in moments when he acts out the role of benevolent superior, as when he says to Hugh, "Look, if you aren't treated okay, you tell me. I can fix it" (Heinlein, *Farnham's Freehold*, 170), but when he thinks back to his twentieth-century experience in the Farnhams' house. At the start of the novel, Joe inhabits a position that Brian Wagner describes this way: "To be black means to exist in exchange without being a party to exchange. Being black means belonging to a state that is organized in part by its ignorance to your perspective— a state that does not, that cannot, know your mind" (*Disturbing the Peace*, 1). After the inversion, Heinlein gives readers a different Joe. For instance, when Joe and Hugh are first reunited, he relates how close Hugh and Duke were to being castrated. This moment is one of the rare times in the book when Joe elaborates on his experience of working for the Farnhams even as it stays true to the Heinlein's inversion:

> Different people laugh at different things. Karen used to use a fake Negro dialect that set my teeth on edge, the times I overheard it. But she didn't mean any harm. Karen— Well, they just don't come any better, and you and I know it and I'll shut up about it. Look, if the vet had gone ahead [with the castrating], without orders, it would have cost him his hands; Ponse sent that word to him. Might have suspended the sentence—good surgeons are valuable. But his assumption was only natural, Hugh; both you and Duke are too tall and too big for a stud. However, Ponse doesn't tolerate sloppiness. (*Farnham's Freehold*, 172)

Joe's complaint is fleeting. He doesn't judge Karen for her racist transgressions, yet he nonetheless notes the impact they had. His words move from honest reflection to accommodation that aims at assuaging Hugh's concern in a paternalistic matter. Here Joe acts out his position from the other side of Heinlein's inversion—he speaks for the dominating race, for Ponse. He reveals the pressures weighing on Ponse and the consideration that the leader must use in making each decision. He also reveals that society is strictly controlled, for both oppressed and oppressor. This way of things, Joe implies, is the natural order.

Later, Hugh pushes Joe as they discuss the way their roles have been reversed. Hugh says, "Joe, do you know what you sound like? Like some white-supremacist apologist telling how well off the darkies used to be, a-sittin' outside their cabins, a-strummin' their banjoes, and singin' spirituals" (ibid., 258). Hugh is stuck in the past. His reach for an analogy to express the domination he experiences is eclipsed by the history of white supremacy in United States. Additionally, the way he describes racialized characters undercuts his point. Thrown forward in time, he has missed the historical emergence of these future humans. He even goes so far as to say to Joe, "You're a Chosen, I'm a servant. Can I fetch your white sheet for you, Massah? What time does the Klan meet?" (ibid.). Hugh's melodramatic appeal to the history of racism in the United States cannot reach Joe, who says, "The shoe is on the other foot, that's all—and high time. I used to be a servant, now I'm a respected businessman. . . . I'm no hypocrite. I was a servant, now you are one. What are you beefing about?" (ibid., 258–59).

In this confrontation late in the novel, Farnham objects to the way Joe refers to his past position with the family as that of a servant: "Joe, you were a decently treated employee. You were not a slave" (Heinlein, *Farnham's Freehold*, 259). At this moment Joe's eyes become "opaque," his visage takes on "an ebony hardness," and he says, "have you ever made a bus trip through Alabama? As a '[n word]'?" (ibid.).[9] This statement overshadows the critical inversion that Heinlein aims for in the novel—not because of its racializing language, but because of the incommensurability of the ongoing history of racial oppression in the United States and the fantastic leaps forward and backward in time in the novel. *Farnham's Freehold* leaps from one steady state of racial oppression to another to offer a lesson about racism. Due to the Farnham's whiteness and the tropes of blackness on display in the novel, this lesson seems to be aimed at white people. Despite the real effort to come to terms with the confining experience of racial oppression, Heinlein's novel falls short. While its inversion could easily be imagined as the vehicle for a radical critique of white supremacy, it instead becomes a study of the recuperative strategies of reactionary forces in the United States in the post-civil rights era. Here, Heinlein uses so-called reverse discrimination,—an all-too-familiar right-wing talking point.

The science fiction critic Sharon DeGraw presents a generous reading of Heinlein's reversal of historical American slavery, writing that "the racial inversion reveals the power, privilege, and normative position of whiteness in western society, attributes normally hidden for white readers by the very privilege attached to their racial classification" (*The Subject of Race in American Science Fiction*, 120). Drawing on Heinlein criticism, she outlines two positions, represented by Philip E. Smith II and Alexei Panshin. Smith reads the ending of *Farnham's Freehold* as validating Heinlein's critical acumen, and Panshin suggests that the text is "a study in the varieties of impotence" (*Heinlein in Dimension*, 109; quoted in DeGraw, *The Subject of Race in American Science Fiction*, 121). Neither position works, according to DeGraw. For a way forward she turns to Gary Westfahl, who claims that critics misread the text because they collapse Heinlein with Farnham too quickly. Thus, in DeGraw's words, they miss "Heinlein's indictment of his own racism, through the more extreme racism embodied in his protagonist" (*The Subject of Race in American Science Fiction*, 121). But this interpretation does not satisfy DeGraw, nor does it satisfy me. Rather, the racialized and gendered dynamics of the novel amplify one another. Westfahl, DeGraw argues, leaves two key moral reasons for Karen Farnham's death out of the discussion: her pregnancy occurred out of wedlock, and she had an interracial relationship as she became romantically interested in Joe: "In breaking these sexual and romantic taboos, Karen incurs the extreme societal punishment of death" (ibid., 122). Moreover, Karen's pregnancy and subsequent death during labor, DeGraw argues, prevents her from consummating a relationship with Joe, which serves to avoid controversy for Heinlein and the science fiction community and maintain Joe's "overt celibacy" (ibid.). In the end, DeGraw makes her position clear: though Heinlein is certainly capable of self-criticism, "this project is sabotaged by the very racism supposedly being critiqued" (ibid., 124). She adds, "Heinlein closes off the possibility, the threat of this racially inverted future, while paving the way for the new, improved Anglo family" (ibid., 126).

Aiming for a critique of racism, *Farnham's Freehold* instead targets slavery, and it does so through a series of racist tropes. The first sign of the limit of Heinlein's inversion strategy is that the novel does not actually tell Joe's story, despite the fact that he may be the character best positioned to recognize the inversion of his present in the future into which he and the Farnhams are dropped. Moreover, the inversion does nothing to reeducate Hugh Farnham: indeed, there is little in the way of *bildung* to be found here. Instead, the novel does no more than show how Hugh, the white patriarch, can plot his and his (new) family's way out of this most compromising of situations.

Because the novel begins in medias res, Heinlein is able to include two mysteries—first, how the unsuspecting characters have been launched forward in time by the bomb, and second, why the world they enter has racially inverted social relations. Curiously, the novel leaves blank the part of the story it seems so desperate to present. Hugh and Barbara make it back to the night of the bomb just in time to interrupt the game of bridge that their past selves are playing and to steal Barbara's car. They get out of town and take shelter in an abandoned mine, which they build into the freehold of the novel's title. This narrative closure—in which inversion is avoided and a new couple and new children replace the old ones—skips over any genuine historical change, all the while hinting that Hugh's descendants would stave off the rise of black culture and white slavery. The novel says none of this directly, yet the closure of *Farnham's Freehold* resists the precise inversion on which its story was founded and celebrates the restitution of the social order through a new family. In this way, the novel forecloses the possibility of a future (thinkable or not) without white patriarchy. Ruling out any other possible future, it produces what I would describe as an enclave and a reduced future at the same time. It presents the critical inversion as an opportunity for the characters to learn from the future and play out their restored time line differently, yet Heinlein's lessons all point toward a radically antiblack future rather than anything approaching the desegregation of the future or even a critique of the domination of the remainders of whiteness and white power.

BLACK FUTURES IN *AFTERMATH*

Burton's *Aftermath* employs a complex apocalyptic conceit to present a fairly straightforward thriller plot. The story begins in a fictional 2011, with a climate scientist at the National Aeronautics and Space Administration, Leon Cane, publishing an alarming article in *Scientific American*. He writes about the orbital, research-focused space station and the impact shuttle traffic is having on the ozone layer. In light of his findings, funding for the space station is canceled. Meanwhile, the first black president of the United States is assassinated only days after his election. The United States begins to collapse due to racial resentment. In orbit meanwhile, the scientists in the now-defunded space station are stranded and left to die. To prevent all-out civil war, a black US general attempts to seize control of the military. His failure sparks a race war that lasts for three years: "Millions die, millions more are left homeless. Food shortages. Nationwide famine. Widespread disease. Neighborhoods become walled communities as everyone tries to hold on to what little they have. Many towns and cities no longer have electricity or running water" (Burton, *Aftermath*, xii). The war ends in 2019 with the signing of a peace treaty.

All of this information is provided in bullet-point form at the opening of the novel, which is related to the practice that Stephen King and Octavia E. Butler mention using to track current events as they were writing *The Stand* and *Parable of the Sower*, respectively. Burton offers in list form what King and Butler draw on to form the backdrop of their storyworld versions of the United States. If the thriller genre is characterized by a series of punctual event, each grander and more spectacular than the last, then Burton's bullet-point world building provides *Aftermath* with superb momentum for its post-apocalyptic thriller plot. Moreover, the considered series of events and their thorough description produce verisimilitude: Burton connects the events of the novel with the 1990s, when he was writing the novel, thereby giving *Aftermath* a startling reality. This move contrasts with David Brin's prologue to *The Postman*, where "it hardly mattered anymore what had done it" (n.p.), and pushes back against

King's disconnected and vague politics. One need only look at US history during the first decades of the twenty-first century to see that Burton's imagined future time line is a highly prescient one. He not only anticipates the election of the first black president, but he also senses the oncoming financial crisis, the return of entrenched antiracist struggles, deepening ideological conflict between the left and the right, the compromising of public funding for space exploration, anthropogenic climate change, and so on.

The plot of the novel revolves around another problematic. The world of the novel is one in which whites fear the sun, while blacks are better able to withstand the ultraviolet light. Dr. Rene Reynolds—one of the protagonists—is a black neuropsychologist who has created a device called the Neuro-Enhancer that can unlock the brain's full potential and use the body's own systems to cure diseases, from neurological ailments to cancers. Uninterested in a technological fix, Dr. Randall Sinclair—a white scientist who is the antagonist—performs illegal skin treatments to graft black skin onto white flesh.[10] Neither of these approaches addresses the systemic problem of solar radiation. The introduction of this conflict signals a departure from the conflicts summarized in the chronology. Rather than taking a societal and collective approach, the novel focuses on the threat of one evil man, Sinclair, and the efforts of a ragtag group of unlikely heroes to put a stop to his evil plan to capture black bodies and steal their flesh.

The novel shifts from bullet points about collective history in a mode reminiscent of medieval annals to a plot that tracks five characters drawn together by circumstance. Sinclair captures both Reynolds and the Neuro-Enhancer. Cane, the disheartened and now homeless author of the *Scientific American* article, witnesses the kidnapping. Reynolds hands off a crucial part of the Neuro-Enhancer to Cane, forming a mental link between them in the process. After this the novel follows five narrative strands: those of Cane, Reynolds, an orphaned white girl named Amy, a Lakota elder named Jacob Fire Cloud, and a Filipino delivery-truck driver named Danny. Over the course of the novel, Reynolds is able to link each of them telepathically through a kind of passive connection. The group of characters comes together in the final pages of the novel just in time to save Reynolds from a skinning operation run by Sinclair. Fire Cloud sacrifices himself so the group can succeed, enacting the trope of the racialized martyr.

The novel ends with Cane heading out to track more skinning operations, Reynolds traveling to Fire Cloud's reservation, and Danny adopting Amy. The characters' telepathic connection provides a conceit that is not in either Stewart's or Heinlein's novels. The characters from those books, Farnham and Williams, both operate as vigilantes and patriarchs, not trusting the people who surround them. The sharing of impressions between Reynolds, Cane, and the others puts not only people of color but a woman of color at the forefront of the imagined struggle for the future. In contrast to the segregated future of Williams's abiding Earth or the patriarchal law that imbues Farnham with self-righteous certainty, Burton's characters have different occupations, histories, and backgrounds. Through an unforeseen side effect of the Neuro-Enhancer, they are in mental dialogue with one another.

Given the politically troubling representation of race in Heinlein's novel, Burton's approach—what I would first describe as one based on the liberal multicultural politics of representation—displays the possibility that the post-apocalyptic novel need not tell white peoples' stories exclusively. Indeed, as Delany and others have argued, the politics of representation can accomplish a great deal in rectifying the whiteness of science fiction.[11] While Burton's diverse cast of characters align is aligned with a liberal politics of inclusion and diversity, his storyworld is one that returns racial difference to starkly biological terms. Racial difference in *Aftermath* divides those who are more or less adapted to a depleted ozone layer, conjuring up a decidedly eugenicist vision of racial fitness. The competing science-fictional solutions to this oddly genetic environmental inversion of white privilege become, in this frame, metaphoric constructions of two distinct responses to a racial inequality that is bluntly literalized by a world inhospitable to one phylogenetic group: the first uses a technology that creates a universal humanist solution (the Neuro-Enhancer), and the second (Sinclair's skin transplant procedure) literalizes the exploitation of the European slave economy, using the skin of people of color to extend the life and well-being of the white population.

Burton's narrator lays bare the absolute brutality that inheres in the novel's racially oppressive shadow economy. White skinners steal homeless black people, discarding their flensed bodies. Cane nearly stumbles over a pair of bodies as he approaches Sinclair's base of operations. The description of this moment combines the narrative strategies of plot-driven storytelling and the fact-fueled time line from the start of the novel: Cane "had heard stories from others on the street, whispered stories told around late night fires about evil men who hunted and murdered people of color, selling their skin for illegal medical grafts. In some cases their internal organs were also taken and sold" (Burton, *Aftermath*, 219). The first sentence features a character's knowledge, and the second slips into the narrator's confirmation of that knowledge. The way *Aftermath* represents the illicit skin trade connects surplus populations with what the literary critic Kevin Floyd describes as "*capital's* abstraction of life, its tendential reduction of living labour to living inertia, to life at once subsumed by capital and externalised from it" ("Automatic Subjects," 80; emphasis in the original). Floyd's claim connects—indirectly, yet with complexity—the racialized bodies caught in the aftermath of a race war in a future version of the United States that is buffeted by solar radiation to the shaky ground of the social organization of labor in this fictionalized moment. Burton's novel shows in clear detail the contradictory way that black lives have historically come to matter in the United States. His imagined post-apocalyptic future hinges on the theft of black people's skin for the ongoing well-being of whites, which complicates the nineteenth-century cultural practice of blackface minstrelsy that Eric Lott has described with the memorable phrase that is the title of his 1993 *Love and Theft*. Moreover, the grisly image of white people wearing the stolen skin of black people hides the system of mass incarceration and police violence behind a brutal metaphor for white anxiety, fragility, and fear. In this figure, Burton's novel expands my initial characterization of its liberal multiculturalism. The novel moves toward what Jodi Melamed has strikingly described as the guiding tendency of racial capitalism: to, in the words of her title, *Represent and Destroy* (2011).

In *Aftermath* the few glimpses of social life are found in scientific laboratories, a diner, Danny's delivery truck, and in the shadow economy of Sinclair's skinning operation. The future projected by Burton is not one without circuits and technocrats of capital. Burton's novel shows this world from the bottom, from the vantage point of the homeless (Cane and Amy), the precariously employed (Danny), the dispossessed (Fire Cloud), and the captured (Reynolds). These characters stand in for other survivors caught in the aftermath. They represent what Floyd describes as forms of "labour . . . disinterred from life, increasingly hollowed out, leaving behind what is, for capital, a vital remainder" ("Automatic Subjects," 81). Floyd's argument hinges on the fact that all capital has left are remainders, and in a world where capital is incapable of producing value, labor suffers as well. All that remains are value fumes, little more than traces of the productive capacity of capital. His argument is presented with an option: quoting Nancy Scheper-Hughes ("The Last Commodity," 145), Floyd writes, "Organ scarcity having once been a serious problem, there is now 'no shortage of desperate individuals willing to sell a kidney, a portion of their liver, a lung, an eye, or even a testicle for a pittance'" ("Automatic Subjects," 81). There are two ways to read Burton's post-apocalyptic shadow economy that are not even mutually exclusive. One is as metaphor, and the other is as political-economic forecast. Though Floyd tracks the volatility of capital in the real world, Burton's bullet-point extrapolation projects a future in which the fictional aftermath and the real aftermath of capitalism are one and the same. The novum of the Neuro-Enhancer is the science-fictional element of Burton's storyworld, and the rest hauntingly characterizes the United States of the early twenty-first century.

There is a long history of black apocalyptic writing. Bould draws on Mark Sinker's list of black science fiction writers ("Loving the Alien"), which includes artists who tend to be considered by race (that is black artists, performers, writers, and so on), rather than by the genres in which they work (that is, treating black creators as science fiction artists, performers, writers, and so on). The lineage of black apocalyptic writing makes clear that Burton's text offers an innovation in the post-apocalyptic mode. In retrospect, the seemingly easy years of anxiety about the atomic bomb have ended. The novel's plot would not make sense without the chronicle of events at its start. The series of events are so interlaced and so contingent that the destruction wrought on the United States in *Aftermath* cannot strictly be considered to have a singular cause. Instead of one punctual event with apocalyptic consequences—as in Stewart's and Heinlein's novels—Burton unleashes a cascade of apocalyptic crises. In framing his novel with such a list of apocalyptic narrative conceits, Burton provides a further point of differentiation between his novel and Heinlein's: *Farn-*

ham's Freehold has a singular, atomic origin that irrevocably changes suburban life (even as it obliterates the inner city), while the apocalypse of *Aftermath* displays historical nuance.

Burton's novel touches on a topic of some debate in American literature and politics: what does, or can, the apocalypse mean? It could, as in the Cold War world of Stewart and Heinlein, represent the looming threat of nuclear annihilation. This definition of what constitutes an apocalypse presents *the* apocalypse, in James Berger's sense (*After the End*), as a totalizing event: it affects everyone almost everywhere. *Aftermath* demonstrates that there is more unevenness to apocalypse than the definite article indicates. Writing about such unevenness, Maxine Lavon Montgomery makes a crucial distinction between two US political agendas, arguing that black Americans and white Americans have "conflicting notions of what constitutes an apocalypse" (*The Apocalypse in African-American Fiction*, 1).[12] The distinction is one between the economic productivity of the state and capital, on the one hand, and the livelihood of people, on the other hand. The same apocalyptic event may threaten both the state and the people, but the way a government responds to the event typically favors profitability over livelihood. This distinction takes on more force in Montgomery's argument because she follows it as it separates the white state and black citizens. In this context Montgomery argues that for the black tradition, "writing an apocalyptic novel is a socially symbolic act with a meaning often hidden from the eyes of those outside the culture, because the novelist uses language in an effort to inscribe a future that challenges the beliefs present in the American mythos" (ibid., 2–3). As is the case in American literature and culture more generally, in the post-apocalyptic novel, race becomes a locus of contest with social implications that are not always evident or clear to every reader.

Apocalypse signifies differently depending on the author and the audience. Better than Heinlein's inversion, which reproduced racial categories of dominance rather than critiquing them, Burton's novel could fit in Montgomery's black apocalyptic tradition. She writes, "In apocalypse, then, there is evidence of the crisis-ridden African-American experience: the movement from country to city, the change from a rural or agrarian to an urban or industrialized environment, and once history disappointed hope for progress, the search for a tenable response to continued racist oppression" (*The Apocalypse in African-American Fiction*, 1–2). The enumeration of contingent disaster at the start of *Aftermath* introduces a new form of post-apocalyptic narrative: Burton's aftermath, then, is not the aftermath of a singular event such as a war, a nuclear detonation, or the spread of a virus. Instead, it occurs in the wake of the extrapolation of racial oppression in the United States from the mid-1990s into the twenty-first century. Burton's use of the thriller plot, preceded by bullet points, provides a genuine attempt to track racial strife through 1990s multi-cultural discourse. The inclusion of the race war as part of the chronicle of events leading to the plot indicates its political import: Burton implicitly draws on histories of dispossession and discontent, as well as on urban resistance and the work of black-power groups, to project a future breaking point.

Aftermath contests the whiteness of the post-apocalyptic tradition on multiple levels at once. On the level of plot and representation, the novel is about people of color working together to stop a white man's skinning operation. On the level of form, it extrapolates a post-apocalyptic storyworld from the erasures and inequalities of real-world history. Rather than targeting the conceptual shortcoming of freedom through critical inversion as Heinlein does, Burton imagines a storyworld in which things have gotten worse for everyone. Race matters differently in post-apocalyptic narratives than in science fiction because it shows us the limits of whiteness as a neutral category, and in doing so, it creates an opportunity for a sense of the reckoning required to begin dismantling white supremacy. The whiteness of the genre cannot be addressed simply by critical inversion or by including characters of color, though the latter is a viable first step to take. The history of the post-apocalyptic mode is a history of imagining that white people survive the apocalypse. Burton's book continues to make the argument set out by Du Bois and Butler and repeated by Public Enemy and others by insisting that black people already have survived it. Understanding this fact is merely the first step.

6
The Reproductive Imperative

> *They sat at the window and ate in their robes by the candlelight a midnight supper and watched distant cities burn. A few nights later she gave birth in their bed by the light of a drycell lamp. Gloves meant for dishwashing. The improbable appearance of the small crown of the head. Streaked with blood and lank black hair. The rank meconium. Her cries meant nothing to him. Beyond the window just the gathering cold, the fires on the horizon. He held aloft the red body so raw and naked and cut the cord with kitchen shears and wrapped his son in a towel.*
> —CORMAC MCCARTHY, *The Road*

To those familiar with Cormac McCarthy's work, it should come as no surprise that his Pulitzer Prize–winning novel *The Road* (2006) has a troubled relationship with gender. In the epigraph above, the man feels nothing about the woman's cries.[1] Severing one connection as he forges another, he thinks of the woman as "her," while the newborn child is "his son." Yet why is it that the woman's role as giver of life, so central to this novel, is pushed to the side by the narrator and critics of the novel? An answer to this question can be found in the same passage. Characters tell a personal story about gender, and the objects they use tell another. In the birth scene, the tools of housework have been as incredibly repurposed as everything else has after the apocalypse: with "gloves meant for dishwashing" and kitchen shears turned into surgeon's tools, the intended use of objects has become as irrelevant to survivors as the paper money littering the streets. In the apocalyptic scenario, the man discovers a more direct usefulness in the objects around him. "Her cries meant nothing to him" because the narrator has instrumentalized the woman. Building on these insights, this chapter argues that she plays a double role in *The Road*, as both a symbol of what must be left behind and the guarantor of the idea of the future. Put in the idiom I have been advancing, *The Road* grapples with the idea of the woman as a remainder, but here my reading of the novel develops the concept of the reproductive imperative.

The Road can be added to a list of post-apocalyptic novels about and often focalized through male characters who openly display the genre's obsession with survival. This list includes Jack London's *The Scarlet Plague* (first published in 1912), George R. Stewart's *Earth Abides* (first published in 1949), Robert A. Heinlein's *Farnham's Freehold* (first published in 1964), Stephen King's *The Stand* (first published in 1978; the unabridged version was published in 1990), and Peter Heller's *The Dog Stars* (2012).[2] The ways survival happens in these novels vary. It could take place in the past, as in London's novella—in which the protagonist tells the story of his survival to his grandchildren from the safety of restored order. In Stewart's novel, the character's survival is tracked moment by moment until the point when the linguistic and cultural regression of the next generation leave them nearly unrecognizable to the protagonist. Of the books in this list, Heinlein's novel perhaps best portrays an attempted return to small-scale agriculture, which is a sure route to survival. Alternatively, in *The Stand* survival is based less on nutritional needs than on spiritual and social needs: survival is first something that just happens (that is, the surviving characters were not infected by disease) and later becomes a reason to gather and fight. Heller's book is perhaps the least interested in how the characters managed to survive in the early years after the apocalyptic event, as it features a pair of men who manage post-apocalyptic survival quite well, yet the protagonist begins to feel a need for something more than the passage of years. Characters in such works ask, "why am I doing this?"—in effect, why fight to survive? Characters in each example start from the position of surviving the apocalypse and the immediate situation it created (the lingering presence of a disease, a new landscape, a different sociality), and from there they turn to questions about futurity. Even in novels narrated by mothers or other female characters, such dynamics hold sway, as in Carola Dibbell's *The Only Ones* (2015), Edan Lepucki's *California* (2014), and Octavia E. Butler's oeuvre.[3]

The answer to the question "why am I doing this?" often arrives in the form of the family, or procreation. The struggle to carry on is often framed by the need to protect children and guarantee their future well-being. This move of the post-apocalyptic novel—to set the gateway to the future in the form of the possibility of future generations—confuses the character-level struggle for survival with the species-level fight against extinction. For the most part, post-apocalyptic novels enact in the realm of narrative what Lee Edelman described in the realm of the political as reproductive futurism. Edelman's critique opposes the futurism of compulsory heterosexuality with a radical queer slogan of "no future" founded not in affirmation, but in radical negativity. Writing about P. D. James's novel *The Children of Men* (first published in 1992), in which the crisis is the end of fertility *tout court*, Edelman quotes James's protagonist, who whines, "'without the hope of posterity, for our race if not for ourselves, without the assurance that we being dead yet live, all pleasures of the mind and senses sometimes seem to me no more than pathetic and crumbling defences shored up against our ruins'" (James, *Children of Men*, 9, quoted in Edelman, *No Future*, 12). Edelman asks, "How better to characterize the narrative project of *The Children of Men* itself, which ends, as anyone not born yesterday surely expects from the start, with the renewal of our barren and dying race through the miracle of birth?" (*No Future*, 12). Writing in direct opposition to the combination of future possibility and heterosexual procreation, Edelman calls for a queer insistence that "we are the advocates of abortion; that the Child as futurity's emblem must die; that the future is mere repetition and just as lethal as the past" (ibid., 31).[4] For all its negativity, Edelman's critique cuts only one way. Edelman's conceptualization of reproduction as a mode of procreative normativity remains exclusively focused on heterosexual intercourse, while it leaves untold "our daily reproduction in the service of capitalism" (Parvulescu, "Reproduction and Queer Theory," 89). *The Road*, as a post-apocalyptic novel fixated on the possibility of a future rising out of the ashes of the blasted world, makes vivid the limits of both reproductive futurism and of Edelman's critique.[5] It emphasizes survival and reproduction, and it demonstrates the slippage between the two concepts that happens in the post-apocalyptic mode.

In this chapter, I discuss the role of the woman in *The Road* differently from the way that other critics have done. To do so, I read critics' focus on style and ethics in *The Road* as a way of avoiding political readings of the novel. My reading does not draw prescriptive lessons from fiction. Rather, it focuses on the capacity of post-apocalyptic narrative to express the entanglement of gender and futurity and to grapple with the imperative that this entanglement imposes. *The Road* employs the post-apocalyptic survival narrative in three different ways:

(1) From the man's perspective, the world seems to be set against him. The story that the man tells is one of failure—the past is too distant and alien, and the future is not guaranteed.
(2) The second perspective—the boy's—is revealed only at the novel's close. Ethical readings of *The Road* tend to pull on this thread, which leads to the boy's fundamental openness to the world, his desire to help others, and his interest in finding other "good guys" (McCarthy, *The Road*, 77) like him and the man.
(3) Third is what I see as a third path through the novel—the woman's aborted narrative—which is addressed by few critics.

Though the woman's story remains crucial to the cohesion and successful completion of the plot, the novel does not present it. For example, the woman's suicide is the causal event that moves the plot of the novel forward, but it is never represented, and its profound motivating force in the story is registered only in its effects. The problem here is that *The Road* effectively banishes the woman from its pages, despite the fact that she is necessary to the flourishing of the man and the boy. The novel works as narrative precisely because of the aborted emplotment of the woman and the appearance of the new woman at the plot's end. Put differently, the novel makes the woman the bearer of the power of creation, but this power can be contained only by excluding her from the story. The triangulation of *The Road*'s implied argument reveals a simultaneously individualized and universalized demand placed on people with internal reproductive organs and those who appear to be such people—the demand that they must reproduce. The focus of this chapter, then, is what I call the reproductive imperative and the way McCarthy's highly praised and widely taught novel—as well as much of the attendant criticism—works to efface its gender problematic.

BEYOND ETHICAL READINGS

Compared to many of the texts I discuss in this book, *The Road* has a significant body of critical work. In the fifteen years since its publication, it has also been taught in countless graduate and undergraduate classrooms. Moreover, a search on August 24, 2020, of the MLA International Bibliography Database for items containing both the terms "McCarthy, Cormac" and "*The Road*" generated 161 English-language results.[6] In light of the proliferation of writing on *The Road*, this chapter engages with criticism of the novel.

A great many critics emphasize ethics in their readings of *The Road* by describing the novel's stylistic impasse as a clash between the dissolution of language in the storyworld and the power of fiction in the novel form.[7] The language used to describe the novel varies wildly. Critics describe *The Road* as an adventure story (Chabon, "Dark Adventure"), a "classic hero story" (Cooper, "'There Is No God and We Are His Prophets,'" 135); a "garden variety dystopia" (Jameson, "On the Power of the Negative," 72); a mix of environmental and Christian apocalypse (Coyle, "Morels and Morals," 286); modernist irony (Adiutori, "*The Road* Is Mapped"); a "post-9/11 male sentimental novel" (Sullivan, "The Good Guys"); a depiction of a "post-abundant reality" (Kollin, "'Barren, Silent, Godless,'" 160); and as both a post-apocalyptic novel and definitely not a post-apocalyptic novel.[8] This much critical work on the title produces a descriptive churn around the novel's generic status. More must be made of the novel than a battleground for critics to work out their arguments about genre or style. Style remains of central importance to grasping the implications of the novel, but it is not the end. What makes McCarthy's post-apocalyptic novel so appealing must be the way it rests at the crux of both a generic divide (between literature and genre) and a conceptual one (between ethics and politics).

The ethical approach to reading *The Road* takes a step toward addressing the deep inequalities of the novel's storyworld.[9] In moral terms, Lydia R. Cooper argues that in *The Road* "symbols may be shorn of their referents, but the attempt to reunite the symbol with ethical action is of paramount importance" ("'There Is No God and We Are His Prophets,'" 132–33 and 142–43). The ethical parameters hinge on the man's and the boy's referring to themselves as the good guys and the man's multiple suggestions that they are "carrying the fire" (McCarthy, *The Road*, 83, 129, and 216). Paul Patton elaborates this point: "We might understand the fire in *The Road* as a metaphor for some kind of moral order and the guarantee of a future humanity that is clearly intended, at least in the eyes of the father to be borne by the son" ("McCarthy's Fire," 142). Ethical readings of the novel carry more persuasive force by moving beyond a vaguely moralistic understanding of the good and grounding their ethical readings in environmentalism. For instance, Laura Gruber Godfrey persuasively describes the landscape of the novel as "an environment well past the point of ecological crisis" ("'The World He'd Lost,'" 166), and George Monbiot has famously claimed that *The Road* is "the most important environmental book ever written" ("Civilisation Ends with a Shutdown of Human Concern"). Critics opposed to reading the ethics of *The Road* such as Madison Smartt Bell argue that "the order of the universe does not require our survival" ("A Writer's View of Cormac McCarthy," 10), while Dana Phillips claims that "to read *The Road* for signs of hope and redemption is to misread it" ("'He Ought Not Have Done It,'" 188). Building on the observations of Bell and Phillips, I argue that ethical approaches to the novel tend to miss the pivotal role of gender in the novel's relationship to the future.

Nell Sullivan is one of the few critics to take up gender as a critical lens for reading *The Road*.[10] In "The Good Guys," Sullivan argues that the book should be read as a male sentimental novel that, by placing the man and the boy outside of the domestic sphere, allows them to develop a paternal-filial bond. Women are excluded from the story as a way of building male sentimental affection and maternal power so these male characters begin to transcend masculine stereotypes.[11] The male relationships in the novel make clear that "the filiation theme" in *The Road* needs at least one character with internal reproductive organs, "a womb to produce fruit" (Sullivan "The Good Guys," 90).

Here, the novel opens a gap that allows critics to misidentify a political struggle over gender as an ethical one. *The Road* invites ethical readings because it connects the future to the reproductive capacities of the uterus and then scrutinizes the reproductive choices of the absent female character in particular. Taking such scrutiny into account makes it possible to read the novel in a way that grasps its audible post-apocalyptic imperative: reproduce!

FROM THE INACCESSIBLE PAST TO THE IMPOSSIBLE FUTURE

I open my reading of *The Road* with the final exchange between the man and the woman. In this exchange, the woman identifies the future she inhabits as coterminous with a choice: will one endure the present in the hope of a future or give in to that future's seeming impossibility?

> You talk about taking a stand but there is no stand to take. My heart was ripped out of me the night he was born so dont ask for sorrow now. There is none. Maybe you'll be good at this. I doubt it, but who knows. The one thing I can tell you is that you wont survive for yourself. I know because I would never have come this far. A person who had no one would be well advised to cobble together some passable ghost. Breathe it into being and coax it along with words of love. Offer it each phantom crumb and shield it from harm with your body. As for me my only hope is for eternal nothingness and I hope it with all my heart. (McCarthy, *The Road*, 57)

The woman's suggestion to "cobble together some passable ghost" binds the work of maternal care to her proposed absence. The woman could be understood in terms of a post-apocalyptic or postpartum depression or exhaustion: her attachment to the world and her son becomes unbearable in a way that reveals the gendered dimension of her familial role, a role she ultimately rejects.[12] The ghost she prescribes for the man seems to both offer and need the nurturing, feeding, and caring demanded of her as a woman and a mother. Her ghost is not meant as her replacement, nor is her conciliatory suggestion aimed at justifying her evident longing for "eternal nothingness." Michael Chabon claims that "in this impossible land the mother's choice is clearly the only sane one, and nothing that occurs in the course of the novel up to the death of the father argues against the suicide that . . . he repeatedly ponders" ("Dark Adventure," 101).

Readers who reorganize the man's scattered memories of the woman may start to recognize the woman's absence through other passages of the novel. Rearranging the plot in this way, I came to understand that the woman must have been waiting to take her life and must have stayed with the man and the boy until just before the opening pages of the novel. This scene from a little way into the book is the hinge between her presence and her absence: "She was gone and the coldness of it was her final gift . . . in the morning the boy said nothing at all and when they were packed and ready to set out upon the road he turned and looked back at their campsite and he said: she's gone isn't she?" (McCarthy, *The Road*, 58). Here, *The Road* reveals more of its conflicted nature: its plot begins after the woman's death, rather than immediately after the apocalyptic event. The novel gives credence to the woman's position even after her death: its opening pages take place in the long wake of her suicide. The plot of the novel is inaugurated as much by the end of the couple as it is by the apocalypse.

McCarthy's characters work through a problem for which the solutions appear as false alternatives: survival in the name of an impossible reproductive futurity or death. *The Road* subtracts maternal care from the present of the novel, leaving such care behind in the inaccessible past. Maternal care returns only at the novel's close, when the future—in the form of the family—is restored as a possibility.

The different temporalities at play within *The Road* shape its characters' relation to survival as deeply spatial in nature. Without the woman and until the death of the man, he and the boy appear to be stranded in a perpetual and inhospitable present. Characters chart time through survival rather than through their prior knowledge or their longing for a return to normalcy. In fact, the novel presents such a return as impossible. Although the characters are mobile, time appears to be frozen. The novel describes the apocalypse as a punctual event: "The clocks stopped at 1:17. A long shear of light and then a series of low concussions" (McCarthy, *The Road*, 52). The time of the event becomes forever marked as "1:17," and the time of apocalyptic novum demarcates the pre- and post-apocalyptic periods. The man's memories flow from the former, and the boy, born after the apocalyptic event, knows only the latter. The time of the event consistently threatens to make space the dominant characteristic of the narrative: the characters' reliance on the road signals this spatialization.

Always marked by where the man and the boy are on the road, the perpetual present of the narrative deepens the spatial sense of time: in the absence of temporal orientation, there is only spatial mapping. The chipped and charred blacktop serves as their guide and ultimately signals the danger of their struggle. In a strong sense, then, the road is the narrative present, and moving along it becomes a brand of survival, continuance, inertia, and the slow shuffle toward one's destination. The road never presents an end point of its own, though it certainly promises to deliver weary travelers to their hearts' desire. In this way, the novel subverts an expected journey that is at once practical and spiritual, offering instead only the literal road. The three other ruined modes of transportation that the man and the boy encounter—a stalled train, a wrecked tractor trailer, and a reefed boat—similarly signify that time has been derailed, left stranded in a fully spatial present.

This temporality of the now is the strongest one in *The Road*, leaving the future nearly as inaccessible as its second strongest, the past. The perpetual present contains no whispers of futurity other than the soft suggestion of joining the woman in her fate. While locked into their journey, the man and the boy remain frozen in time. Without access to the way things were and with no sense of the way they could be, the man and the boy are stranded in a limited, threatening present with only the dead weight of the world around them: a workable shopping cart, a pistol with only a few bullets, and a wallet full of memories.

SURVIVAL AND THE REPRODUCTIVE IMPERATIVE

The Road carefully negotiates its own terms for survival. The man's role in the obliteration of the past and his heightened sense of the present unfolds as he recalls episodes with the boy's mother: "We're survivors he told her across the flame of the lamp," and she replies, "What in God's name are you talking about? We're not survivors. We're the walking dead in a horror film" (McCarthy, *The Road*, 55). The man's and the woman's understandings of the present are disconnected. Though the woman expresses a different sense of the post-apocalyptic landscape, the man's perceptions are privileged in the novel. Their disagreement about survival is one way of delimiting narrative possibility in the novel: one is either for or against survival. The man describes the woman's insistence on ending her life as "talking crazy," as it remains an entirely untenable position for him.[13] The woman offers an opposite form of action:

> I should have done it a long time ago. . . . I didnt bring myself to this. I was brought. And now I'm done. I thought about not even telling you. That would probably have been best. You say you would die for us but what good is that? I'd take him with me if it werent for you. You know I would. It's the right thing to do. (ibid., 56)

As she outlines the reasons for her decision, she paints a picture of the cannibals catching, raping, and eating them. In the face of this fate, one truth of the man's insistence on survival, and particularly on her survival, emerges when he says, "Please don't do this . . . I cant do it alone" (ibid., 57).[14] The novel implies that without the care or labor of a woman, the man and the boy are capable only of reproducing the present. The burned-out afterimage of what came before appears like a mirage, visible long enough to show that something did indeed come before but vanishing before it can provide any information about how to rebuild the world. Nothing is left for the present but survival. The novel stages a world where reaching the future should not be possible and suggests that the woman is to blame for not being able to set things right.

The real-world relationship of survival and reproduction is complex and indirect. On the one hand, survival has a particular sense of immediacy. It implies a focus on basic needs. To survive means to live through a life-threatening event, such as disease or warfare; to scavenge or forage for sustenance; to locate safe shelters; and to get away from the people who threaten one's life.[15] On the other hand, reproduction names the process of maintaining a particular effect or situation. It also names a gendered problem particular to capitalism. It is in this sense that reproduction is taken to mean the procreation and rearing of children, as well as the work of care in the home (cooking, cleaning, nurturing, supporting, and so on) that has typically been (and in many ways still is) carried out by women as unwaged work.[16] Reproduction describes an ongoing process necessary to life, but it has also become the name for a political process: the social reproduction of the worker under capital. Thus, survival and reproduction are related to, yet distinct from, one another.

However carefully defined, in post-apocalyptic narratives the two terms often collapse into one set of imperatives. Since the present is so often under threat in post-apocalypse stories, the imperative to survive the world-destroying effects of the apocalyptic event slides into the imperative not only to reproduce life as it was before the apocalypse, but also to reproduce it in the same manner. Survival in the post-apocalyptic mode becomes the normative ground from which these novels project their visions of the future.

Essentially felt as a reproductive imperative, this conceptual form of futurity takes a political question about the collective destiny of humanity and turns it into an ethical or moral question about particular people's lives, ensuring repetition by downloading collective responsibility to such people—especially women. As Natasha Hurley argues, "Nowhere are women more idealized or policed than as mothers, despite our collective failure to provide the social and financial supports necessary to child-rearing" ("Reproduction/Non-Reproduction," 154). The problem is that the imperative to have children, despite its collective meanings and effects, is felt on an individual basis. Yet today the reproductive imperative is itself a remainder. In North America, birth rates have been declining. In August 2016, Madison Park reported that in the first three months of 2016 the US birth rate fell to the lowest level since 1957: just below 60 births per thousand women ("US Fertility Rate Falls to Lowest on Record").[17] This rate is similar to that reported for the first quarter of 2015 and less than half of the 123 births per thousand reported for 1957. Indeed, as Robert Brenner and others have argued, we collectively find ourselves in a long downturn—a so-called secular crisis of capital (*The Economics of Global Turbulence*). In a moment when the requirements of labor to support industry are sharply in decline, both in the United States and elsewhere around the world, why have babies? Hurley provocatively suggests that "the era not only of new technologies for producing new generations of humans but also, arguably, of the capitalist enterprise, one that has never been able to do without reproducing new generations of labourers" ("Reproduction/Non-Reproduction," 151), may be reaching a close, replaced by "the age of non-reproduction" (ibid., 154). *The Road*, with its reproductive imperative and gutted future, simultaneously imagines what is to come and recoils from it.

Early in the novel, the man and the boy encounter a group of "bad guys" and see them pass "two hundred feet away, the ground shuddering lightly. Tramping. Behind them came wagons drawn by slaves in harness and piled with goods of war and after that the women, perhaps a dozen in number, some of them pregnant" (McCarthy, *The Road*, 92). *The Road* raises social form as a fundamental question: how is survival even possible in the face of the limited capability for the reproduction of daily life and nightmarish visions of sex slavery and cannibalism? Characters in the storyworld of *The Road* survive in cannibalistic gangs (a mode the novel cautions ought to be strictly avoided), in small units like the man and the boy, or in small groups of seemingly benevolent people like the family group that emerges at the end of the novel. Characters are torn between the security of known self-reliant others and the risk of a collective full of members with uncertain motivations. The woman's absence from the present, on the one hand, and the man's desire for a break from the past, on the other hand, further complicate the future in the novel. Her suicide acts as a refusal of further care and further children. Alternatives do exist in a collective form—the new family, a known collective invested in the future, stands apart from its shadowy other, the "bloodcults" (ibid., 16).

The reduction to the present in *The Road* extends from the limited frame of survival in the novel to its more expanded dimension of reproduction. Aside from the remembered conversation with the woman, the novel comes closest to illustrating the absolute destruction of nature's fertility in the two bunker scenarios. The grisly truth of the bunkers appears in this first scene, where the man and the boy find a bunker in the form of a cellar filled not with preserves but with human cattle: "Huddled against the back wall were naked people, male and female, all trying to hide, shielding their faces with their hands. . . . Help us, they whispered. Please help us" (McCarthy, *The Road*, 110). The man and the boy flee from the old farmhouse, pursued by four men and two women—the keepers of the bounty of human flesh. Later, the man and the boy come upon an abandoned campfire with everything taken except "whatever black thing was skewered over the coals," which the boy identifies first: "a charred human infant headless and gutted and blackening on the spit" (ibid., 198). These two moments of explicit cannibalism relate differently to the problem of survival: the first is organized, planned, and orchestrated, while the second paints a scene of desperation. Earlier, the two malnourished travelers had found a different cellar filled with what seems like a limitless bounty: "Crate upon crate of canned goods. Tomatoes, peaches, beans, apricots. Canned hams. Corned beef. Hundreds of gallons of water in ten gallon plastic jerry jugs. Paper towels, toilet paper, paper plates" (ibid., 138). Is this bunker a holdover from the early days of the Cold War that has recently been restocked or a new construction? The bunker and the kinds of objects they find in it (especially the Coca-Cola) seem to date the events of the novel after World War II.[18] The appearance of the bunker offers the man and the boy both shelter and food.

The two bunker scenes highlight the fact that humanity has no future. It is literally sustained in the interim only by itself. Inger-Anne Søfting puts it carefully: "there is no future as humanity is not self-sustainable" ("Between Dystopia and Utopia," 713). And Monbiot makes direct reference to the cannibalism of the novel: "all pre-existing social codes soon collapse and are replaced with organized butchery, then chaotic, blundering horror. What else are the survivors to do? *The only remaining resource is human*" ("Civilisation Ends with a Shutdown of Human Concern"). In the moment when the man and the boy discover a baby on a spit, the novel fully reveals the emptiness and infertility of its storyworld: to persist, humans in the world of *The Road* literally have to eat their own young. The novel builds a world in which cannibalizing future generation is the only path toward survival.[19] The two cellars full of shelf-stable goods present the stark options of survival in a strikingly similar form—in the novel, scavenging from what has been left behind or enforcing a harrowing regime of childbirth for food are the only options for survival in the short term.[20] Nothing can be grown in the barren fields, and nothing can be made, so one must feed on either the reserves of a dead world or the dying flesh of the living. Despite these limits to human flourishing, reproduction remains the path to the future in the novel.

At the moment the boy finds himself alone, he is discovered by a new man, a "veteran of old skirmishes" (McCarthy, *The Road*, 281) who turns out to be part of a new family group. Despite McCarthy's endeavor to sever the past from the post-apocalyptic present, the novel reintroduces futurity as a reproductive imperative. The novel's final paragraph reinforces this tension, while it posits the impossibility of civilization's return:

> Once there were brook trout in the streams in the mountains. You could see them standing in the amber current where the white edges of their fins wimpled softly in the flow. They smelled of moss in your hand. Polished and muscular and torsional. On their backs were vermiculate patterns that were maps of the world in its becoming. Maps and mazes. Of a thing which could not be put back. (ibid., 286–87)

Unlike earlier passages that described the man's dreams fading into gray mornings, these visions remain blazoned in the arresting image of trout in a stream, fish that have long since vanished from the world. Here, the narrator offers not only descriptions of sights and smells but also figures of totality, so many "maps and mazes." What follows does not banish these visions; instead, it acknowledges the impossibility of the return of their subjects. By dividing the final two sentence fragments in this passage—"Maps and mazes" and "Of a thing which could not be put back."—McCarthy inscribes a threshold between these ideas that cannot be crossed. Such remainders gesture toward their context of origin, yet they also signal their own removal from that previous situation and their alienness in the current one. The most thoughtful post-apocalyptic stories endeavor to situate and historicize remainders.

The family form in *The Road*, though relegated to the pre-apocalyptic past in the nostalgic memories of the man, seems also to represent utopian possibility in the novel. Nancy Armstrong identifies the family as a marker of a particularly novelistic problem: can the novel today imagine a collective scale beyond the family? The family in post-apocalyptic novels acts as a stable structure around which all of the challenges to the storyworld take place, so that even though everything appears to have changed, these texts rarely provide, in Armstrong's words, "imaginative access to what comes after the family" ("The Future *in* and *of* the Novel," 9). As Søfting suggests, "In order to intimate the possibility for future procreation the presence of female characters is important; the sole presence of a father and his son as the characters to carry the world on is surely in a very literal sense a dead end" ("Between Dystopia and Utopia," 712). At the end of the novel, a family unit—a man, a woman, and some children—discovers the boy just as he leaves his dead father behind. Furthermore, in John Hillcoat's 2009 film version of *The Road*, the boy is discovered by a man who is the head of a nuclear family complete with a dog, in a world that is supposedly devoid of nonhuman animals. The boy must choose: should he go with the strangers or go off on his own? The choice does not seem bizarre against the backdrop of the rest of the novel, but the appearance of the new woman in this group makes this encounter a deeply problematic moment in the text. The family approaches the boy only after his father, the defender of the last bastion of self-reliance and mistrust, has died.

In this moment, the reproductive imperative delivers its strongest signal. The new woman shares her own ghostly theory about reproduction, which recasts the absent woman's remembered monologue in a positivistic light:

> The woman when she saw him put her arms around him and held him. Oh, she said, I am so glad to see you. She would talk to him sometimes about God. He tried to talk to God but the best thing was to talk to his father and he did talk to him and he didnt forget. The woman said that was all right. She said that the breath of God was his breath yet though it pass from man to man through all of time. (McCarthy, *The Road*, 286)

This passing on "from man to man" emphasizes the reproductive imperative and the absent presence of the mother. However enshrined and radiant this passing on appears to be, it does not represent what takes place in the novel. Without the woman and her womb, the fire could not pass from the man to the boy. This rewriting of the absent woman's indictment effaces her existence and her labor. Sullivan decodes the new woman's message: "The waiting mother's function in *The Road* is clear: her daughter ensures that the boy can engender a new generation to 'carry the fire,' without which Papa's suffering would be in vain. She thereby also satisfies narrative exigency" ("The Good Guys," 97). While the arrival of the family at the end of the novel could be read as a sign of hope, I argue that it is doubly symptomatic of the book's reproductive imperative: it effaces the maternal role and simultaneously relies on gendered reproductive labor to create the links "from man to man."

The Road does away with the complexities of life in the present, leaving life simpler (though far deadlier) than before the apocalypse. However, it takes this process a step further. In *The Road* all that remains are the residues of the pre-apocalyptic world. In the novel, the ideology of gender is at the heart of the fantasy of beginning anew. Survival itself depends on re-creating the situation that allowed one to experience the previous day and stay alive. In the face of the impossibility of human life continuing into the storyworld's future, *The Road* still clings to the hope that rearing the next generation can make some sort of change in the world. The need for the entangled fate of humanity and futurity to come through reproduction is descriptive fact. Interpreting *The Road*—or worse, teaching it—without taking into account the structural role of the absent woman passes over the gendered nature of the novel's post-apocalyptic plot. This novel does not tell a story about humanity, its future, or its ethics. Instead, it tells a story about men. *The Road* narrativizes the impossible desire for a patriarchy without women or mothers.

McCarthy's novel is both divergent from and faithful to the development of the post-apocalyptic mode. It diverges stylistically, which is what people tend to love about this book: its tone, rhythm, and imagery do not conform to those of other texts classified as post-apocalyptic. Yet as I have been arguing throughout, this distinction is a generic one. For all of its stylistic pomp, McCarthy's novel cleaves to the post-apocalyptic narrative mode. It tells a story that could exist alongside David Brin's *The Postman* and Kim Stanley Robinson's *The Wild Shore*.[21] *The Road* stands apart from these other titles because of how it focuses on the filial relationship and infrastructure rather than on the human mechanisms of the state. *The Road* dramatizes the casting out of the man and the boy, misrecognizing their abandonment by the state as the woman's leaving them.[22]

Put differently, McCarthy's novel works through the long-term effects of the neoliberalism implemented in the 1980s and already considered by earlier post-apocalyptic titles.

Much as W.E.B. Du Bois's "The Comet" did against Stewart's *Earth Abides* (see chapter 5), Butler's post-apocalyptic writing can be described as a critique that pushes back against its own descendants.[23] Her *Parable of the Sower* critiques *The Road*'s inward-looking, libertarian, masculinist hand-wringing in advance, showing that vague fears of the end of the world are most often expressed from the vantage point of the realm of power and dominance under threat. Butler's elaborations take into account the specific ways that people might mistreat but also come to rely on one another and have more to offer our understanding of catastrophe in the real world than the misguided fears of McCarthy's protagonist. And Richard Matheson's last man trope comes preformed with a critique of self-reliance.

In light of their ready response to *The Road*, Butler's Parables books complement and extend the critical concept of the remainder. They deepen the dialectical way I want to use the term "remainder": on the one hand, *The Road* is a derivative holdover, and on the other hand, Butler's novels offer a critique of it from the past. Drawing from my commentary in chapter 5, I can say that Butler saw the encroaching crisis with clear eyes, while McCarthy cannot fathom any manner of continuance under the conditions he imagines. *Parable of the Sower*, in this sense, is an extrapolative text, whereas McCarthy's is a regressive one. This assessment has as much to do with *The Road*'s latent racial dynamics as it does with its troubling take on family, children, and the future. Conversely, as a figure constrained by reproductive futurity, Olamina's set of choices differ from those of the absent woman in *The Road*. Crucially, those choices are not limited to these individual characters and their uniqueness, but instead light up the divergent narrative possibilities within each text. McCarthy's absent woman had no other choice, and the text frames her taking her own life as the best choice facing someone in that storyworld. Olamina has agency, and the ways it is constrained produce a trenchant, immanent critique of racial capital and the struggles faced by a black woman in navigating it. Olamina's choices in this case echo across the two books we have (*Parable of the Sower* and *Parable of the Talents*) and the one we do not have (*Parable of the Trickster*).[24] Here, once more, is a powerful example of how reading mode against genre can provide insights: these books feature strikingly similar characters, plots, and ways of getting something done, but the something that is accomplished is markedly different. One presents the reproductive imperative as a lament, the other as a warning.

7
Automobility Regression

....

A wave of scholarship during the past decade has made it clear that the history of the United States in the twentieth century remains at best partial without a rigorous account of the role of energy—in particular, petroleum—in solidifying and maintaining US hegemony in the period. Tracking the impact of energy has led to genuinely paradigm-shifting accounts of the global technics, politics, and economics of oil. It has also begun to reveal the degree to which modernity's increasingly dependent relationship to petroleum registers in profound ways in the social and cultural organization of everyday life. I use the term "petroculture" to capture the cultural and social dimension of fossil-fuel use. The term names a wide ambit of concerns that are intended to enclose both the unconscious use of energy production, distribution, and consumption and the profound impact these processes exert on cultural production, social norms, and humanity's creative capacity to imagine and enact varying futures.[1]

The cultural expression of the use of petroleum is brought home by the historiographical thought experiments of post-apocalyptic stories. Most post-apocalyptic novels use changes in the supply of energy as a way to reduce possibilities in the storyworld future. In particular, such tales restrict presumed capacities to move people and goods around the globe at high speeds, focusing instead on a locale or region traversable by slower modes of travel. Unlike the vision of a future relying on technology-driven transportation such as flying cars, interstellar travel, and teleportation found in other science fiction, post-apocalyptic stories subtract fossil fuels from social life, thereby revealing the absolute reliance of the modern subject on those fuels, their by-products, and the habits their use encouraged.[2] As subjects of petroculture, especially those of us in developed countries, we have come to expect a smoothness of conveyance to our destinations, on the one hand, and the reliable delivery of goods to us at home, on the other hand.[3] Post-apocalyptic texts also disrupt global connections. They imagine how characters might respond to new limits on travel and access to goods, and they project future possibilities for the remainders of petromodernity. Such novels serve as a litmus test for survivability and adaptive potential.

The reduction of the scale and complexity of contemporary social life to its imagined core conflicts and contradictions unsurprisingly produces an awareness of energy concerns that has, until quite recently, remained largely absent in the field of cultural production more broadly. Given the infrastructural failure that post-apocalyptic stories typically assume, their characters appear in a world in which aspects of contemporary life, such as automobility, exist only as distant memories or rare luxuries—if they have not been entirely forgotten or changed into some violent spectacle of a fossil-fueled death match amid rubble-strewn wastes.[4] More likely in post-apocalyptic scenarios are futures of scarcity, when the goods and services that required being shipped from afar or the use of energy and communications infrastructures will no longer be available: absent a steady supply of fuel, lines of supply are severed, networks of communication and the attendant sense of social connectivity evaporate, gears seize up and foods rot, and the productivity of all labor is radically constrained.[5]

Rather than focus on one or two exemplary texts, this chapter presents a survey of the post-apocalyptic mode's relationship to thinking about petroculture. Whether suspicious of the fossil regime or nostalgic for the explosive potentials of oil's energic burst (and how could one not feel a little of both?), these texts offer critical lessons about the legacies of fossil capitalism and its impact on US hegemony. What becomes clear in examining this literature is that post-apocalyptic novels develop more compelling scenarios when they imagine what a life without electricity might look like, as opposed to prophesying the end of availability of oil in particular. These energy apocalypse novels better represent both modernity's inertial need for energy and the profound impacts of a life not just without oil but also without extraction and refinement teams, distribution networks, maintenance crews, and technocrats of the energy infrastructure. By imagining what has vanished from an imagined future, post-apocalyptic novels draw attention to what exists in the present.

As early as the 1960s, post-apocalyptic scenarios were considering the impacts of a loss of petroleum and electricity on daily life. For instance, Pat Frank's *Alas, Babylon* (first published in 1959) is set in the town of Fort Repose, Florida, and dramatizes the isolation of such a town during a nationwide red alert: "Like most small towns, Fort Repose's food and drug supply was dependent upon daily or thrice weekly deliveries from warehouses in the larger cities. Each day trucks replenished its filling stations. For all other merchandise, it was dependent upon shipments by mail, express, and highway freight, from jobbers and manufacturers elsewhere" (117). Even in 1959, before just-in-time production and the green revolution, small towns and urban centers relied on industrial agriculture. Frank's novel traces the chain from stores' shelves and fueling stations' reservoirs through delivery fleets and drivers back to implied warehouses and gasoline refineries.[6] What the post-apocalyptic story does that other fictions do not is to shock the awareness of energy into being through a focused, subtractive gesture. The disappearance of items from store shelves—or rather the shelves' lack of replenishment—signals the fossil-fueled character of their logistics.

Frank does not stop there. He uses the focal point of Fort Repose to represent what must be going on elsewhere across the United States. The novel conducts a thought experiment premised on removing the supply chains that keep any given town or city fed and fueled: "With the Red Alert, all these services halted and at once. Like thousands of towns and villages not directly seared by war, Fort Repose became an island. . . . [I]ts inhabitants would have to subsist on whatever was already within its boundaries, plus what they might scrounge from the countryside" (Frank, *Alas, Babylon*, 117). The importance of transportation and what has since become known as logistics is striking in Frank's description of how Fort Repose "became [like] an island."[7] What might be presumed to be a constantly stable and plentiful supply of food in the supermarket or gasoline at the pump is actually under constant movement—goods are sold or thrown out, and gasoline is pumped into vehicles and then burned. One of Frank's characters realizes that "one thing he certainly should have foreseen . . . was the loss of electricity" (ibid., 151). This realization seems obvious in retrospect, but rather than stocking nonperishable foods, the characters gather fruit and meat.

In adhering to some aspects of reality, the post-apocalyptic story can make evident an obvious, though unrealized, truth:

> Even had Orlando[, Florida,] escaped, the electricity [in Fort Repose] would have died within a few weeks or months. Electricity was created by burning fuel oil in the Orlando plants. When the oil ran out, it could not be replenished during the chaos of war. There was no longer a rail system, or rail centers, nor were tankers plying the coasts on missions of civilian supply. . . . Even those sections of the country which escaped destruction entirely would not long have lights. Their power would last only as long as fuel stocks on hand. (Frank, *Alas, Babylon*, 151)

Asking how a town might go about living through the aftermath of a nuclear attack also addresses an unremarked upon feature of daily life. The petrocapitalist reliance on the ceaseless circulation of commodities generates a population that is profoundly unprepared for any kind of catastrophe and particularly ill-equipped for the nuclear crisis imagined by Frank. If energy input is measured by how oil fuels infrastructures, the development of machinery, and everyday life, then an attentive critic might be able to read traces of the energy regime alongside the remainders of capital in post-apocalyptic fiction.

Subsequent post-apocalyptic novels include the disappearance of fuel as part of their thought experiments. In the 1990s, Octavia E. Butler's *Parable of the Sower* makes gestures similar to those in Frank's novel. Butler's scarcity-wracked United States of 2024 is one in which massive social and cultural changes have taken place, yet such changes have no single source—rather, decline and enclosure characterize this future. Butler reveals the lack of transportation before sharing the animating conceit of the protagonist: Lauren Oya Olamina has a drug-induced condition known as hyperempathy. In *Parable of the*

Sower, automobiles cease working as gasoline is diverted to other uses. "To the adults," Olamina writes in her journal entry dated Sunday, July 21, 2024, "going outside to a real church was like stepping back into the good old days when there were churches all over the place and too many lights and gasoline was for fueling cars and trucks instead of for torching things" (Butler, *Parable of the Sower*, 8). Butler counts the loss of old habits using a conjunctive rhythm to end this sentence: "and . . . and . . . for . . . and . . . for . . . ." In this case, such habits are not Olamina's: they belong instead to her elders, who equate burning gasoline in internal combustion engines with bounty and see this arrangement as the way things ought to be. Along these lines, Olamina adds, "They never miss a chance to relive the good old days or to tell kids how great it's going to be when the country gets back on its feet and good times come back" (ibid.). Butler ominously suggests that in her storyworld gasoline has not run out or stopped being refined and distributed, but rather that it has been put to more violent uses. The lack of automobiles becomes important again later in *Parable of the Sower*, as Olamina travels away from her walled community of Robledo in search of a place to found a new homestead.

Before this journey, Butler includes other important references to the waning of automobile transportation. In her journal entry dated Saturday, March 29, 2025, Olamina writes, "The Moss rabbit house is a converted three-car garage added to the property in the 1980s according to Dad. *It's hard to believe any household once had three cars, and gas fueled cars at that.* But I remember the old garage before Richard Moss converted it. It was huge with three black oil spots on the floor where three cars had once been housed" (Butler, *Parable of the Sower*, 73; italics in the original). Those three spots signify the absence of fossil-fueled mobility and the relations that it supported; they are remainders of powerful forces that no longer exist in the narrative present. For adults in Butler's storyworld, those three stains indicate a lost wealth that might someday return. To Olamina and others of her generation, they signal a difficulty in understanding memories of a reminder of the fossil regime, which has been erased by the economic decline that caused a transition away from petrocultural logistics. By subtracting oil from the storyworld, post-apocalyptic storytelling moves beyond positive claims about the social meaning of oil and begins to imagine a reduced future that simultaneously addresses the deep energy commitments of the real-world present and hints at the possibilities for a post-petrol future. Post-apocalyptic novels that take the question of fuel sources and energy infrastructures into their calculations of character survival perform a useful form of speculative reasoning.

In the analyses that follow, I look specifically to futures of scarcity and those depicted as lacking or having little oil. After the energy apocalypse, the neat routines of middle-class life have become nearly impossible to maintain: working late most weeknights, running errands on the weekend, enjoying a meal with friends, and so on. Deep-seated patterns remain in place. Some characters still behave as though the lights will come back on or the shipments of food will begin to arrive once more. These behaviors reveal in the negative what a life lived in energy abundance is like, and once that life has been stripped away, one can begin to see the profound inequalities that structure it. Reading post-apocalyptic novels with energy in mind means attending to the presence of abundant energy, the effects of having it, and strategies for coping with it as well as those for coping without it.[8] In what follows, I analyze four recent novels that feature a regression of automobility: James Howard Kunstler's *World Made by Hand* (2008), Emily St. John Mandel's *Station Eleven* (2014), Peter Heller's *The Dog Stars* (2012), and John Varley's *Slow Apocalypse* (2012).[9]

SUBTRACTING OIL

Kunstler's post-oil novel *World Made by Hand* reduces social relations into manageable units, exploring a world that has come to resemble that of the mid-nineteenth century.[10] The novel's social dimensions present an odd incompatibility between ecological concerns and other emancipatory politics, which function in the story as two related forms of desire for an egalitarian future. While Kunstler's novel ultimately fails to resolve the incompatibility. The construction of his post-oil storyworld and the ambivalent desires that it seeks to embody fall short of the capacity of novelistic form to address oil as subject and the critical potential of the post-apocalyptic mode. Such a reading of Kunstler helps situate the limits of this form in imagining and depicting the future of our modern, oil fueled world.

In a 2011 article, Kunstlers reflects on a kernel of the ethical and political project at the foundation of *World Made by Hand*:

> There are a lot of ways of referring to American-style suburbia, but these days I favor the greatest misallocation of resources in the history of the world. You can say that because it's clear that we are not going to be able to run it in a very few years ahead as the nation's oil supply gets more restricted and we have to face the disappointing reality that so-called alternative energy will not come close to offsetting our oil losses. Suburbia therefore represents a living arrangement with no future. ("Farewell to the Drive-In Utopia," 82)

This lack of a plausible way forward is the motivating crisis for *World Made by Hand*, which is arguably as much an effort to jump-start the dying engine of American futurity as it is an answer to the peak-oiler's question, "where will humanity end up without oil?" Kunstler's novels and his other nonfiction work *The Long Emergency* address concerns of an early twenty-first-century energy crisis that would result from reaching global peak oil production. According to Matthew Schneider-Mayerson, "Between 2004 and 2011, hundreds of thousands of Americans came to believe that impending oil scarcity would lead to the imminent collapse of industrial society and the demise of the United States" (*Peak Oil*, 1). Reading this passage in the present, one is struck by the absolute reversal of fortunes that fracking (high-volume hydrogen fracturing) and other unconventional means of accessing and extracting fossil fuels have brought about. Indeed, as Gerry Canavan writes: "To the extent that liberals and the left took up Peak Oil as a slogan, they have therefore missed entirely the much more significant threat to the common good originating not from having too little oil, but from having too much" ("Peak Oil after Hydrofracking, " 306). Since 2008, Kunstler's post–peak oil apocalyptic novel has become part of the realm of mere fantasy as a result of the technological developments and advances of fossil-fuel science.

Kunstler's story of the transition to a world without oil throws society back into the age of dependence on wood for energy: neither coal nor the fat or muscle of nonhuman creatures are employed in the novel (save for the New Faithers' use of mules). He imagines a civilization regression that can easily ignore or work beyond the impact of oil on collective decision-making practices.¹¹ Fossil fuels are absent in *World Made by Hand*: there is no coal, no oil, nor the systems they once fueled. Kunstler positions the breakdown of the global circulation of commodities and resources as the leading cause of civilization's regression.

Effectively, *World Made by Hand* stages a post-petrol scenario in which human beings come to live in harmony with the landscapes surrounding them by turning back to a life before dependence on oil. The post-apocalyptic scenario in the novel originating with the possibility of terrorism causes major problems for foreign exchange, which severs the global relations of the United States: no one wants to trade with an overly securitized nation that checks every single container coming into its ports. In this way, the novel considers automated logistics incompatible with the idea of terrorism. Kunstler uses the storyworld of his novel to present an alternative to the fossil regime, a world made by hand. He provides a thicket of apocalyptic problems fueled by peak oil—global terrorism, virulent disease, and economic crisis—as the backdrop for his solution to the ills of oil dependency and its attendant technologies in the real world. Like David Brin, for Kunstler, "it hardly mattered anymore what had done it" (Brin, *The Postman*, n.p.). The subtraction of oil and subsequent return to a pre-oil society present a logical leap reminiscent of the French utopian socialist Pierre-Joseph Proudhon's desire to address the ills of an emerging capitalism by simply eliminating money (*What Is Property?*). Proudhon and Kunstler each mistake a form of capital—money and oil, respectively—for commodities. Yet like money, oil is not simply a thing: indeed, it is a social relation, and subtracting oil from the world suddenly makes that fact inescapable.¹² In the reading of the novel I advance here, I map the connections among the characters and find little evidence of those connections being determined or even influenced by oil.

The novel follows its protagonist, Robert Earle, through one eventful summer in his life to a turning point for the small community of Union Grove, in Washington County, New York. Earle is a fiddler, carpenter, lover, and rationalist, and he eventually becomes the mayor of Union Grove. His carpentry links him to the community, the novel's title, and the fuel of choice after oil: wood. One reason that the civic politics Earle epitomizes have the most potential as a social form is largely because they include professionals and knowledgeable citizens capable of repairing, rebuilding, diagnosing, treating, and maintaining a healthy population; good shelter; and the democratic process—three elements that the novel shows in relation to one another. The townsfolk whom Earle represents in both spirit and, later, in his capacity as mayor form the privileged one of the four groups that drive the plot of the novel.

Three groups are arrayed around the townsfolk: the New Faithers, the trailer park denizens, and the plantation owner and workers. Each group in Union Grove is represented by a main figure and—with the exception of the townsfolk—is located at a distance from the town's core. Wayne Karp, leader of the trailer park residents, and Stephen Bullock, leader of the plantation group, represent opposing types of social order. Karp stands for libertarian lack of regulation, while Bullock is the closest thing to an official lawmaker in Union Grove. Identified by their geographical or ideological distinction from the neutral townsfolk, each offers a different take on what post-oil life might look like. Here, Kunstler uses a post-apocalyptic move first deployed by Leigh Brackett in *The Long Tomorrow*: he develops a map of the community groups that outlines the varied responses to social life in post-apocalyptic times.

The trailer park is poised beside the Union Grove dump. Providing salvage and goods for the general store, the dump is a resource that must be accessed through handiwork. Located just outside of town, its inhabitants are fiercely territorial about their treasure trove. Earle describes Karp as a muscled tough guy who loves rock 'n' roll and wears camouflage tees: "on the rare occasions when I saw Wayne, the phrase *with his bare hands* always echoed in my mind" (Kunstler, *World Made by Hand*, 42; emphasis in the original). Earle identifies Karp as a tough guy who has a different aesthetic than the townsfolk as well as, crucially, a different resource: the dump. These two features are linked through the physical remainders of salvage and the connection they provide to the pre-apocalyptic world. Earle and Karp are different not in mode, but in kind: they use the same means but different materials and have divergent political aspirations. Later in the book, Karp emerges as a violent antagonist who must be dealt with by the law of the town. In staging this conflict, the novel asks whether it will be the carpenter's hands or the fighter's that shape what is to come.

Bullock stands in balanced distinction to the first two social groups. He possesses over two thousand acres of arable land, which he maintains well after the breakdown of American society. He offers protection, food, shelter, and purpose in exchange for hard labor. The novel lists his manufacturing accomplishments—"the creamery, the smokehouse, the brewery, the harness shop, the glass shop, the smithy, the laundry" (Kunstler, *World Made by Hand*, 78)—which are actually the result of his capacity to organize and manage those who join his complex. This arrangement allows Bullock to accomplish feats that the other groups can only imagine: he generates electricity, runs motors, and produces fine food and drink—hot dogs, hamburgers, mustard, cider, and whiskey. Bullock's compound presents a remainder from past post-apocalyptic narratives by once again glorifying the return of feudal social relations.

As their designation suggests, the New Faithers are deeply religious. They purchase an old school on the outskirts of Union Grove through an arrangement with the mayor at the time and without the knowledge of the townsfolk. Their use of mules as a favored animal in the field signals their reliance on animal labor over the wood fires and boilers featured in the town or Bullock's compound, respectively (Kunstler, *World Made by Hand*, 79). The New Faithers' version of a world made by hand is not opposed to those of the townsfolk or Bullock. They do not seek to dominate or indoctrinate anyone. In the novel, the townsfolk, Bullock, and the New Faithers work together to share resources and support one another's initiatives.

With these groups and characters as the principal actors, the novel develops two entwined plots. First, a friend of Earle's is shot outside of the trailer park's general store in broad daylight. The murder acts as a catalyst for the complacent townsfolk to form a more cohesive social body and demand justice. Second, Earle and some of the New Faithers travel to Albany as part of a trade deal: the New Faithers need new concrete poured and Bullock wants to find out about a missing trade ship he has been expecting. They find that Albany has become a lawless place. They return to Union Grove, which serves to reassure the characters and reader that, no matter how dangerous, residents of the small community have much more potential to thrive than do people in the big city.

This overview brings to light the fact that civic life rather than oil is the central problem of the novel. The groups become the principal units of action in the story. Abiding in an older small town means that the necessary building repair can be done by hand: local decisions and efforts emerge from a combination of individual willingness and group need. For instance, food is produced locally—with cornmeal, eggs, honey, and cow's and goat's milk being easily obtainable, while sugar and wheat are not. The descriptions of and reflections about food preparation and meals locate food production, preparation, and consumption as its most vital moments.[13] Unlike the mapping that Frank's *Alas, Babylon* does through the subtraction of capitalist food logistics, Kunstler provides his characters with plentiful regional fare. Once again, a book seemingly concerned with imagining a post-oil future instead projects a pre-oil fantasy space.

Focusing on the small town rather than the urban space of the city also marks an assumed absence of linguistic and cultural difference. One of the New Faithers, Joseph, a former marine, describes what is left outside the community and the narrative:

> There's grievances and vendettas all around at every level. Poor against whatever rich are left. Black against white. English-speaking against the Spanish. More than one bunch on the Jews. You name it, there's a fight on. Groups in flight everywhere, ourselves among them. I haven't seen black folks or Spanish in Union Grove so far. You got any, sir? (Kunstler, *World Made by Hand*, 149)

Joseph presents critical grievances and brutal conflict outside of Union Grove. His description divides the United States along racial and linguistic lines that do not entirely take geography into account. For Joseph, conflicts in the post-apocalyptic United States are intensified and divided across multiple classes and racialized cultural or linguistic groups. Earle responds:

> Some black families lived in that hollow down by the Wayland Union Mill, the old factory village. There was a fellow named Archie Basiltree who worked in the Aubuchon hardware store when we first came. The store is gone and so is Archie. Another black man worked on the county road crew. (ibid.)

Though the end of America was purportedly caused by a terrorist attack, the novel makes no mention of terrorism in Union Grove. Instead, Earle's response knits together Joseph's divisions by identifying black families with a factory village, Basiltree with a hardware store, and another black man with road maintenance work. The point is not that there were so few people of color that he could almost count those he considered nonwhite on one hand, but rather that his knowing them is decidedly mediated by pre-apocalyptic social relations, and that at their core, the post-apocalyptic social relationships Kunstler imagines—in a world built by hand, rather than by oil—explicitly do not include everyone living in and around Union Grove. A question raised in chapter 5 reverberates once more: Why is it that the post-apocalyptic future (imagined by a white, cisgender male author) must be suspiciously white as well? And why does focusing on ecological problems, not only for Kunstler but for other authors as well, trigger such a sharp return to racialized and gendered hierarchies? If one can accept the apocalyptic conceit of the novel, then it offers a realistic account of how a small community might go about making civic decisions in the absence of anything but the memory of legal procedures, property law, and civil rights. If one cannot, then it projects an idealized return to society before the combustion engine through a kind of magical subtraction or type of time travel that leaves characters (and thus the reader) able to see that life without fossil fuels and electricity is just life better lived. In either case, the novel offers a handful of lessons—whether intended or not—by thinking about energy in fiction.

In *World Made by Hand*, the goal seems to be to make a powered-down future along the path of least resistance, which could be why the novel snaps back into racialized and gendered hierarchies. This observation shifts the meaning of Kunstler's critique of suburbia: "The project of suburbia rolled out as any *emergent*, self-organizing system will under the right conditions. It elaborated itself as neatly as an algorithm" ("Farewell to the Drive-In Utopia," 83; emphasis in the original). On the one hand, Kunstler's ecological impulse seeks a smooth transition to carbon-free social relations. On the other hand, the well-worn and ready-to-hand characterization and narrative approach of the novel makes it especially susceptible to systemic racialization and patriarchal rule.

In attempting to picture the effected transition to a post-oil model of sociopolitical organization, *World Made by Hand* contains a particular conservative logic common to post-apocalyptic fiction and environmentalist writing that can either be taken up by peak oilers and proponents of a local lifestyle as a maintenance of the status quo (that is, humanity can survive, if only things could stay a particular way) or as political warning signs (if we continue along this path, this destruction is what will happen). Despite its compelling focus on the minutiae of municipal and civic life, Kunstler's novel falls short of providing even an imaginary solution to the slick contradictions of fossil capital in the twenty-first century. *World Made by Hand* simply makes oil disappear and erases racial and cultural diversity. It then places the leadership of the community firmly in the hands of white men.

The novel's fantasy hinges on the wonder of forgetting the complexities of modern life, of erasing the haunting feeling that the goods of petromodernity come at the price of the exclusion of some people today and the devastation of generations tomorrow, and of assuaging the liberal guilt at not having a locavore diet. Kunstler's novel posits an energy future in which the coordinates of possibility are still delimited by the shortcomings of the ecological imaginary of the present. Though the title, *World Made by Hand*, can be read as a name for the attempt to wrest freedom from necessity and to choose the polis over the global empire, the real takeaway lesson is that the production of goods can no longer be shored up by low-cost, high-consequence energy. Instead, Kunstler makes clear that in the post-petrol world he has fashioned, human labor returns as the dominant force of production. Kunstler envisions an intensely unproductive project that employs absolutely everybody, since without cheap energy everything must be accomplish by the laborious work of human hands. But what about post-apocalyptic novels that more carefully mediate the loss of modernity—not through oil in particular, but through the loss of the energy regime?

ENERGY'S APOCALYPSE

Mandel's *Station Eleven* captures a feeling of powerlessness so acutely that, if only for a moment, the full gravity of losing power is fully conveyed to the reader. Twenty years after the Georgia flu has massively reduced the world's population, a character flips a light switch:

Kirsten closed her eyes for just a second as she flipped the light switch. Naturally nothing happened, but as always in these moments she found herself straining to remember what it had been like when this motion had worked: walk into a room, flip a switch and the room floods with light. The trouble was she wasn't sure if she remembered or only imagined remembering this. (150)

This passage implies that the expectation of something happening when a character flips a switch is unnatural. It connects grasping for the light to a memory that cannot be accessed, yet this feeling is one that Kirsten Raymonde has attempted to reach before. She attempts to access what Patricia Yaeger has called "the touch-a-switch-and-it's-light magic of electrical power" ("Editor's Column," 309), and all she can find are her own uncertainties. In the novel, it has been twenty years since the power failed. Though the novel explicitly addresses energy, it omits the cause of energy failure. It invites assumptions about what has taken place. At least, that is the assumption I make about the status of energy infrastructure in this novel. A disease has ravaged the population of North America, and perhaps little could be done to get the dams, nuclear power plants, and the coal furnaces running once more.

The narrative recounts the experiences of several characters before, during, and after the outbreak of the disease, alternating between multiple moments—leading up to the outbreak, immediately following it, and a moment twenty years later. The novel moves between the past in Los Angeles, year zero in Toronto, and year twenty in the Great Lakes region and at the Severn City Airport. In year zero, an emergency medical technician named Jeevan Chaudhary holes up with his brother to wait out the collapse brought about by the disease. In year twenty, the focus jumps back and forth. One group makes a home in the airport, using the space provided and the food stored there to get themselves on their feet.[14] Raymonde is part of another group: an orchestra and theater troupe that continues to tour the Great Lakes region. The group's members take every opportunity to explore the ruins of modernity, such as houses and old schools.

Raymonde's encounters defamiliarize spaces and actions that are familiar to most readers—from the routine of flipping a light switch to that of going to school. The structures are still in place, but instead of producing electricity and orchestrating social activities, these remainders have been repurposed either as useful in new ways or as startling reminders of the technological evolution of human culture. The strain of remembering slips between certainty and fancy, and it signals the principal work that the post-apocalyptic mode does in relation to thinking about energy: it allows for the imaginary subtraction of energy's use. Even the half-remembered, half-forgotten ways energy used to touch the lives of characters living in the wake of societal collapse face this reduction, marking all the more strongly the bizarre yet normalized ways that modern humans interact with energy on a daily basis.

In a revelation remarkably similar to the one experienced by one of Frank's characters in *Alas, Babylon*, one of Mandel's characters realizes the human motive power that is required to keep a city moving:

> On silent afternoons in his brother's apartment, Jeevan found himself thinking about how human the city is, how human everything is. We bemoaned the impersonality of the modern world, but that was a lie, it seemed to him; it had never been impersonal at all. There had always been a massive delicate infrastructure of people, all of them working unnoticed around us, and when people stop going to work, the entire operation grinds to a halt. No one delivers fuel to the gas stations or the airports. Cars are stranded. Airplanes cannot fly. Trucks remain at their points of origin. Food never reaches the cities; grocery stores close. Businesses are locked and then looted. No one comes to work at the power plants or the substations, no one removes fallen trees from electrical lines. (Mandel, *Station Eleven*, 178)

Characters caught in post-apocalyptic stories often have the revelation of life's altered rhythm, it seems. Of course, post-apocalyptic texts attempt to produce this awareness for readers as well. Frank's work portrayed a preparedness movement in the United States and presented the practical steps that could be taken to ready oneself for a nuclear strike. Mandel does not outline a program for survival here, so much as she reproduces the profound insight that despite the illusion of a dearth of work, many must labor every day to make sure that people in a city can move and be fed, clothed, and kept warm. It is not too much of a stretch to equate Mandel's work here and that of other post-apocalyptic writers with producing a kind of organic Marxism. The passage above clearly highlights the secret of the commodity: it is human labor that Chaudhary discovers in his musing. The fact that it takes a rupture—even an imagined one—in the steadily moving, fossil-fueled city signals both the way oil as a motive force has become hidden in plain sight and the efficacy of imagined scenarios to make such facts plainly legible once more.

Distinct from the above considerations of a regression in automobility, post-apocalyptic novels also lament other things lost after a catastrophe. Early in *Station Eleven*, Mandel takes an entire chapter to list places one can no longer go and things one can no longer do, mapping in the manner of making an itinerary:

> No more diving into pools of chlorinated water lit green from below. No more ball games played out under floodlights. No more porch lights with moths fluttering on summer nights. No more trains running under the surface of cities on the dazzling power of the electric third rail. No more cities. No more films, except rarely, except with a generator drowning out half the dialogue, and only then for the first little while until the fuel for the generators ran out, because automobile gas goes stale after two or three years. Aviation gas lasts longer, but it was difficult to come by. (31)

The order of things in Mandel's list is worth considering. The list transitions from the heady days of summer—with swimming pools, baseball, and warm nights—to public transport, and its theme hangs on a thread of electric power. The list also moves from concrete immediacy to increasingly abstract and general phenomena: "No more cities." The real loss here is dissimilar to that explored by Chaudhary or by Frank's characters in *Alas, Babylon*. Here it is the petrocultural experiences of modernity that Mandel's list laments.

The second part of Mandel's list cleaves to the theme of energy for entertainment: "No more screens shining in the half-light as people raise their phones above the crowd to take photographs of concert stages. No more concert stages lit by candy-coloured halogens, no more electronic, punk, electric guitars" (Mandel, *Station Eleven*, 31).

The list is associative and grounded in a location: the concert hall. The specificity of the references to "electronic, punk, electric guitars" informs the reader that this list could only be Raymonde's if it was someone else's first, as Raymonde was too young to have memories of such things. The regression of automobility entails the development of a keen sense of nostalgia for the things a younger generation never even had the chance to experience, which echoes Butler's description of the three oil patches in the garage. The occasion of the novel provides Mandel with an opportunity to process the gravity of a loss of power in the way it might come to shape intergenerational relationships and culture.

As much as these losses communicate, it is the central paragraph of Mandel's list that is most crucial to the project of figuring postapocalyptic survival: "No more flight. No more towns glimpsed from the sky through airplane windows, points of glimmering light; no more looking down from thirty thousand feet and imagining the lives lit up by those lights at that moment. No more airplanes, no more requests to put your tray table in its upright and locked position" (Mandel, *Station Eleven*, 31). It is not the loss of connection that troubles the list maker the most, but the experience of flying. The list captures the affective, embodied experience of being on a plane, even though one of its central characters struggled to recall what used to happen after flipping a light switch. The list maker interrupts themselves: "but no, that wasn't true, there were still airplanes here and there. They stood dormant on runways and in hangers. They collected snow on their wings. In the cold months, they were ideal for food storage. In summer the ones near orchards were filled with trays of fruit that dehydrated in the heat. Teenagers snuck into them to have sex. Rust blossomed and streaked" (ibid.). The speaker here must be either a narrator, who exists outside the time of the storyworld, or one of the characters who transform the Severn City Airport into a livable space for a community. The group of survivors holed up in the airport uses the airplanes exactly as described in the above passage. Once used to convey passengers around the world, planes now serve more mundane purposes as climate-controlled or at least private spaces close to home, yet far enough away to make them useful. The airport group not only makes use of one of the most profoundly liminal and alienating spaces of modernity, but its members also found a museum dedicated to memorializing petroculture. The Museum of Civilization commemorates the past, accepting MP3 players, magazines, and other items for its collection. As Diletta De Cristofaro makes clear, this museum elegizes the "bygone hyper-globalised world" in a way that ultimately refuses "to paint the old world as worthy of a destruction" ("Critical Temporalities").

Subtracting oil is not like removing any other commodity from the storyworld. That difference becomes legible only in stories, such as post-apocalyptic ones, in which oil is gone—and as it turns out, with it goes just about everything else.[15] If energy input is measured in the form of how oil fuels infrastructures, the development of machinery, and everyday life, the very items in Mandel's lists, then the traces of the energy regime are right there on the surface as surely as are the remainders of capital in post-apocalyptic fiction. Briohny Doyle, a critic of that fiction, argues that such remainders "form the substance of the postapocalyptic imagination" ("The Postapocalyptic Imagination," 101). I argue that by subtracting oil from the storyworld, post-apocalyptic storytelling such as Mandel's moves beyond positive claims about the social meaning of oil and begins to imagine a reduced future that simultaneously addresses the deep energy commitments of the real-world present and hints at the possibilities for a post-petrol future. *Station Eleven* envisions a world from which the detritus of late capitalism has not vanished. Instead, the physical traces of an energy regime, such as the light switch in the passage quoted above, serve as useless reminders of half-forgotten memories. The touring group of performers has even converted the cabs of old cars into sleighs to be pulled along with them. Thus, the remainders of the fossil regime persist as memories or in the repurposing of old objects for new ends. *Station Eleven* effectively communicates the loss of the fossil regime precisely because it does not take oil as its object. It sets out to tell a story leading to and flowing from the massively fatal Georgia flu. Rather than imagining what good life would be possible without oil, it subtracts the energy regime by necessity. Without the people in place to maintain the system, attend to the infrastructure, and monitor the pipelines and reactors, these systems simply break down. *Station Eleven* is a novel useful for thinking about energy precisely because it takes other stories as its focus: the exploration of abandoned homes, the litany of lost experiences, and the people who make a home out of an airport. The energy regime's absence can also be registered in the few places it still shows up: for instance, in a portable, refined form of fossil fuel, as discussed in the next section.

FUEL AS A RESOURCE FOR *THE DOG STARS*

In Heller's *The Dog Stars*, the protagonist lives at a small airfield, which he describes as a superb place to live, given the post-apocalyptic conditions:

> On a big creek, check. So water, check. Anyone who read anything knew, too, that it was a model for sustainable power, check. Every house with panels and the FBO run mostly on wind. Check. FBO means Fixed Base Operator. Could've just said the Folks Who Run the Airport. If they knew what was coming they wouldn't have complicated things that much. (9)

Hig is a knowledgeable pilot: he understands the short life span of unleaded gasoline, where to find the freshest airplane fuel, and how best to extend its shelf life. At one point, he imagines that the supply will last him as long as he needs: "In ten years the additive will no longer keep the fuel fresh enough. In ten years I'll be done with all this. Maybe" (ibid., 10). The novel accounts for the continued use of fossil-fueled vehicles in a thoughtful way, which is not to say that it is focused on energy. Rather, it constructs its concern about fossil fuels as background ambience. Concern about fuel registers through an older sense of economy (as in household accounting). Unlike *World Made by Hand* and *Station Eleven*, *The Dog Stars* considers fuel as a resource. There was no fuel to speak of in Kunstler's and Mandel's novels, as the former ignored energy altogether and the latter tracked its absence.

Heller's novel shifts between the main character's internal dialogue and metacommentary. The book's aphoristic form makes this distinction clear: it does not have chapters; instead, there are sections separated by asterisks. A section can be a sentence, a paragraph, or longer. Hig often thinks in short bursts of rhetorical glee: "I still got a mild kick out of free gas" (Heller, *The Dog Stars*, 152). As the sections accumulate, this form becomes not just the presentation of Hig's thoughts but a more complete picture of the storyworld—one in which an airplane pilot survives the apocalypse, lives on an air field, and has an airplane with plenty of fuel. Unlike Raymonde, Hig is still a creature of the pre-apocalyptic world. Though he has to adjust his habits, he does not have his own light-switch moment—a fact that I will argue can be traced to the way the remainder of fuel is framed as the central issue here, rather than energy as a social form.

The novel blends post-apocalyptic tropes with explanatory information about fuel. In a sense, it teaches a kind of post-apocalyptic energy literacy: "I fuel up. The pump runs off its own solar panel. Used to use a battery and inverter but the battery died so I wired it directly to the inverter and now can only fuel up if the sun is shining which it is. I have a hand pump if I need it, but it's a pain" (Heller, *The Dog Stars*, 74). Hig has access to three kinds of energy: stored, solar, and kinetic. His work is taxing but ultimately enjoyable. He climbs a stepladder to fill the tanks "through capped intakes at the top of each wing." He complains that "it's a real pain to be on the ground and pump and keep track of the fuel level which is checked by climbing up and looking straight down into the bladder through the fill hole." He can fuel up his plane, but the procedure requires focus. Though he can "estimate and get it close," it is "easier just to stand up there and pull the trigger on the pump hose and hear the reassuring electric hum and the clicking of the numbers rolling on the meter like filling up a car use to be." In filling the plane's tank, Hig expresses nostalgia for the ease of automated pumps and electric sensors—doing things by hand and eye is challenging. Ultimately, he communicates his own expertise and capacity as a pilot.

Hig interrupts such nostalgic longing. He notes the fuel's shelf life: "Plenty of gas still out in the world but problem is the auto gas went stale and bad a year or two after. 100 low lead, which I burn, is stable [for] something like ten years" (Heller, *The Dog Stars*, 74). In this way, Hig shares his intimate knowledge of how to treat a fossil-fueled machine and how much longer he has until the fuel runs out. He continues: "I expect to lose it one of these days. I can add PRI [fuel stabilizer] and nurse it along for ten more years probably. Then I'll have to look for jet fuel which is kerosene and lasts for basically ever. I know where it is, the closest. I know that right now I'm the only one alive who knows, or at least knows how to get it out." But Hig's ruminations in this passage are not entirely for the sake of energy literacy. They also play on the convention of the post-apocalyptic mode, raising risky propositions and mentioning resource wars and the dangerous lengths one will go to for fuel: "Every time I land at Rocky Mountains Airport I feel vulnerable in ways I never do at other stops. It's too big. A big old jetport with scores of buildings, hangars, sheds and the pumps and the steel fill plates out in the open." The fuel situation at the Hig's air field recalls the past way of doing things, and as he struggles with awkwardly fueling his plane, he forecasts the future fortunes of his fuel supply. Fuel is in short supply, which raises the tension for Hig and his companion Bangley, a former military man. How will they resupply themselves if forced to do so by land?

Each trip to survey their small territory is limited by the amount of fuel required to get home again safely—that is, by a point of no return, beyond which Hig cannot go. *The Dog Stars* doesn't stop at that limit. On one of his trips around the perimeter, Hig intercepts a brief signal from a distant control tower. It is choppy and cuts out, but it leaves him with a slowly mounting dilemma. Indeed, it takes a full three years before he decides to act. The novel poses the question of whether or not he should investigate this message in several ways: Should he trade his life of repeated tasks for the unknown? Should he heed Bangley's insistence that he not get lost in "Recreating" (Heller, *The Dog Stars*, 56)? Is Hig's curiosity just nostalgia for a world of mobility and travel, or is it something new? Should he chase this ghostly faint signal of a new, different situation?[16] As Hig tries to decide whether to continue on short excursions to gather more supplies or to take the chance on a long flight, chasing an alien signal to see if there is another way of living, his dilemma echoes that faced long ago by Daniel Defoe's Robinson Crusoe.

In the meantime, Hig's dog dies. Hig mourns. He survives an attack by some miscreants. Bangley picks off his attackers at long range with deadly precision. Hig and Bangley presume that the attackers were coming to take their supplies and shelter. Shaken, Hig decides to take a chance on the trip. For all of its consideration of fuel as resource, *The Dog Stars* concludes by offering a standard conclusion to its post-apocalyptic plot. Hig follows the signal and finds love, using his cunning and ingenuity along the way. This novel does not end up imagining a future energy transition as much as it bears witness to one man's processing the trauma of surviving the loss of the love of his life and then the death of his dog. Loss is sad, true—but *The Dog*

Stars offers little more than that fact. Its relation to energy is still imagined in much the same way as Robinson Crusoe's record keeping, only Hig attends to airplane fuel rather than driftwood and food.[17] The post-apocalyptic conceit in Heller's book presents fuel as a resource and encourages the idea that with the right knowledge, training, and equipment, the right person could continue to fly in a world where fossil fuel extraction, refinement, and distribution has come to a standstill. In this way, *The Dog Stars* plays out the last man trope without the strong, social dimension of community mapping that we see in the other examples presented here.

Finally, I turn to a text that deploys the subtraction of future reduction by simply removing oil from the storyworld rather than leaving some fuel behind to see what happens. The move leaves behind the vast infrastructural and social constructs of the fossil-fuel regime so that the characters navigate without access to fuel or electric energy produced by fossil fuel.

SLOW APOCALYPSE IN ENERGY'S ABSENCE

Like the characters in Mandel's and Heller's novels, those in Varley's *Slow Apocalypse* must consistently check if their old habits and patterns of movement make sense. After holing up in their suburb, the central characters set out to discover if Los Angeles (LA), once the land of highways and automobility, is passable in the aftermath of a massive earthquake. Varley's protagonist, Dave Marshall, thinks to himself, "the map is not the terrain" (190). His discovery that many of LA's landmark buildings are absent or in ruins after the earthquake rocked the city seems to prove him correct. Moreover, the community militias make previously traversable roadways impassable with barricades. The ease of movement that motor vehicles granted vanishes along with highway maintenance crews, traffic cops, and drive-through restaurants. *Slow Apocalypse* narrativizes the process of cataloguing each no longer usable feature of modern life like so many blocked or dead-end streets. Late in Varley's novel, Marshall; his wife, Karen; daughter, Addison; and Addison's horse, Ranger, join with a few of Marshall's friends to escape LA. They manage to do so at a slow crawl in an Escalade and two retrofitted *Mad Max*–type vehicles: a U-Haul truck and a school bus, each equipped with an engine that burns wood chips and armor plating stuffed with books.[18]

The plot of *Slow Apocalypse* relies on Marshall's role as a Hollywood screenwriter. This fact means he is woefully ill-suited for the events of the novel, but it is also what gives him the chance to be prepared for the worst. At the novel's opening, Marshall is doing research for a science fiction thriller, and a retired military man warns him of a top-secret scientifically manufactured supervirus that is capable of rendering the world's oil reserves inert. *Slow Apocalypse* is Marshall's writing, which is part journal and part manuscript: in the epilogue, readers discover that, not unlike Kim Stanley Robinson's *The Wild Shore*, they have been reading a character's firsthand account all along—which also ties *Slow Apocalypse* to Isherwood Williams's catalogue of post-catastrophe America in *Earth Abides*. The virus itself first appears as a device in a Hollywood film treatment described by a former military man, but it turns out to be true. The single science fiction element in *Slow Apocalypse* causes the breakdown of modern life. The virus is thus a literary conceit in the truest sense: if readers can accept it, the rest of the story follows. The novel, set in motion by the event of the petroleum virus, does not reveal any more than Marshall can see or describe. Instead, the novel stages a geopolitical event that it then mediates through the particular senses of a single character caught in LA. On the surface, the apocalyptic event that rocks LA is an earthquake, yet Marshall has insider information, so the reader knows that the quake is a result of the solidification of oil reserves.

Slow Apocalypse reads like an amalgamation of Kevin J. Anderson and Doug Beason's *Ill Wind* (1995) and Albert Brooks's *2030* (2011), and it ends like Kunstler's *World Made by Hand*. In *Ill Wind*, a microbe dubbed "Prometheus" that was designed to clean up a massive oil spill devours not just oil but all petroleum products, causing the regression of civilization. In *2030*, Los Angeles suffers a major earthquake, but the US government is destitute and cannot respond. Finally, as discussed above, in *World Made by Hand*, upstate New York has been cut off from communication not only with the rest of the world but also with the next state, a small town becomes a hub of activity, and its denizens work together to survive. *Slow Apocalypse* is also derived from the classic science fiction monster trope of the blob, and the plot is developed in the same kind of way, with a mad scientist and a runaway invention.

The storyworld of *Slow Apocalypse* takes on the remainders of an LA remade by the narrative act of world destroying, of previous apocalyptic plots, and of varying approaches to both the subtraction of oil and the consideration of energy after the apocalyptic event. In a review of the novel, T. S. Miller makes an astute point: "at this point in the universal saturation of all forms of culture with apocalypse, it can be exceedingly difficult to produce an end of the world that we haven't already seen before" ("Slow Apocalypse by John Varley"). This synthesis offers a better vantage point on the working of the postapocalyptic mode than on the cultural logic of the fossil regime. In the same review, Miller writes that *Slow Apocalypse* "narrates the gradual diminishment of the world, the forced reduction of modern globalized society to a collection of impossibly distant localities" (ibid.). The novel not only forcibly removes oil from the storyworld, causing literal and figurative shock waves, but it also tracks the profoundly isolating effect that both the earth's tectonic upheaval and reduced vehicle availability can have. Before this point gets lost, I want to note that both of Miller's observations about Varley's book refer to the same phenomena: the fossil-fuel regime and its culture of transportation both enable and produce a cultural milieu wherein the stories we tell are many and multiple and appear varied, yet closer inspection reveals a repetition compulsion in both the arena of travel and the domain of narrative.[19] More work needs to be done on the correspondence drawn in Varley's storyworld between an "end of the world that we haven't already seen" and the "forced reduction of modernized global society to a collection of impossibly distant localities." The lived experience of such a transformed social and political space would prove profoundly unique and challenging when compared to the suburban experience of Marshall and his family.

In their trip away from the Hollywood hills, Marshall and his family pass crowds of refugees gathered in Anaheim in parking lots. One of Marshall's companions reports: "There are refugees, thousands of them penned up behind chain-link fences all along [California State Route] 91. They're being guarded by what look like Anaheim cops and armed civilians. There's no shelter I could see, just bare concrete. I don't know what they're doing with those people" (Varley, *Slow Apocalypse*, 360). They travel on to Buena Park, where there are also refugee camps, but fewer of them, and speak with a police officer who tellingly says, "'Ain't it the shits? Did you ever think you'd see Americans . . .' He couldn't go on for a moment" (ibid., 363). They encounter similar situations throughout their trip. Communities cannot take any more people in, and the people who have gathered have nowhere to go but empty lots, where they try to piece together meals from what has been left behind. Marshall's companions soon discover people with flu symptoms, and several of them come down with the flu. Marshall and his companions have also heard tales of the ships at the coast that offer transport away from LA to thousands of refugees crowding the shore. The message behind these conditions and the characters' response to them is crystalized in the words spoken by the Buena Park cop: seeing Americans living in conditions faced by other refugees forced out of their homes for economic, environmental, or political reasons is emotionally devastating—even unspeakable.

The repeated narrative act of subtracting oil and the fossil regime from imagined futures emphasizes the longevity and tenacity of oil's modernizing promise. In Kunstler's, Mandel's, and Heller's attempts to imagine an energy-scarce future, I still find a world of abundance. Whether these novels include food, art, culture, and community or not-yet-stale airplane fuel, they do not capture the scarcity of food and resources imagined by Varley. *Slow Apocalypse* demonstrates that it is increasingly difficult to produce a new end-of-the-world story, not because of its generic remainders and plot repetitions, but because its city-street verisimilitude and refugee-crisis imaginary present a near-future extrapolation founded in a real world that does not seem to need science-fictional destruction of oil reserves to threaten collapse. To paraphrase William Gibson, that future is already here—it's just not evenly distributed.[20]

Varley's post-apocalyptic imaginary can be tied to the cultural horizons of capital, especially once capital has become entirely reliant on fossil fuels. Fredrick Buell describes scarcity thinking as a possibly revelatory way of imagining oil culture's current dominance: "oil's possible collapse, as imagined today, provides both motivation and a heuristic for asking many interesting questions about oil's relationships with culture, *both* in the past and the present" ("A Short History of Oil Cultures," 70; emphasis in the original).[21] Drawing on the work of the environmental sociologist William Catton, Buell forms his argument around twin poles: "Fossil-fuel culture can be, in short, described as an 'age of *exuberance*'—an age which is also, given the dwindling finitude of the resources it increasingly makes social life dependent on, haunted by *catastrophe*" (Catton, *Overshoot*, 36 and 159, quoted in Buell, "A Short History of Oil Cultures," 71).[22] Buell tracks a nuanced unfolding of the fossil regime between these two poles of exuberance and catastrophe. As he explains, they do not describe discrete periods; rather, they are coeval: "Exuberance and catastrophe materialized as historically specific forms of capitalist triumph and oppression, of environmental domination and destruction, and of human liberation and psychic and bodily oppression" (Buell, "A Short History of Oil Cultures," 74). This sense of the present entangles the raw potential with the unbridled destructiveness supplied by burning oil to produce electricity.[23] The dance between the two moments will always entail the experience of the dominant moment's opposite: there can be no moment of exuberance without catastrophe, and vice versa.

On Buell's account, oil fuels a cultural vision of reality through the entwined logics of catastrophe and exuberance—which, on my account, take on the role of the two percussive narrative beats found in post-apocalyptic writing. They appear in the plot as separated moments, but Buell argues that they should be considered parts of a larger whole. Through the dialectic of exuberance and catastrophe, Buell presents two variants of a reactionary logic that are not different periods in the history of fossil-fueled capitalism. These moments are not phases, and they do not follow on each other's heels. Instead, they operate in a manner similar to what Max Horkheimer and Theodor Adorno identified as the dialectic of enlightenment: socialism and barbarism all in one (*Dialectic of Enlightenment*). Driving a car on a freeway, getting an ultrasound in a doctor's office, or eating food shipped from the other side of the planet—each moment provided by oil's liquid energy is entangled in the misery of oil. Such misery can be seen not only in gushers and pipeline bursts, but also in the blanket of carbon dioxide warming the planet and the violent conflict for control of oil fields, pipelines, and refineries. But the connections are not balanced, and to use Mika Minio-Paluello and James Marriot's language, there is a vast carbon web (*The Oil Road*, 6) that is created and maintained not by individual choices, but by corporate, government, and institutional action (Taylor and Watts, "Revealed"). Buell's analysis attends to the impacts of oil in fiction, which allows us to understand how such narratives frame real-world cultural and social relations to fossil fuels.

Alas, Babylon, Parable of the Sower, World Made by Hand, Station Eleven, The Dog Stars, and *Slow Apocalypse* stage complex relations to energy as a regime. Frank imagines what happens to Fort Repose not after the bomb strikes, but once it has become like "an island," cut off from the shipment of goods and delivery of electric energy. Butler imagines the United States in a steep economic decline that has forced many people to fend for themselves in a world where gasoline is no longer the cheap, subsidized commodity it is in the real world. Kunstler's novel uses the end-of-oil conceit to project an idyllic, patriarchal civic life. Mandel extrapolates the embodied feelings of living in a world without energy except in half-glimpsed memories. Heller's novel usefully considers fuel as a resource but in doing so loses sight of the energy regime itself. Varley combines elements of Mandel's storyworld with Heller's attention to transportation. He imagines stopgap solutions to the loss of automobility at the same time as he maps the changing terrain of Los Angeles. The fuel innovation and preparedness of the protagonist serve to protect his family from the fate suffered by the masses—forced into camps, crowded onto boats, and shipped to an unknown future.

Varley's energy apocalypse reveals a guiding fantasy at the heart of the post-apocalyptic mode: that the masses of real-world refugees, forced out of their homes by the state, economic decline, war, and climate change, would simply disappear in the world-destroying apocalyptic event. In *World Made by Hand*, the New Faithers need a home, so they purchase the abandoned school. In *Station Eleven*, one group of people takes shelter in the airport, where there is enough room for each of them. In *The Dog Stars*, any people approaching the hanger are dealt with by Bangley, gruesomely and at a distance. In *Slow Apocalypse*, however, the refugees do not disappear. The hungry wander the streets, the thirsty congregate in buildings hollowed out by economic depression, and the tired keep watch in shifts. After a showdown with some bikers who were terrorizing a mountain town, Marshall and his crew eventually settle there. Yet the boats crowded with refugees seem to be forgotten by the novel's end. Massive refugee populations and incredible armies of the unemployed and unemployable are social problems raised by Varley's book, but the narrative cannot solve them. As many people as the fossil-fueled energy system can support in this golden era of energy abundance, there are still many left outside in the dark.

Conclusion
Remainders of the American Century

> *Up and down the island the buildings collided, they humiliated runts through verticality and ambition, sulked in one another's shadows. Inevitability was mayor, term after term, yesterday's old masters, stately named and midwifed by once-famous architects, were insulted by the soot of combustion engines and by technological advances in construction. Time chiseled at elegant stonework, which swirled or plummeted to the sidewalk in dust and chips and chunks. Behind the façades their insides were butchered, reconfigured, rewired according to the next era's new theories of utility. Classic six into honeycomb, sweatshop killing floor into cordoned cubical mill. In every neighborhood the imperfect in their fashion awaited the wrecking ball and their bones were melted down to help their replacements surpass them, steel into steel. The new buildings in wave upon wave drew themselves out of the rubble, shaking off the past like immigrants. The addresses remained the same and so did the flawed philosophies. It wasn't anyplace else. It was New York City.*
> —COLSON WHITEHEAD, *Zone One*

This passage above from early in Colson Whitehead's *Zone One* (2011) reframes the apocalyptic event of the novel as simply another in an ongoing history of urban reformation. The consecration of each rising generation of urban planners and architects by the previous, the marks left by automobile use, the shift from labor-heavy industry to the cognitive burden of creative industries, and the crash of wave after wave of new immigrants eager to become American—everything is here. For Whitehead, each of these items becomes contained in the vastness of the New York skyline.[1] The evolution of New York City from the beginning of the twentieth century to the 1960s and 1970s provides a history leading up to the post-apocalyptic present of Whitehead's novel. The places remain the same, and in many cases so do the names, but everything seems different now. *Zone One* simultaneously depicts the complexity of urban development and the churn of remainders from the pre-apocalyptic moment in the post-apocalyptic mode.

In this realm, no apocalypse is complete. The narrator describes one of the people Mark Spitz (the novel's protagonist, who is nicknamed after an Olympic athlete) has to work with, framing the characters' relationship to the post-apocalyptic mode with a metafictional gesture:

> He was one of those apocalypse-as-moral-hygiene people, with a college-sophomore socialist slant. The dead come to scrub the Earth of capitalism and the vast bourgeois superstructure, with its doilies, helicopter parenting, and streaming video, return us to nature and wholesome communal living. . . . The human race deserved the plague, we brought it on ourselves for poisoning the planet, for the Death of God, the calculated brutalities of the global economic system, for driving primordial species to extinction: the entire collapse of values as evidenced by everything from nuclear fission to reality television to alternate side of the street parking. Mark Spitz could only endure these harangues for a minute or two before he split. It was boring. The plague was the plague. (Whitehead, *Zone One*, 124–25)

Stephen Joyce reads this passage as a parody on Whitehead's part, one that Joyce labels ironic ("Convergence Publishing and Prestige Niches," 135). I agree, but I would emphasize the internal irony that Whitehead deploys over any sense that it might be unexpected for a post-apocalyptic novel to make fun of literary criticism. This passage allows Whitehead to make such an interpretive commentary and make it well—while disavowing it altogether through Spitz's reaction. If anything, this passage might demonstrate some self-doubt on the part of the author. The critiques here may be cute, but they are precisely mimicked in a way that betrays a level of familiarity or closeness to the position, whereas Spitz's dismissal is underexamined and undertheorized. Readers might identify with this desire for an overarching explanation and be self-doubting, too, or even bored with it at the same time.

Zone One shows, once more, that the literary history of the post-apocalyptic mode is one fueled by remainders. The concept of remainders is a capacious one. It is related to yet distinct from Raymond Williams's three terms for describing the cultural process in terms of its residual components that are repurposed elements from a previous moment, dominant components that pervade and shape the cultural process, and those emerging components that have not been fully articulated and can be sensed only subtly (*Marxism and Literature*, 121–27). Yet the term "remainders" names elements of the cultural process in the post-apocalyptic storyworld that may well have been emerging features as much as they could have been dominant or residual ones. In this sense, remainders are the result of a profound reordering. Here is a review of how I have used the term in this book: it describes what gets left behind in the process of future reduction; it names the techniques of post-apocalyptic writing transmitted from text to text; it makes the books that have gone unsold and unread reappear; it captures the specific ideological leanings of these imagined futures; and it renders historical the structures that make up the American century. To be a remainder is to be between two types of usefulness, to be in want of productive force, and to wait for innovation. The symbolic function of remainders might be thought of asymptotically, to use a figure from mathematical analysis that describes limiting behavior. Becoming ever closer to the representation of US hegemony, remainders can never fully depict the extent of such a system of force and power. Focusing on one particular residuum pushes the rest into the background. The post-apocalyptic mode is ultimately describable as a narrative form that imagines how remainders are made and repurposed.

To dive into a mass of zombies is Spitz's final decision in Whitehead's *Zone One*: "In the stream of the street the dead bobbled in their invisible current. . . . These were the angry dead, the ruthless chaos of existence made flesh. These were the ones who would resettle the broken city. No one else" (258). Up to this point in the novel, Spitz had been working for Project Phoenix to clear skels out of high-rise buildings in New York City.[2] As Spitz ponders his decision, he imagines the tide of flesh moving on to the "next human settlement, and the one after that, where the barrier holds until you don't need it anymore" (ibid.).

Though the original Mark Spitz was an Olympic swimmer, Whitehead's Spitz cannot swim. As Andrew Hoberek points out, "the moment late in the novel when we find out that Mark Spitz is black occurs when he is telling [his companion] Gary his Last Night story, and Gary—otherwise an encyclopedia of "racial, gender, and religious stereotypes" (231)—fails to recognize the one (black people can't swim) that adds an additional element of irony to Mark Spitz's nickname" ("Living with PASD," 412). In the end, Spitz cannot seem to shake the impulse to dive, one he finds almost irresistibly funny: "Fuck it, he thought. You have to learn how to swim sometime. He opened the door and walked into the sea of the dead" (Whitehead, *Zone One*, 259). Spitz's plunge into a "sea of the dead" offers a new finale for the narrative movement of the post-apocalyptic mode. In the face of a return to the same, he decides to dive in, to become a new kind of post-apocalyptic subject. His decision to embrace the mass flies in the face of the post-apocalyptic mode: more specifically, his gruesome decision to "learn how to swim" shakes the foundation of the repetition compulsion and the focus on the individual demonstrably found in the post-apocalyptic novel. It closes a critical look at character in the post-apocalyptic mode that was opened by Richard Matheson's *I am Legend*.

Zone One's long architectural passage gains new significance in light of Spitz's dive. The narrator may be describing the changing urban plan of the city and the social relations that undergird it, but in providing a theory of the urban metabolism, the narrator also gestures to a deeper connection between history and the post-apocalyptic mode. The figurative slippage of *Zone One*'s narrator creates an informal history of literary transformation that is not strictly limited to the city. In this reading, the narrator offers a metahistory of cultural forms: "Up and down the island the buildings collided, they humiliated runts through verticality and ambition, sulked in one another's shadows" (Whitehead, *Zone One*, 5). Moreover, I read the passage as a description of the rise of the post-apocalyptic mode through the tumultuous changes in publishing described in chapter 3: the effects wrought by writers' creating their visions of what happens after the end are replaced as "time chiseled at elegant stonework, which swirled or plummeted to the sidewalk in dust and chips and chunks" (ibid., 6). *Zone One* raises questions about expression and transmission, race in America, what comes next for the beleaguered hegemon, and whether the struggle to rebuild the old world from its ashes is one worth undertaking. At the same time, it furnishes the conceptual tools to pursue answers to those question. Perhaps, *Zone One* seems to say, perhaps there are other struggles worth undertaking. Spitz's dive, seen in this light, is a radical break with the typical outcomes of other texts written in the post-apocalyptic mode. Perhaps counterintuitively, there is something here that validates and encourages a transformation of what the post-apocalyptic mode can do and be, perhaps suggesting that another text, a genre text, might offer a different path forward than the one Spitz takes.

In this regard, one post-apocalyptic–adjacent or –related tale stands out from the rest. N. K. Jemisin's Broken Earth trilogy is the first to have won a Hugo award based on fans' votes for each novel. *Obelisk Gate* (2016) and *The Stone Sky* (2017) also won the Nebula award for best novel, and *The Fifth Season* (2015) was nominated for that award. These books have won more than acclaim; they also represent a triumph of progressive elements in the science fiction community. In light of the success of people of color and women as authors of books chosen by fans for Hugo awards, two slates of reactionary science fiction fans (known as the Sad Puppies and Rabid Puppies) sought to take the fan-chosen awards by fiat. Both groups believe that speculative fiction writing has grown too diversified and have campaigned against what they perceive to be a leftist bias in science fiction writing and culture. They coordinated the nominations of authors they think represent more conservative values.[3] Progressive fans rallied, and the Puppies' plans were thwarted. The nomination of the final book in Jemisin's trilogy for the Nebula award ratified the view of the progressive science fiction fans who defended the Hugo awards from an organized regressive faction. Moreover, not only have Jemisin's books won awards, but they also use the end-of-the-world narrative frame to tell an exciting story that is rich with social commentary. They push the threat of total environmental destruction to its limits. For instance, the first novel in the trilogy, *The Fifth Season*, introduces the Stillness, a land where world-shattering tectonic plate movement threatens established cities and a subjugated people wields immense power over the geologic movement of the planet. *The Fifth Season* begins: "Let's start with the end of the world, why don't we? Get it over with and move on to more interesting things" (1). Jemisin's opening lines address the tiredness of world ending as a fictional premise, and in retrospect they rebuke the regressive protestations of the Puppies. They also echo Spitz's tired thought that "the plague was the plague." Jemisin's trilogy constructs a storyworld in which history has long been buried and people struggle under false pretenses, misinterpreting the capacities of those around them as reasons to be fearful and mistrusting. Here the remainders of a civilization that has been dead for millennia still disrupt the lives of everyday people and the gifted, earth-bending orogenes alike.

Though we may agree with Whitehead's and Jemisin's narrators and admit a certain level of tiredness with fiction about the end of the world as we know it, today multiple post-apocalyptic futures compete for dominance. In *The Postman* and *The Wild Shore*, the movements of the protagonists on the mail route or on the way to discover the return of technology in the city make evident possible configurations of the social. Remainders of the national imaginary float with the ash from the frontier. In *Farnham's Freehold*, the critical inversion of the relations of chattel slavery results in a freehold dedicated to preventing a black-dominated future, while in *Aftermath*, the representation of the ongoing apocalypse of white supremacy and antiblackness generates a new critical direction for the post-apocalyptic mode. The politics of survival in *The Road* unfold spatially, rather than temporally, which serves to reinforce the long-held grip of the reproductive imperative on futurity. *Station Eleven*, *The Dog Stars*, and *Slow Apocalypse* build on a tendency of the post-apocalyptic mode to depict the breakdown of energy infrastructure and automobility. They depict the aftermath of the fossil-fuel regime, yet theirs is a vision with no carbon dioxide blanketing the planet—a remainder of the long, steady burning of coal and crude oil. In each of its figurations of space and time, the post-apocalyptic mode grounds possible futures in already existing communities. Following this line of reasoning, we could think of post-apocalyptic storyworlds as a desire for the future as disruption.[4] The post-apocalyptic mode imagines that success comes after failure, in the sense that it offers a glimpse of a possibly different future. These futures are about struggle. There might be a conflict about re-forming the state or a contest over the representation of race. This book has attempted to show that intuitive readings of post-apocalyptic stories are not incorrect: these tales do express contemporary cultural anxieties, yet these anxieties are far from universal.

Remainders of the American century are part of a long and ongoing project of settler colonialism—people stolen from Africa, lands stolen from Indigenous peoples, and everyone free to subscribe to the tenets of liberty. The apocalypse has already happened, and we all live in its the long shadow of colonization and capital, although their effects are uneven.[5] In this sense, the term "remainders" also names a form of surplus, an excess incomprehensible to groups such as the Project for the New American Century and the 2016 presidential campaign of Donald Trump with its slogan "make America great again." Post-apocalyptic writing often obscures this surplus, yet as a critical term "remainders" strives to make apparent the structures of thought and feeling that radiate from such stories. Subtraction works in particular ways in the post-apocalyptic mode. Attend to who gets left out of your crisis-prone future forecasting and be wary of fellow travelers with exclusive systems for survival. My hunch is that we will all weather the ongoing crises by learning how to trust one another. I would urge us all to consider a fuller and more just mathematics of survival and persistence during the long decline of US hegemony and the time that will follow it.

Notes

Introduction: Post-Apocalyptic Novels in the Age of US Decline

1. Claire P. Curtis, John Hay, and others use the adjective "postapocalyptic." I prefer to indicate the narrative sequence involved by using a hyphen to describe the post-apocalyptic mode, as Diletta De Cristofaro does (see *The Contemporary Post-Apocalyptic Novel*). The *Oxford English Dictionary* defines the adjective "post-apocalyptic" in this manner: "*(a)* of or relating to the time after the revelation of St John . . . 1); *(b)* following an event regarded as an apocalypse, *esp.* following a nuclear war or other catastrophic event; (of a science fiction film, book, game, etc.) set in a period following such an event" ("Post-, prefix"). The use of "post-apocalyptic" dates to a 1982 review of *The Road Warrior* in the *New York Times*. I am grateful to John Hay for sharing this useful terminological detail. See Hay, *Postapocalyptic Fantasies in Antebellum American Literature*.

2. These books do not tend to begin with proactive characters. In post-apocalyptic storytelling, the apocalyptic novum makes a reactionary stance the most obvious response that a character can have. Even Octavia E. Butler's Lauren Oya Olamina develops Earthseed—an arguably ambiguous utopian enclave—in response to the deterioration of ecological and social relations (see *Parable of the Sower*). This kind of reactionary position can all too easily become a kind of political conservatism or insularism that seeks to maintain a status quo. Even when these texts are utopian or revolutionary, they often still find purchase within such reactionary political thinking. Compare, for example, Rebecca Solnit's *A Paradise Built in Hell*, a sociological study of how people react generously and humanely rather than selfishly and with violence to real crises. Solnit's cases studies include the San Francisco earthquake and fires of 1906, the Halifax explosion of 1917, the Mexico City earthquake of 1985, the events of September 11, 2001, and the aftermath of Hurricane Katrina. Rather than the clichéd, Hobbesian narrative of crisis in which a society becomes fragmented into tribes competing for scarce resources, Solnit finds humans in the wake of a crisis working together to make a better life for one another. She writes, "In the wake of an earthquake, a bombing, or a major storm, most people are altruistic, urgently engaged in caring for themselves and those around them, strangers and neighbors as well as friends and loved ones. The image of the selfish, panicky, or regressively savage human being in times of disaster has little truth to it. . . . Decades of meticulous sociological research on behavior in disasters, from the bombings of World War II to floods, tornadoes, earthquakes, and storms across the continent and around the world, have demonstrated this. But

belief lags behind, and often the worst behavior in the wake of a calamity is on the part of those who believe that others will behave savagely and that they themselves are seeking defensive measures against barbarism" (ibid., 2). While this manner of behavior is most encouraging and I would not discount it, it does name the response of people to a specific crisis event rather to the ongoing assault on social programs, the environment, and conflict-ravaged countries by the US government—an ongoing and slow-burning series of crises to be sure, which are all too easy to pass over in silence.

3. For an excellent account of post-apocalyptic film in the twenty-first century, see S. Trimble, *Undead Ends*.

4. See John Adams, "Post-Apocalyptic Science Fiction."

5. That playbook might be, in Richard Hofstadter's words, those of "the paranoid spokesman" who "sees the fate of conspiracy in apocalyptic terms—he traffics in the birth and death of whole worlds, whole political orders, whole systems of human values. He is always manning the barricades of civilization. He constantly lives at a turning point. Like religious millennialists he expresses the anxiety of those who are living through the last days and he is sometimes disposed to set a date [for] the apocalypse" ("The Paranoid Style in American Politics"). Hofstadter's diagnosis has long been set aside by historians for its basis in secondary sources rather than archival material and its lack of focus on the work of women and people of color, yet both the fictional Jarret's and the real Trump's words use a perceived sociocultural decline and an apocalyptic turning point to motivative social movements. As Hofstadter puts it, "the modern right wing . . . feels dispossessed: America has been largely taken away from them and their kind, though they are determined to try to repossess it and to prevent the final destructive act of subversion. The old American virtues have already been eaten away by cosmopolitans and intellectuals; the old competitive capitalism has been gradually undermined by socialistic and communistic schemers; the old national security and independence have been destroyed by treasonous plots, having as their most powerful agents not merely outsiders and foreigners as of old but major statesmen who are at the very centers of American power" (ibid.). See also Kathryn Olmsted, "A Conspiracy So Dense."

6. Hay cites John Van Ness Yates and Joseph White Moulton's *History of the State of New York* (1824) as one of the earliest examples of post-apocalyptic fantasy (*Postapocalyptic Fantasies in Antebellum American Literature*, 1). Outside of the United States, the first example likely to come to mind is Mary Shelley's *The Last Man* (first published in 1826). But there is also Jean-Baptiste Cousin de Grainville's *Le dernier homme* (first published in 1805, with an anonymous translation published in 1806 as *The Last Man or Omegarus and Syderia, a Romance of Futurity*), which spurred a series of similar tales—including Lord

Byron's poem "Darkness" (1816), Thomas Campbell's poem "The Last Man" (1823), and Shelley's novel.

7. Other examples of apocalyptically inflected stories contemporary with *Caesar's Column* include John Ames Mitchell's *The Last American: A Fragment from the Journal of Khan-Li* (1889), Agnes Bond Yourell's *A Manless World* (1891), Frona Eunice Colburn's *Yermah the Dorado* (1897), and Stanley Waterloo's *Armageddon: A Tale of Love, War, and Invention* (1898). I am indebted to Julie Fiorelli for these references. See also Lyman Sargent, *British and Utopian Literature*; Kenneth Roemer, *The Obsolete Necessity*.

8. In a 2004 article on US post-apocalyptic writing, Matthew Wolf-Meyer lays the groundwork for a study of the genre in the aggregate, writing, "individual [post-apocalyptic] novels are unexceptional in their effects: They postulate ambiguously utopian futures without finding resolution in the thematic elements present in the narrative. When coupled with other novels that interrogate similar thematic elements, as well as the trope of post-apocalyptic America, the reader is positioned at a nexus of dialectical opposition, required to identify which of the futures holds more personal truth, and more importantly, which is more *American*" [emphasis in the original].

9. I understand Rieder's description of genre with its emphasis on practice by way of mode: genre, too, has a way of getting something done. The argument that he incubates about genre here is clearly what he hatches in *Science Fiction and the Mass Cultural Genre System*. See also Andrew Milner, *Locating Science Fiction*.

10. Again, see Rieder, who writes, "A masterpiece might encapsulate an essence, if science fiction had one, and it certainly can epitomize motifs and strategies; but only intertextual repetition can accumulate into a family of resemblances" (*Colonialism and the Emergence of Science Fiction*, 19).

11. Hollinger's words are reminiscent of Samuel R. Delany's claim in the conclusion to "About 5,750 Words" that "any serious discussion of speculative fiction must get away from the distracting concept of sf content and examine precisely what sort of word-beast sits before us. We must explore both the level of subjunctivity at which speculative fiction takes place and the particular intensity and range of images this level affords" (15).

12. Readers gain access to the storyworld through the text. Indeed, the interaction between the reader and the text generates the storyworld. Aubrey Isabel Taylor argues that any text must maintain a "certain level of the real," adding that "speculative fictions are able to play with this reality in ways more mimetic literature does not" (*Patricia A. McKillip and the Art of Fantasy World-Building*, 15). Crucial to the perception of a work of science fiction, world building describes the aggregated effect of a narrative that allows a reader the sense that the imagined world presented is not only graspable, but also plausible.

13. As with *The Handmaid's Tale* (1985), Atwood sets *Oryx and Crake* in the United States, while later novels in the trilogy have a wider national scope. Though produced by a Canadian author and featuring multiple generic tendencies (literary fiction, dystopia, and speculative fiction), I would argue that texts such as *Oryx and Crake* fit the post-apocalyptic mode as I describe it. Post-apocalyptic texts may do any number of other things, yet when read in aggregate against the crises of US capital in the late twentieth and early twenty-first centuries, their interpretive horizons shift away from the individual concerns of specific texts and toward US hegemony.

14. For a strong, situated argument against distinguishing between dystopian and post-apocalyptic stories, see Paula Barba Guerrero, "A Vulnerable Sense of Place."

15. A conceptual gulf that Berlant identifies in this passage separates people from individuals and especially from characters. The first could be taken as a neutral term for a human being, while an individual is a legal entity and ideological construct and characters are literary and dramatic figures. The ruptures of the ongoing disaster engulf each entity at different moments.

16. For a series of examples of crisis as a capitalist mode, see Naomi Klein, *The Shock Doctrine*. Karl Marx wrote about the contradiction at the level of the circulation of commodities: "If the assertion of their external independence proceeds to a certain point, their unity makes itself violently felt by producing—a crisis. There is an antithesis, immanent in the commodity . . . between the conversion of things into persons and the conversion of persons into things; the antithetical phases of the metamorphosis of the commodity are the developed forms of motion of this immanent contradiction. These forms therefore imply the possibility of crises, though no more than the possibility" (*Capital*, 209).

17. Whether or not the American century has come to an end and what that might mean have long been topics of dispute. This book does not intend to settle these disputes, which will nevertheless intrude from time to time from the margins of my investigation. Rather, the American century serves as a useful historical index of US hegemony, itself a world and worldview that provides the most compelling symbolic frame for an analysis of the post-apocalyptic narrative as it has evolved since 1945.

18. Luce's article, published in *Life*, proposes a program of US development on the world stage that embraces its hegemonic potential and demands that Americans rise to the challenge of being a world leader.

19. Each systemic cycle of accumulation moves from a phase of production to a phase of circulation that features an expansion of financial capital. Founding his theory on an assessment of territorial control and political power, Arrighi identifies what he calls long centuries of capitalist development, each of which is grounded

in a particular zone of accumulation—typically a state or statelike entity. Arrighi identifies Genoa, Holland, Britain, and the United States as previous centers.

20. Cumings bases this point on the work of Joseph Schumpeter—specifically *The Theory of Economic Development*, first published in 1912.

21. Cumings writes, "To be an American [was] to be maxed out" ("Still the American Century," 276). It still is. As credit-card balances overall grew by 135 percent between 1989 and 1995, they increased by 400 percent among the poorest fifth of the US population (ibid.). In 2014, Canadians had the highest household debt relative to income, at 166.1 percent, while Americans were in fourth place, at 113.4 percent (Gordon Isfeld, "Canadians' Household Debt Climbs to Highest in G7 in World-Beating Borrowing Spree"). See also Annie McClanahan, *Dead Pledges*; Leigh Claire La Berge, *Scandals and Abstraction*.

22. From 1930 to 1939 the United States spent an average of $8.3 million a year on the military. Compare this to the average $288 million a year spent from 1940 to 1949 for a sense of the massive increase in military spending that bolstered the growth of the US armed forces. The amounts are in 2000 dollars (Max Roser and Mohamed Nagdy, "Military Spending"). Today, "the US military accounts for 40 percent of global military spending" (Genevieve LeFranc, "A Century of Defense Spending in the United States").

23. Since the 1950s the size of the military has ranged from just under 1.5 million to 3.0 million personnel on extended or continuous active duty, a number that excludes reserves on active duty for training (Christopher Chantrill, "Defense Spending").

24. With the introduction of intercontinental bombers and then intercontinental ballistic missiles, as well as atomic and then thermonuclear bombs, Franklin could include the shift from explosive concussion to guided precision as the reigning logic of drone warfare.

25. According to David Vine, "While there are no freestanding foreign bases permanently located in the United States, there are now around 800 US bases in foreign countries. Seventy years after World War II and 62 years after the Korean War, there are still 174 US 'base sites' in Germany, 113 in Japan, and 83 in South Korea, according to the Pentagon. Hundreds more dot the planet in around 80 countries, including Aruba and Australia, Bahrain and Bulgaria, Colombia, Kenya, and Qatar, among many other places. Although few Americans realize it, the United States likely has more bases in foreign lands than any other people, nation, or empire in history" ("The United States Probably Has More Foreign Military Bases Than Any Other People, Nation, or Empire in History"). See also Catherine Lutz, *The Bases of Empire*; Vine, *Base Nation*.

26. I am thinking of the Korean War, the deposing of Mohammad Mossadegh, and Operation PBSUCCESS, respectively.

27. Though Brenner's political-economic approach does not mesh easily with Arrighi's more power-inflected assessment of global hegemony, both authors identify a breaking point in the 1970s.

28. This quotation was made available to Joshua Clover in typescript, which is why I have not taken it directly from the source.

29. According to Aaron Benanv and John Clegg, "in its subsequent abandonment of Bretton Woods and its policy of 'benign neglect' of the deficit, the US used this threat of dollar devaluation to impose a new flexible dollar reserve currency standard on the rest of the world, effectively delegating the job of stabilizing the dollar to foreign central banks who would be compelled to spend their surplus dollars on US securities in order to maintain the dollar value of their own currencies. This to all intents and purposes removed budgetary constraints from the US, allowing it to run up deficits and issue dollars at will, knowing that foreign nations would have no choice but to recycle them back to US financial markets, particularly into US government debt which quickly replaced gold as the global reserve currency" ("Misery and Debt," 601).

30. This logic gets reproduced in state- and municipal-level spending on policing. The same logic that the United States perfected abroad has been implemented at home, with racialized communities overrepresented as the target for the murderous force of weaponized law enforcement.

31. According to Franklin, "although the stupendous American arsenal of superweapons could easily annihilate any nation or group of nations, it has not secured an American victory in the Korean War, the Vietnam War, or the Iraq War. Nor has it secured America itself, as demonstrated on September 11, 2001" (*War Stars*, xi).

32. See also Christoph Scherrer, "Reproducing Hegemony."

33. The US Department of Defense is the world's largest institutional user of petroleum and thus the greatest emitter of carbon dioxide. It is no wonder the United States broke records for fossil fuel extraction in 2018. See Neta Crawford, "Pentagon Fuel Use"; U.S. Energy Information Administration, "The U.S. Leads Global Petroleum and Natural Gas Production with Record Growth in 2018."

34. Compare calls for a Green New Deal by Representative Alexandria Ocasio-Cortez of New York and Senator Edward J. Markey of Massachusetts, which do propose a Keynesian approach to the climate crisis and unemployment (Lisa Friedman, "What Is the Green New Deal?").

35. I am indebted to Marija Cetinic for insisting that I read Haggluund's work.

36. A more contemporary example might be found in the 2017 report that the Svalbard "doomsday" seed vault had flooded due to permafrost melt (Da-

mian Carrington, "Arctic Stronghold of World's Seeds Flooded after Permafrost Melts"). Here the total destruction of the archive is remainderless to the degree that one reconfigures one's sense of the content of this archive. The vault was not completely compromised, but as in Derrida's nuclear example, the threat invades the present.

37. The publishing market indirectly determines which books get remaindered. As Dan Sinykin writes, "At each stage of publishing—in the hands of the agent, the editor, the publisher—a text must now, more rigorously than ever, demonstrate its potential profitability" ("The Conglomerate Era," 472). See chapter 3. The Warwick Research Collective stated that "we are further enjoined . . . to grasp reading and translating as themselves social rather than solitary processes, and thereby to attend to the full range of social practices implicated: writing as commodity labour, the making of books, publishing and marketing, the social 'fate' of a publication (reviews, criticism, the search for, creation and cultivation of a readership, etc.)" (*Combined and Uneven Development*, 28).

38. De Witt Douglas Kilgore has commented that "what has seemed for so long a 'white' expressive form has become, in retrospect, less a straightforward projection of particular caste interests and more an aesthetic expressive of a complex multiethnic society. As such it should not be surprising that the genre is capable of serious engagement with contemporary arguments around race yet is able to sustain (some might say to withstand) critical scrutiny of its record vis-à-vis race and its relations ("Difference Engine," 18).

39. Sinykin quotes Loren Glass's *Counterculture Colophon*—"The New York publishing world had been an insular community of (mostly) men, all of whom knew each other and most of whom shared a commitment to literary culture that, they felt, distinguished their industry and their product from others" (quoted in "The Conglomerate Era," 464)—when he lists the men who dominated New York City publishing houses in the 1960s and 1970s: "Alfred Knopf, Bennett Cerf, Donald Klopfer, Harold K. Guinzburg, Dick Simon, Max Schuster, Leon Shimkin, William Warder Norton, Horace Liveright, and James Laughlin" (ibid.). Juliana Spahr and Stephanie Young attended roughly two hundred readings between 2010 and 2015 on "college and university campuses, [in] living rooms and back yards, museums, imperiled collective arts spaces founded 30 years ago, new community centers affiliated with free schools, and independent bookstores," and they reported that "in almost every case, the readings . . . took place in a mainly white room" ("The Program Era and the Mainly White Room").

40. Writing in the context of world literature, Emily Apter asks, "Is the interdependency of narrative markets—crucial to a Wallersteinian model of literary

world-systems—now simply the economic symptom of literary survivalism? Is a genre's travel the measure of its aliveness, its drift the gauge of force required to break open the bounds of a closed world-system?" ("Untranslatables," 593). See also Apter, *Against World Literature*.

41. The pronoun "we" here might function along class lines, but just as surely one might read it as a marker of whiteness or cisgender identity.

42. See Kyle Powys Whyte, "Our Ancestors' Dystopia Now"; Lawrence Gross, "The Comic Vision of Anishinaabe Culture and Religion."

43. I also want to be careful not to conflate patriarchy, white supremacy, and settler colonialism (though they do find a compelling synthesis in the figure of the settler white man). Such structures persist too in remaindered form in post-apocalyptic stories.

44. It has always struck me as odd that more post-apocalyptic novels have not featured bicycles as a reliable form of transportation. Butler's *Parable of the Sower* opens with a bicycle ride, but its characters eventually rely on walking. Kim Stanley Robinson's ecotopian novel *Pacific Edge* features cyclists prominently. John Varley's novel *Slow Apocalypse* stands out for its inclusion of bicycles as a primary mode of transportation. There is no good reason why other post-apocalyptic texts do not include this mode of transport more often. Mountain bikes, especially, would be useful for any terrain and are easy to learn how to maintain, and presumably—depending on one's location—bike shops and thus spare parts would be abundant.

45. Here I am drawing on Gerry Canavan's reading of the trilogy. See Canavan, *Octavia E. Butler*.

46. During the COVID-19 pandemic Bayo Akomolafe writes of cancer cells: "And die we must. If our cells are functioning properly, they are constantly dying. We lose millions of cells every day, every second. A cancerous cell is, by definition, a cell that has refused to die" ("I, Coronavirus").

47. Margaret Ronda illustrates the concept of the remainder in a remarkably similar way to that used in the current study, while drawing on a completely different archive of materials: US poetry of the American century. She writes that "remainders operate as a means of considering the relations between ecology, history, and form as they become newly visible in the devalued remains of capital's circuits of production, circulation, and production" (*Remainders*, 13). Ronda counterposes the remainder against the elliptical shard and the fragment, positing that the remainder "evokes the ongoing and intensifying processes that characterize natural-historical entanglements in this period" (ibid.). For Ronda, remainders might be "obsolescent commodities," "polluted air," and "toxic matter," and they convey "the strange temporalities and phenomenologies of socioeconomic life in turmoil" (ibid., 5). The archive Ronda

works with situates "nature itself as a remaindered category of poetic thinking" (ibid., 9). She even remarks that "one image this study's title evokes, *Remainders*, is that of the remainders table at a bookstore, an image of the decidedly equivocal value of the literary in this period" (ibid., 17).

48. The science fiction critic M. Keith Booker characterizes the long 1950s as running from 1945 to 1964 (*Monsters, Mushroom Clouds, and the Cold War*).

49. While I use the term "world destroying," other critics of post-apocalyptic fiction use terms taken from narratology. For instance, Marco Caracciolo draws on the narratologist David Herman's concept of world disruption, explaining that "world disruption and narrative world-making are two sides of the same coin: narrative world-making is triggered by events that destabilize the status quo of a world, and are therefore surprising and highly tellable" ("Negative Strategies and World Disruption in Postapocalyptic Fiction," 223).

50. Mathias Nilges describes this as the "post-apocalyptic industry" ("Neoliberalism and the Time of the Novel," 372). Meanwhile, concerns related to genre and market are also being asked in markedly different contexts. For instance, see Ghosh, *The Great Derangement*.

51. The science fiction critic Patrick B., Sharp emphasizes the durability of racializing cultural narratives in the US imaginary, especially noting two nineteenth-century remainders—the frontier as a reemerging setting and the US cultural fixation with civilized whiteness as opposed to racialized savagery (*Savage Perils*, 7). See also Kilgore's elaboration of the continued frontier in *Astrofuturism*.

Chapter 1. Post-Apocalypse Tropes

1. I use the term "trope" in the sense that David Mikics gives it when he writes that "tropes can generate traditions" (*A New Handbook of Literary Terms*, 301). M. H. Abrams defines tropes as "figures of thought" (*A Glossary of Literary Terms*, 96), and he also acknowledges their origin in the church, where a trope was an often repeated aside during dramatizations of the liturgical service. The more common, secularized usage today implies a behavior, event, or situation that is common to a particular genre of storytelling. For instance, a wise old character appears to guide the protagonist, as in Joseph Campbell's discussion of the quest narrative (*The Hero with a Thousand Faces*).

2. Before authors became obsessed with imagining the rent world of rubble and shadows that the bomb would bring about, science fiction writers had anticipated it: H. G. Wells predicted the invention of atomic weapons in a story that the Hungarian physicist Leo Szilard, the originator of the Manhattan Project, claims to have read in the 1930s. David Seed and other science fiction critics situate Wells's *The World Set Free* (first published in 1914) as a precursor to

the bomb. Seed, in particular, describes Szilard's surprise at Wells's "depiction of nuclear war" and how it suggested "the possibility of a chain reaction he was able to apply in the planning of the first atomic bomb" (*American Science Fiction*, 5). See also Brent Ryan Bellamy, " . . . or Bust: Science Fiction and the Bomb, 1945–1960"; Seed, *Under the Shadow*; Patrick Sharp, *Savage Perils*, 4–5.

3. For a detailed discussion of the whiteness of the atomic project and its representational shockwaves, see Paul Williams, *Race, Ethnicity and Nuclear War*.

4. The convention of dividing science fiction production into ages corresponds loosely with Isaac Asimov's stages theory of American science fiction, as described by Fredric Jameson: "Stage One (1926–1938), adventure dominant; Stage Two, (1938–1950), technology dominant; Stage Three (1950–?), sociology dominant . . . we can probably date the end of Stage Three from the mid-'60s, and add a fourth stage ('aesthetics dominant') [a] 'new wave' [preoccupied] with myth and language" ("Towards a New Awareness of Genre," 323). Roger Luckhurst offers a parodic history of science fiction in "The Many Deaths of Science Fiction" that I reproduce here, in juxtaposition to Jameson's more clinical overview, for its dynamic energy: "SF is dying; but then SF has always been dying, it has been dying from the very moment of its constitution. Birth and death become transposable: if Gernsback's pulp genericism produces the 'ghetto' and the pogrom of systematic starvation for some, he also *names* the genre and gives birth to it for others. If the pulps eventually give us the 'Golden Age,' its passing is death for some and re-birth for others. If the New Wave is the life-saving injection, it is also a spiked drug, a perversion, and the onset of a long degeneration towards inevitable death. If the 1970s is a twilight, a long terminal lingering, the feminists come to the rescue. But then the feminists are also partially responsible, Charles Platt argues, for issuing one final vicious twist of the knife. And what of cyberpunk? Dead before it was even born—or rather dead *because* it was named. 'Requiem for the Cyberpunks' aims to finally kill the label. And what now? Christina Sedgewick asks 'Can Science Fiction Survive in Postmodern, Megacorporate America?' A new decline, or rather a circling back: SF dying because of its *re*-commercialization" (35).

5. Another post-apocalypse trope worth considering is one that comes from John Rieder's account of Richard Jeffries's *After London; or, Wild England* (1885), which he argues inverts core and periphery in a manner still recognizable in such texts as J. G. Ballard's *The Drowned World* (1962) and Kim Stanley Robinson's *The Wild Shore* (1984) (Rieder, *Colonialism and the Emergence of Science Fiction*, 147). For an extended discussion of *After London*, see ibid. 125–35.

6. For instance, although Stephen King was clearly influenced by *Earth Abides* when he wrote *The Stand* (first published in 1978), he complains that "the first half of Stewart's long book is riveting; the second half is more of an uphill push—too much ecology, not enough story" (*Danse Macbre*, 370). Yet King's assessment cannot diminish the critical importance of Stewart's novel. Apocalyptic criticism such as Eric Rabkin and coeditors' *The End of the World*—a collection in which each nearly every essay refers to Stewart's novel—and more recent ecocritical work such as *Green Speculations*, a monograph by the literary critic Eric C. Otto, underline the lasting importance of Stewart's novel for post-apocalyptic fiction.

7. Other works feature this kind of jump forward in time as well: Miller's *Leibowitz* novellas each jump forward hundreds of years into the future, and Octavia E. Butler's Xenogenesis trilogy (alternatively titled *Lilith's Brood*) features a leap forward in time and a dive into the story of a new protagonist with each novel in the trilogy.

8. Stewart's novel mentions this connection: "The road led on across the wide spaces; U.S. 66 read the signs beside the pavement. It had been a great highway, he remembered, in the old days, the road of the Okies to California" (*Earth Abides*, 52).

9. Stewart also includes what he calls "inter-chapters" that he introduces at the end of chapter 8 in this way: "*Here ends Part 1. The inter-chapter called* The Quick Years *follows, after a time interval of one year*" (*Earth Abides*, 117).

10. To anticipate an argument that I make in chapter 5, the moments when Williams does encounter others are some of the most striking in the text. For instance, when he meets a trio of racialized characters by the roadside, Williams's response and the narrator's both convey white fragility and overcompensation for it.

11. For a discussion of the middle-of-the-road hero, see Georg Lukács's description in *The Historical Novel* of Sir Walter Scott's *Waverly* (first published in 1814).

12. "So uneven development (that is, these same phenomena of displacement and condensation observable in the development process of a complex whole) is not external to contradiction, but constitutes its most intimate essence. So the unevenness that exists in the 'development' of contradictions, that is, in the process itself, exists in the essence of contradiction itself" (Althusser, *For Marx*, 213).

13. For instance, Hannegan, the mayor of Texarkana, forms alliances, defeats the nomadic warriors who have been plaguing the countryside, and declares war against New Rome.

14. As noted above, Jean-Baptiste Cousin de Grainville's *Le dernier homme*

was first published in 1805, and an anonymously translated English version was published in the following year. The original and translated versions inspired a series of last man stories. See A. J. Sambrook, "A Romantic Theme."

Chapter 2. Reduced Futures

1. See Marco Caracciolo's explanation of the negative strategies of the post-apocalyptic text: "the postworld emerges as the narrative negates (i.e., subtracts or pares down) some of the salient characteristics of the pre-world—features with which readers are familiar through their everyday reality. Thus famine negates the availability of food and other resources, the postapocalyptic wasteland negates the organized urban environments of the pre-period, widespread violence contradicts the rule of law, and so on" ("Negative Strategies and World Disruption in Postapocalyptic Fiction," 224–25).

2. Wolfe's celebration of the kind of clarity that the end-of-the-world story offers readers (and presumably authors) rankles: he declares that features such as "individual effort" and "courage" are able to converge in post-apocalyptic characters, and he asserts that power gathers in a "natural aristocracy" for those "uninhibited by political and economic complexities" ("The Remaking of Zero," 4). Here, Wolfe's phrasing rings alarm bells signaling authoritarian ideology. He imagines a storyworld where the politics become clear as storyworld elements are removed.

3. After the release of *Soylent Green* (directed by Richard Fleischer), soylent came to connote cannibalism. Recall Charlton Heston's infamous lines: "The ocean's dying, the plankton is dying. It's people. Soylent Green is made out of people."

4. In this passage, Jameson addresses two of Ursula K. Le Guin's science fiction novels, *The Left Hand of Darkness* (first published in 1969) and *The Dispossessed* (1974).

5. The reduced ecologies of the environmental humanities scholar Ursula Heise find an analog in post-apocalyptic novels that strip away the contingencies of economic, political, and social life ("Reduced Ecologies").

6. For a different view on the origins of the post-apocalyptic mode, see Hay, *Postapocalyptic Fantasies in Antebellum American Literature*.

7. The apocalyptic has long signified as a moment of revelation, particularly in eschatological thinking. The word "apocalypse" means both unveiling and ending. It anticipates a moment of judgment when the faithful and the penitent will be rewarded and the rest, the heathen masses, will be damned.

8. Kermode was probably referring to Festinger's 1956 *When Prophecy Fails*.

9. It is important to note that I am not interested in generic distinctions for their own sake. There may very well be a compelling argument to be made for

how and why something fits in or stretches a definition, and thus I would prefer to avoid hard-and-fast definitions.

10. If post-apocalyptic fiction is a subset of science fiction, then it is also a subset of a narrow range of terrestrial science fiction.

11. See Evan Williams, *Combined and Uneven Apocalypse*; Peter Paik, *From Utopia to Apocalypse*. Both accounts focus on films and graphic narratives rather than on novels.

12. See David Ketterer, *New Worlds for Old*.

13. Since a narrative's beginning, middle, and end are relative terms made meaningful within their particular context, the relationship of story to plot determines the beginning, middle, and end in each case. The apocalypse as a plot event could occur at any point, depending on how an author tells a story—or, to borrow a term from Hayden White, the way the author emplots it ("The Question of Narrative in Contemporary Historical Theory," 44). This process is part of what White terms emplotment: "the way by which a sequence of events fashioned into a story is gradually revealed to be a story of a particular kind" (*Metahistory*, 7). However, the terms of the post-apocalyptic story dictate that the apocalypse act as an origin, not a middle or ending. Here the distinction between the end of the plot (that is, closure) and the apocalyptic end (that is, the origin) gives sense to what I mean by a narrative that begins after the end. Whether or not the plot of the post-apocalyptic novel begins in medias res, the characters always look back to the apocalyptic end as a moment of beginning, the moment when things changed.

14. Fisher evokes what the Russian formalist Viktor Shklovsky dubbed *ostranenie* (defamiliarization) in *Theory of Prose*.

15. For an account of the relation between post-apocalyptic writing and twenty-first-century developments in the historical novel, see Brent Ryan Bellamy, "Figuring Terminal Crisis in Steven Amsterdam's *Things We Didn't See Coming*."

16. Novels from the feminist strain of science fiction—including Samuel R. Delany's *Dhalgren* (first published in 1975), Le Guin's *The Left Hand of Darkness* and *The Dispossessed*, Marge Piercy's *Woman on the Edge of Time* (1976), and Joanna Russ's *The Female Man* (1975)—use world building as a generative moment to establish new collectivities based on a turning away from patriarchy or a turning toward a subversion of the gender binary. Delany unsettles the reader's capacity to fully grasp the events, people, and places of his novel—which is set in Bellona, a midwestern city cut off from the rest of the United States by an unidentified catastrophe. By making the real world seem strange yet plausible, Delany addresses oppressive elements of life in the real world. Le Guin posits alternative evolutionary and political developments for Gethen,

the planet called winter, and Anarres and Urras (Tau Ceti's twin inhabited worlds). Piercy places her utopian community, Mattapoisett, in the future. It features a mindful ecology, the abolition of gender, communal living, a more humane lifestyle, the defeat of racism, the encouragement of art, the reconfiguration of the family, and new life cycle rituals. Russ uses multiple interwoven time lines to defamiliarize characters' gender assumptions and the very concept of normative gender. These texts offer positive critiques (saying to the reader "see how things could be otherwise") and pessimistic indictments ("look at how messed up the world really is"). Each approach uses generative utopianism to rework science-fictional tropes of alien planets, time travel, and parallel worlds.

17. Despite its eugenics, *The Gate to Women's Country* reveals that beginning a novel with an egalitarian women's collective raises the question of whether these novels can be consider post-apocalyptic at all. I read them as utopias in light of their combination of social melodrama and societal blueprint, but they also employ the post-apocalyptic mode to posit such utopias because they rely on a world-destroying event to establish the storyworld.

18. All of this is made more complicated by the fact that Brome is actually cursing Sushannah for getting pregnant despite his wishes, which I point out to show the ways women are afforded agency in the text even when they are not the focus of the narrative.

19. Berger writes: "We often see in the post-apocalypse two rival groups. One is somewhere between barbaric and fascistic, centered around a charismatic leader, and employing violence not only for strategic, practical ends, but also in ritual and purely sadistic ways. The other group might be characterized as 'liberal.' It attempts to function through consensus, though often a strong leader emerges who helps them through their inevitable crises. For the liberal group also, however, violence is essential to survival" ("'The Voice of the Bridegroom and the Bride Shall be Heard No More,'" 130–31).

20. King wrote: "I saw a *60 Minutes* segment on CBW (chemical-biological warfare). I never forgot the gruesome footage of the test mice shuddering, convulsing, and dying, all in twenty seconds or less. That got me remembering a chemical spill in Utah that killed a bunch of sheep (these were canisters on their way to some burial ground; they fell off the truck and ruptured). I remembered a news reporter saying, 'If the winds had been blowing the other way, there was Salt Lake City.' This incident later served as the basis of a movie called *Rage*, starring George C. Scott, but before it was released, I was deep into *The Stand*, finally writing my American fantasy epic, set in a plague-decimated USA. Only instead of a hobbit, my hero was a Texan named Stu Redman, and instead of a Dark Lord, my villain was a ruthless drifter and supernatural mad-

man named Randall Flagg. The land of Mordor ('where the shadows lie,' according to Tolkien) was played by Las Vegas" ("The Stand Inspiration").

Chapter 3. Remaindered Books

1. Morec enforces a humorless, state-produced culture. The book's title, *The Man Who Japed*, refers to Purcell, a Morec packet producer (that is, the producer of a media show), who plays a practical joke (a "jape") that lands him in prison by the novel's end.

2. Hokkaido has not been restored since the war: "The island had been saturated during the war, bombed and bathed and doctored and infested with every possible kind of toxic and lethal substance. Moral reclamation was useless, let alone gross physical rebuilding. Hokkaido was as sterile and dead as it had been in 1972, the final year of the war" (Dick, The Man Who Japed, 7).

3. This moment characterizes an emerging postmodern culture that is stirring at the height of modernism. Critics argue that Dick was a forerunner of the transition from modern to postmodern culture in the United States. See M. Keith Booker, *Monsters, Mushroom Clouds, and the Cold War*.

4. See Mark Steven and Julian Murphet, "Introduction."

5. Stephen Joyce contributes to the sense of post-apocalyptic worlds as hostile to the codex: "Post-apocalyptic fiction often anticipates a world where books have no meaning because they take part in a conversation that has ceased. There will be no future readers or writers and thus the great treasure store of world knowledge, the heritage of civilisation, becomes effectively worthless" ("Convergence Publishing and Prestige Niches," 121).

6. Vintage Books was an imprint of Knopf (founded in 1915), which in turn became an imprint of Random House in 1960 when Knopf was acquired by the larger publisher.

7. Though McCarthy is staunchly averse to giving interviews and making public appearances, he agreed to be interviewed by Oprah Winfrey when she selected *The Road* for her book club in 2007.

8. Ursula K. Le Guin has used the term "genrefication" to explain the trend she sees in literary fiction (see Alexander Moran, "The Genrefication of Contemporary American Literature," 230–31). Susan Watkins—writing on Margaret Atwood's *Oryx and Crake* and *The Year of the Flood* (2009); Jeannette Winterson's *The Stone Gods* (2007); Doris Lessing's *Mara and Dann* (1999) and its sequel, *The Story of General Dann* (2005); Maggie Gee's *The Ice People* (2008) and *The Flood* (2005); and Liz Jensen's *The Rapture* (2009)—claims that "despite the long tradition of women's speculative writing and the respectability of the 'literary' tradition of apocalyptic writing, there still seems to be some question about whether women writers can move between these genres with the

same success as men, for women's writing within the genre is sometimes dismissed as preachy agitprop" ("Future Shock," 119). See also S. Watkins, *Contemporary Women's Post-Apocalyptic Fiction*.

9. The results are based on a search of worldcat.org.

10. The big five are Hachette, HarperCollins, Macmillan, Penguin Random House, and Simon and Schuster (Sinykin, "The Conglomerate Era").

11. Sinykin traces the tendency for literary writers to adopt generic conventions to the 1970s, when "the [publishing] industry began to think newly about the possibilities of making literary fiction commercial," and "earnestly taking up genre was one salient way" to do so (Sinykin, "The Conglomerate Era," 480). Sinykin uses Don DeLillo and Thomas Pynchon as key examples of this maneuver, adding that it "is not that Pynchon and DeLillo set out deliberately to adopt generic conventions in response to conglomeration; instead, they worked from within a milieu under pressure from conglomeration's rationalization and mediation, which produced ripe conditions for the emergence of a new aesthetic form, of which their novels are emblematic" (ibid., 479).

12. Kim Stanley Robinson's dissertation "The Novels of Philip K. Dick" situates these novels as postholocaust novels. Robinson argues that in each case Dick uses nuclear war "to disengage history" and "take it where he will," which leads him to "dystopian societies much like ones that in other novels are linear extensions of our history, that require no cataclysm" (ibid., 57).

13. Belmont was founded in 1960 and merged with Tower Publications in 1971 to become Belmont Tower—which went under in 1980.

14. A midlist title is one that sells between 10,000 and 100,000 copies (Sinykin, "The Conglomerate Era," 471). Charles Platt glosses midlist science fiction authors as writing the "most interesting science fiction," what he calls "too adult or complex to be sold as downmarket trash, too conformist to be make it as bestseller material" ("The Vanishing Midlist," 49).

15. Dick's *The World Jones Made* was published with Margaret St. Clair's *Agent of the Unknown*, and *Vulcan's Hammer* was published with John Brunner's *The Skynappers*.

16. In 1970, three of the six nominees for the Nebula Award for best novel were from the Ace Science Fiction Specials series: Ursula Le Guin's *The Left Hand of Darkness*, Roger Zelazny's *Isle of the Dead*, and John Brunner's *The Jagged Orbit*. The other nominees were Norman Spinrad's *Bug Jack Barron* (published by Avon), Robert Silverberg's *Up the Line* (Ballantine Books), and Kurt Vonnegut's *Slaughterhouse-Five* (Delacorte Press).

17. The New Ace Science Fiction Specials series included Marion Zimmer Bradley's *Endless Voyage* (1975) and Stanislaw Lem's *The Invincible* (1975).

18. The average costs of an item in the Ace Doubles series and one in the Ace

Science Fiction Specials series would be around $3.50 and $8.00, respectively, in 2019 dollars.

19. "Ace [was] acquired by Grosset & Dunlap in 1972, who in turn was purchased by G. P. Putnam's Sons in 1982, which itself was purchased by Penguin in 1996. Throughout these changes Ace was the SF [science fiction] imprint for each of these companies" (Internet Speculative Fiction Database, "Publisher: Ace Books").

20. Doubleday published Dick's *The Stigmata of Palmer Eldritch* (1964), *Now Wait for Last Year* (1966), *Do Androids Dream of Electric Sheep?*, *Ubik* (1969), *A Maze of Death* (1970), *Flow My Tears, the Policeman Said* (1974), and *Deus Irae* (1976, coauthored with Roger Zelazny).

21. Doubleday was the largest US publisher in 1947. It published Richard Matheson's *I Am Legend* in 1954, Stephen King's *The Stand* in 1978, and Colson Whitehead's *Zone One* in 2011 (as an imprint of Knopf, with which it had merged in 2009).

22. This list is somewhat wishful and reductive. It might also include agents, publishers' marketing departments, literary awards and festivals, reviewing outlets, and so on. See John Thompson, *Merchants of Culture*.

23. Sinykin explains that "after World War II, with the GI Bill, a soaring economy, and the turn to paperbacks, the market for books boomed" ("The Conglomerate Era," 464). See also Mark McGurl, *The Program Era*.

24. Dystopian writing has an inverse trajectory to those of science fiction and post-apocalyptic fiction, going from well-known literary writers and being taught in high school and college classes to a dominant mode of writing for novels targeted at teen and young adult readers.

25. In 1986 Ballantine would rerelease Leigh Brackett's *The Long Tomorrow*. Ballantine is also the imprint of Alan DeNiro's 2010 *Total Oblivion, More or Less* and Justin Cronin's trilogy—*The Passage* (2010), *The Twelve* (2012), and *The City of Mirrors* (2016)—the first volume of which was a *New York Times* best seller. On Cronin, see Maria Lindgren Leavenworth and Van Leavenworth, "Fragmented Fiction."

26. In a 2013 interview, Charnas described the struggle of trying to get the book published. She reported that editors would say things such as "SF [science fiction] is written for young boys, and you have women and horses having sex. Turn them all into men and we'll take it in a minute," "There's no story here, there's no action, there's only women," and "I would take this book in five minutes if the characters were all male. We could really sell this. It would be a big thing" ("Suzy McKee Charnas Interview").

27. Berkley was founded in 1955 and acquired by G. P. Putnam's Sons in 1965. It published Tom Clancy's *The Hunt for Red October* in 1984. It also pub-

lished the work of such authors as the best-seller Patricia Cromwell, the science fiction author Frank Herbert, and the literary writer Vladimir Nabokov.

28. The series was published in four volumes—*Tales of Nevèrÿon* (1979), *Neverýona, or: The Tale of Signs and Cities* (1983), *Flight from Nevèrÿon* (1985), and *Return to Nevèrÿon* (1987)—and consists of eleven stories.

29. Bantam was founded in 1945 by Walter B. Pitkin Jr., Sidney B. Kramer, and—interestingly—Ian and Betty Ballantine, with funding from Grosset and Dunlap and the Curtis Publishing Company.

30. Arbor House was an independent publisher that was founded in 1969 and that became an imprint of William Morrow and Company in 1988, a year after the release of *The Bridge of Lost Desire*. St. Martin's Press was formed as an imprint of Macmillan in 1952. Grafton was a British publishing imprint created in 1981 by Granada Publishing Ltd.

31. Carr did not write an introduction for Richard Kadrey's *Metrophage* (1988), Ted Reynoldss' *The Tides of God* (1989), Claudia O'Keefe's *Black Snow Days* (1990), or Gregory Feeley's *The Oxygen Barons* (1990)—each of which was edited by Damon Knight, though they were still marketed with this text on the cover: "Terry Carr's Ace Science Fiction Specials."

32. According to De Witt Douglas Kilgore, science fiction "work from the 1970s marks an almost joint effort by white writers to bring their genre [into] dialogue with the civil unrest, political activism, and artistic innovation by African Americans in that era. In these circumstances, even the egregious racialism of Niven and Pournelle's *Lucifer's Hammer* (1977) has a place" ("Difference Engine," 18).

33. *Dawn* (1987), *Adulthood Rites* (1988), and *Imago* (1989). The trilogy was republished by Guild America Books under the title *Xenogenesis* in 1989 and by Warner under the title *Lilith's Brood* in 2000.

34. For instance, Farrar, Straus and Giroux published Bernard Malamud's *God's Grace* in 1982; DAW Books published Suzette Haden Elgin's *Native Tongue* in 1984; Charles Scribner's Sons published James D. Forman's *Doomsday Plus Twelve* in 1984; Coronet published James Kunetka and Whitley Strieber's *Warday* in 1984; Henry Holt published James Morrow's *This Is the Way the World Ends* (with its titular nod to T. S. Eliot's *The Wasteland*) in 1985; Pocket Books published Robert R. McCammon's *Swan Song* in 1987; and Viking published William Brinkley's *The Last Ship* in 1988.

35. Auster published *In the Country of Last Things* (1987) with Penguin; Le Guin published the Kesh novel *Always Coming Home* with Harper and Row in 1985; and Vonnegut published *Galápagos* (1985) with the Franklin Library.

36. The intimate relationship between publishing and capital is not a new phenomenon. According to Benedict Anderson (*Imagined Communities*), the printing press has long been a core component of capitalism.

37. King also held the number two spot, with *Four Past Midnight*.

38. That number does not include a prequel, *Encounter*, published in 1999, or another ten titles released in audiobook format only by Graphic Audio between 2016 and 2019. Axler is the author of another series—Outlanders—set after the apocalypse and in the same world as Deathlands, which includes an impressive seventy-five novels published from 1997 to 2015. As in other post-apocalyptic novels, characters in both series must survive in the postnuclear wilderness. Between the two series, Axler released an annual average of seven titles.

39. According to Ron Miles, "This includes the termination of all titles currently published by Gold Eagle—Deathlands, Outlanders, Rogue Angel, Mack Bolan, Executioner, and Stony Man. There are still several more books in the pipeline for each of these series, but 2015 will be the end of the line" ("Gold Eagle Is Shutting Down").

40. In 2014 Permuted Press found itself the target of author scrutiny when it revised its contracts overnight to end the availability of print-on-demand services, something that had meant that it was capable of getting books onto store shelves. See Nate Hoffelder, "Permuted Press"; Brian Keene, "Permuted Press."

41. Moore's cookbook is not to be confused with Tess Pennington's *The Prepper's Cookbook: Essential Prepping Foods and Recipes to Deliciously Survive Any Disaster* (2013), Amilie Dawson's *Prepper's Cookbook: 20 Delicious Survival Recipes to Keep in Mason Jar* (2017), or Daisy Luther's *The Prepper's Canning Guide: Affordably Stockpile a Lifesaving Supply of Nutritious, Delicious, Shelf-Stable Foods* (2017). The titles in Moore's series are *The Journal: Cracked Earth (The Journal Book 1)* (2014), *The Journal: Ash Fall (The Journal Book 2)* (2014), *The Journal: Crimson Skies (The Journal Book 3)* (2015), *The Journal: Fault Line (The Journal Series)* (2016), *The Journal: Raging Tide (The Journal Series)* (2017), and *The Journal: Martial Law (The Journal Book 6)* (2017).

42. *Apollyon: The Destroyer Unleashed* (1998) was on the *New York Times* best-seller list for twenty weeks and was number seven on the *Publisher's Weekly* best-seller list for 1999. *The Mark: The Beast Rules the World* (2000) was number two on the *Publisher's Weekly* best-seller list for 2000. *The Indwelling: The Beast Takes Possession* (2000) was on the *New York Times* best-seller list for thirty-five weeks and was number four on the *Publisher's Weekly* best-seller list for 2000. *Desecration* was number one on the *Publisher's Weekly* list for 2001 and was on the *New York Times* best- seller list for nineteen weeks.

43. It has only been since the mid-twentieth century that logistic practices were even considered, let alone used to name the circulation of commodities: "Logistics was dedicated to the art of war for millennia only to be adopted into the corporate world of management in the wake of World War II" (Deborah Cowen, *The Deadly Life of Logistics*, 3).

44. Apparently, this practice was not always followed in the United States, though it has been in Europe. It was not until the Great Depression of the 1930s that US publishers began adopting sales on a sale-or-return basis in an attempt to prop up sales. See Thompson, *Merchants of Culture*, 18; John Tebbel, *A History of Book Publishing in the United States*.

45. These changes also adversely affect libraries that need access to robust backlists to replace lost or damaged books (Hoffert, "Publishers Are Looking at You!," 146).

46. Returns are frequently as high as 20 percent and sometimes as high as 50 percent.

47. For instance, Amazon.com has expanded to sell household items, music, computer hardware, and so on, just as it extended its activity overseas—creating national services while establishing an increasingly global network of warehouses.

48. Nor does this summary include the growth of the ebooks market and the use of ereaders.

49. Since 2015, journalists and letter writers have been lauding the resurgence of independent bookstores. For a list of approximately one hundred such articles, see American Booksellers Association, "'Independent Bookstores Are Thriving'").

50. On the similar role humanities and literature departments, in particular, play in relation to US universities, see Leigh La Berge, "A Market Correction in the Humanities."

51. The other approach Sinykin identifies in works such as Ben Lerner's *10:04* (2014) is autofiction: : a portmanteau of "autobiography and fiction," which "features protagonists whose characteristics and situations so closely resemble those of the author—often down to their name—that such novels invite readers to mistake fiction for real life" ("The Conglomerate Era," 465 and 474).

52. It is important to note that I do not think including examples of post-apocalyptic novels written by Canadian authors discredits my focus on US hegemony or US written material. In fact, without the US market, Atwood's book might not have had the enormous sales that it achieved.

53. In one of the book's interviews, Fernando Oliveira (a doctor who imports human organs) describes both the fictional spread of the zombie virus and a process of organ harvesting and distribution from our own world: "You remove the heart not long after the victim's died . . . maybe even while he's still alive . . . they used to do that, you know, remove living organs to ensure their freshness . . . pack it on ice, put it on a plane for Rio. . . . China used to be the largest exporter of human organs on the world market. Who knows how many infected corneas, infected pituitary glands . . . Mother of God, who knows how

many infected kidneys they pumped into the global market. And that's just the organs" (Max Brooks, *World War Z*, 27).

54. For perhaps better examples of this comparison, think of Bong Joon-Ho's films *Snowpiercer* (2013) and *Parasite* (2019) or Christopher Nolan's films *Inception* (2010) and *Interstellar* (2014).

55. Self-published titles in print include Holly Jean Buck's *Crossing the Blue: A Post-Petrol, Post-America Road Trip* (2008), W. R. Flynn's *Shut Down: A Story of Economic Collapse* (2011), and John Michael Greer's *Star's Reach: A Novel of the Deindustrial Future* (2014).

56. According to McGurl, "although it is difficult to find exact data, it would appear that more than a million texts have been self-published via KDP and that hundreds of them have sold hundreds of thousands of copies" ("Everything and Less," 449).

57. The ProQuest affiliate Bowker reports the numbers of titles published as 74,997 in 2007; 85,468 in 2008; 111,359 in 2009; 152,871 in 2010; 246,912 in 2011; 393,421 in 2012; and 458,564 in 2013 (Bowker, "Self-Publishing in the United States, 2007–2012" and "Self-Publishing in the United States, 2008–2013"). While these statistics are not quite comparable to those provided by Thompson, they offer a sense of the growth in the self-publishing sector. That growth reaches its highest rate in 2011 and 2012 and becomes steady in 2013.

58. Elison's series has been well-received by reviewers. See Rich Calvin, "Gender and the Apocalypse"; Ian Mond, "Ian Mond Reviews *The Book of Flora* by Meg Elison."

59. Random House published Sosnowski's *Rapture* in 1996, and Simon and Schuster published his *Vamped* in 2004.

60. *Happy Doomsday* has received mixed reviews on Amazon. Sosnowski was criticized for being both an antivaccination ideologue and a critic of President Donald Trump. Several reviews accused him of playing politics with his fiction (Amazon Customer, "The Stand-ish steeped in Irony"; B. Scott, "Flawed in nearly every way"; Paul Cassel, "Politics Where None's Needed"; John, "An OFFENSIVE novel that goes nowhere!"; H. Stiles, "A story with an autistic character written by an anti-vaxxer . . .").

Amazon Customer. "The Stand-ish steeped in Irony." August 24, 2018. https://www.amazon.ca/Happy-Doomsday-Novel-David-Sosnowski-ebook/dp/B0786B4F9F/.

B. Scott. "Flawed in nearly every way." September 18, 2018. https://www.amazon.ca/Happy-Doomsday-Novel-David-Sosnowski-ebook/dp/B0786B4F9F/.

Cassel, Paul. "Politics Where None's Needed" October 13, 2018. https://

www.amazon.ca/Happy-Doomsday-Novel-David-Sosnowski-ebook/dp/B0786B4F9F/.

John. "An OFFENSIVE novel that goes nowhere!" August 15, 2018. https://www.amazon.ca/Happy-Doomsday-Novel-David-Sosnowski-ebook/dp/B0786B4F9F/.

Stiles, H. "A story with an autistic character written by an anti-vaxxer . . ." August 11, 2018. https://www.amazon.ca/Happy-Doomsday-Novel-David-Sosnowski-ebook/dp/B0786B4F9F/.

Two reviews accused him of playing politics with his fiction.

61. As well as Sosnowski's book, 47 North published at least two others that seem post-apocalyptic adjacent: R. R. Haywood's Extracted trilogy, which does feature the end of the world but is arguably not written in the post-apocalyptic mode. Likewise, Christopher Mari's *The Beachhead* (2017) seems to be a post-apocalyptic story, though Amazon reviewers characterize it as moral philosophy than not science fiction.

62. See also Rosen, "Introduction to Ecologies of Neoliberal Publishing."

Chapter 4. Old and New Americas

1. Writing about the western more generally, Carl Abbott extends this observation, explaining that the subtext of the American western, as a genre, is "the advance of civilization through contests with nature, native peoples, and nasty outlaws," and the trope of expanding across the continent encompasses "the dominant national myth of the United States, and it serves as the American equivalent of European imperialism and imperial adventuring" (*Frontiers Past and Future*, 114).

2. See George Caffentzis, *In Letters of Blood and Fire*.

3. For more on the godlike or top-down view, see Donna Haraway, "Situated Knowledges." She writes: "But, of course, that view of infinite vision is an illusion, a god trick" (582). As I noted in a previous work, "A good example of the formal impulse to figure catastrophe from the outside is the flashy apocalyptic cinematography in Roland Emmerich's *2012* (2009). The narrative of *2012* seems to be an excuse to screen a series of daring escapes—these sequences happen at least three times in the film—in which a plane takes off from a crumbling runway, the very ground collapsing beneath it as it dodges flying debris, soaring out of the latest danger zone" (Bellamy, "Figuring Terminal Crisis in Steven Amsterdam's *Things We Didn't See Coming*," 21).

4. M. Keith Booker and Anne-Marie Thomas argue that although "a series of catastrophes occurs . . . the real collapse of civilization is brought about not by the catastrophes themselves, but by the response of right-wing survivalist groups to these catastrophes" (*The Science Fiction Handbook*, 61).

5. *The Postman* is a precursor of a number of western-style post-apocalyptic novels, including Robert Charles Wilson's *Julian Comstock* (2009), which Gerry Canavan describes as "the worst combination of Manifest-Destiny America, feudal Europe, and decadent Rome" ("Science Fiction without the Future," 11–12). The same could be said of Brin's novel.

6. See Curtis, *Postapocalyptic Fiction and the Social Contract*; Manjikian, *Apocalypse and Post-Politics*; Berger "Apocalypse, Critique, and Procreation."

7. As early as 1893 Fredrick Jackson Turner was contending that US democracy was a historical result of the American frontier. He argued that "the existence of a free land, its continuous recession, and the advance of American settlement westward" explained US development, and more succinctly, he described the frontier as "the line of the most rapid and effective Americanization" (*The Significance of the Frontier in American History*, 11 and 13–14).

8. Indeed, a major concern for critical analysts of capitalism—from the revolutionary Marxist Rosa Luxemburg to the Marxist geographer David Harvey—is capital's reliance on spatial expansion. As the spaces that have not yet been enclosed within capitalist social relations of production become increasingly scarce, this fundamental expansive tendency of capital is transformed into an acute problem. Harvey (along with the Marxist feminist Silvia Federici and others) has argued that the emergence of neoliberalism must be assessed against the backdrop of this scarcity of virgin territory into which capital can assert itself.

9. For a discussion of the Declaration of Independence's ongoing relationship with performance as a public text, see Michael Epp, "What Is Living and What Is Dead in the U.S. Declaration of Independence."

10. Unlike Leigh Brackett's *The Long Tomorrow*, *The Postman* imagines the formation of these amendments as part of its plot. Krantz does not encounter them as preordained but forges them himself.

11. Wahunsenacawh was chief during the establishment of Jamestown in Powhatan lands in 1607. He was the father of the woman who came to be known as Pocahontas.

12. Passed from the Ordoliberals of Weimar Germany to the Chicago school of economics, neoliberal policy was employed by the administration of President Jimmy Carter.

13. The result of the crumbling US economic support for the worker was, as Steven High puts it, a "sense of displacement" and the reality of unemployment (*Industrial Sunset*, 41). And in the postindustrial sector, according to Jeffery Nealon, deindustrialization "most immediately signifies the increasing power and ubiquity of privatized corporatization in everyday life" (*Post-Postmodernism*, 10). See also Sherry Linkon, *The Half-Life of Deindustrialization*; Phillip Neel, *Hinterland*.

14. For criticism of the triptych as a whole, see Brent Ryan Bellamy, "Reading Kim Stanley Robinson's Three Californias Triptych as Petrofiction"; Helen Burgess, "'Road of Giants'"; Rebecca Evans, "The Best of Times, the Worst of Times, the End of Times?"; Lisa Garforth, "Green Utopias"; Tom Moylan, "'Utopia Is When our Lives Matter.'"

15. Arrighi writes, "After a decade of deepening crisis, the Reagan Administration initiated the transformation of legitimate protection into a protection racket," changing the character of the US global role and discarding "the United Nations as a source of legitimacy for US hegemony" (*Adam Smith in Beijing*, 257).

16. There is a literature on railroads as the medium of settler nation building, which has focused particularly on Canada (see Harold Innis, *A History of the Canadian Pacific Railway* [first published in 1923]) and more recently on India (see Roopa Srinivasan et al., *Our Indian Railway*) and Kenya (see Phoebe Park, "Kenya's $13 Billion Railway Project Is Taking Shape"). This interest in rail nationalism predates Benedict Anderson's focus on print and the press and has a modern and distinctly colonial settler focus. While the evolution of modern postal services has a deep relationship to that of railroads, it is interesting to note how these two novels focus on two different and equally well studied media of nationalism. Vladimir Ilyich Lenin indicted railroads as a capitalist and colonialist enterprise: "The building of railways seems to be a simple, natural, democratic, cultural and civilising enterprise; that is what it is in the opinion of the bourgeois professors who are paid to depict capitalist slavery in bright colours, and in the opinion of petty-bourgeois philistines. But as a matter of fact the capitalist threads, which in thousands of different intercrossings bind these enterprises with private property in the means of production in general, have converted this railway construction into an instrument for oppressing *a thousand million* people (in the colonies and semicolonies), that is, more than half the population of the globe that inhabits the dependent countries, as well as the wage-slaves of capital in the 'civilised' countries" ("Preface to the French and German Editions," emphasis in the original).

17. This should not be understood to imply that Robinson's novel is responding to *The Postman*, which was published a year after *The Wild Shore*.

18. See Habermas, "Towards a Communication-Concept of Rational Collective Will Formation. A Thought-Experiment."

19. One could read this as an inside joke on Robinson's part, referring to the owl of Minerva or to Hegel.

Chapter 5. Segregated Futures

1. In a discussion of Merian C. Cooper and Ernest B. Schoedsack's *King Kong* (1933), Jason Haslam (*Gender, Race, and American Science Fiction*) finds that

science fiction's notions of gender are explicit, while its construction of race tends to be implicit.

2. In September 1957, Central High School in Little Rock, Arkansas, became the site of contest as nine black students attempted to integrate the leading white high school in the state. Minnijean Brown, Elizabeth Ekford, Ernest Green, Thelma Mothershed, Melba Pattilo, Gloria Ray, Terrance Roberts, Thomas Jefferson, and Carlotta Walls challenged the Supreme Court's "separate but equal" ruling in *Plessy v. Ferguson* (1896). In November 1998, President Bill Clinton designated Central High School a national historic site, noting that the first skirmish was fought over the implementation of the Supreme Court's 1954 decision to end segregation in public schools in *Brown v. Board of Education of Topeka*. Isiah Lavender III describes a visit he made to the site, noting the "deteriorated urban neighborhood surrounding the school" and attributing the present shape of Central High to "white flight coupled with the 'lost year'— Little Rock closed its schools to both white and black students in 1958/59 school year" (*Race in American Science Fiction*, 2).

3. See Morrison, *Playing in the Dark*; Dyer, "The Matter of Whiteness."

4. See Ian Baucom, *Specters of the Atlantic*, Christina Sharpe, *In the Wake*.

5. Lipsitz presents concrete evidence of this kind of urban policy outcome: "From 1960 to 1977, four million whites moved out of central cities, while the number of whites living in suburbs increased by twenty-two million. During the same years, the inner-city black population grew by six million, but the number of blacks living in suburbs increased by only 500,000 people. By 1993, 86 percent of suburban whites still lived in places with a black population below 1 percent" ("The Possessive Investment in Whiteness," 374).

6. "Antiblackness" is a term used by Sharpe and others to characterize the negative valences of white supremacy—not just as a racializing ideology, but as a state of being in which black lives are forfeit. See Benjamin Noys, "Afro-Pessimism Reading List."

7. Steve Barnes, a black author, has published two alternative history books: *Lion's Blood* (2002) and *Zulu Heart* (2003). In these books, Islamic Africans from Egypt colonize America. According to Matthew Schneider-Mayerson, in this alternative America (called Bilalistan), "racial hierarchies are reversed, with Africans and Arabs in positions of power while European slaves are used for manual labor" ("What Almost Was," 78).

8. Matthew Wolf-Meyer argues that "the much decried cannibalism of the future rulers of Earth should be seen as a Swiftian critique of the upper class, not the barbarism of Blacks" ("Apocalypse, Ideology, America") Though the argument has merit, the dialectical point here is that Heinlein produces a critique of power and domination at the same time that he unavoidably racializes

that critique. Class and race are unavoidably caught up in the history of black slavery in the United States.

9. I have chosen not to reprint Heinlein's use of the n-word here because it ultimately is not crucial to the discussion. I acknowledge that the layers here are thick: Heinlein has Joe, a black character, use it to admonish Farnham, a white character. Heinlein was and I am white, so I will seek to distinguish myself from Heinlein by redacting that part of his text and by acknowledging that redaction here.

10. Burton's emphasis on biomedical procedures has a precursor in George Schuyler's 1931 novel, *Black No More*. DeGraw argues that Schuyler "revises the essentialist, biological theories of race common at the time" in an attempt to "reflect the literal melting pot of American society" and that he uses the "speculative technique of science fiction to transform the cultural phenomenon of skin-whitening and hair-straightening products, targeted at African-Americans, into a biological medical procedure" (*The Subject of Race in American Science Fiction*, 58).

11. See Delany, "Racism and Science Fiction"; André Carrington, *Speculative Blackness*.

12. Montgomery draws her primary example from the 1991 Gulf War, when President George Bush described "the new world order" as a governmental response to crisis. This new world order was "a multinational one . . . built upon militaristic aggression, political strength, and world domination cloaked in the guise of democracy," and Montgomery argues that these catchwords validate "the notion of manifest destiny present in the national psyche" (*The Apocalypse in African-American Fiction*, 1). The way Bush described his response to crisis differs wildly from Montgomery's characterization of the responses made by black leaders, who instead emphasized "American's hypocrisy in intervening in a foreign country's dilemma while neglecting the most pressing social, economic, and political problems confronting black citizens at home" (ibid.).

Chapter 6. The Reproductive Imperative

1. I refer to the absent female character as the woman because that is how McCarthy's male character, the man, refers to her. Her identification as a woman is less important here than the way the novel conflates her being a woman with her having internal reproductive organs (that is, potentially able to reproduce). I note this here to indicate that in no way do I wish to advance essentializing or binary claims about gender in this chapter or in this book.

2. David Kuhne offers a comprehensive survey of such works in "Gender Roles after the Collapse."

3. On *The Only Ones*, see Brent Ryan Bellamy, "Violent (Non-)Labour."

4. For a development of Edelman's work on reproduction and narrative, see Heather Latimer, *Reproductive Acts*; Rebekah Sheldon, *The Child to Come*.

5. Because I focus on a speculative novel, I use the term "futurity" rather than "futurism" to indicate the setting of a literary scene rather than a rhetorical argument in the present. Edelman's use of "futurism" implies an orientation toward the future—a desire for what is to come and, in effect, a belief that a cultural focus on a particular social form might bring into being (or, in this case, make impossible) such a future. On the one hand, Italian futurism looked to an aestheticized industrialism as the height of modernity, while on the other hand, Afrofuturism seeks to find purchase for a radically black vision of the future even as it contests and reimagines the present. In contrast, "futurity" implies a fictional state of being, or an imagined state of being that is brought into being. If reproductive futurism represents the relationship of people to their real and ongoing conditions of existence through the possibility of procreation, then reproductive futurity (that is, the form that survival takes in the post-apocalyptic novel) represents the imaginary relationship of characters to their post-apocalyptic conditions of existence through the possibility of imaginary children. This logic becomes strange, especially when we remember that fiction can be told from any number of perspectives beyond the familial.

6. The search was of peer-reviewed articles in academic journals and thus excluded book chapters, dissertation chapters, and book reviews.

7. See John Cant, "Appendix Two," 280; Michael Chabon, "Dark Adventure," 104; Diane Luce, "The Painterly Eye"; Jan Gretlund, "Cormac McCarthy and the American Literary Tradition"; Linda Woodson, "McCarthy's Heroes and the Will to Truth," 23–24.

8. See Dana Phillips, "'He Ought Not Have Done It.'"

9. See Stephen Frye, "Histories, Novels, Ideas"; Donovan Gwinner, "'Everything Uncoupled from Its Shoring'"; Allen Josephs, "The Quest for God in *The Road*"; Ashley Kunsa, "'Maps of the World in Its Becoming.'"

10. In Sullivan's taxonomy of women in McCarthy's novels, she discusses the term "whorish" in *The Road*: "When the term *whore* slips from the confines of dialogue into third-person narration or is used by a female character to label herself, McCarthy gives narrative credence to the perception of women as disposable commodities" ("Gender in McCarthy's Fiction," 200). To illustrate this point, Sullivan describes a scene from the novel in which the man places a photograph of his wife on the road and concludes that since the woman has fulfilled her reproductive function, she has become a "dangerous lure to death" (ibid., 203).

11. In Sullivan's words, "McCarthy's good-guy sentimental undoes an implicitly matriarchal domestic power structure and confers upon the father the

affective power traditionally ascribed to the feminine or feminized sentimental subjects" ("The Good Guys," 81).

12. See Madeline Lane-McKinley and Marija Cetinic, "Theses on Postpartum."

13. Jay Ellis describes the father as "*Homo techne*," arguing that he must act to ensure that his son survives ("Another Sense of Ending," 30).

14. McCarthy tends to avoid using apostrophes and quotation marks throughout his work, which makes the inclusion of an apostrophe in "don't" stand out.

15. The language of survival is also used in discussions of trauma surrounding sexual assault, destructive events, and mass migration, in which it replaces the nomenclature of victimhood.

16. There is a rich literature about the problem of social reproduction. See Silvia Federici, *Caliban and the Witch*; Mariarosa Dalla Costa and Selma James, *The Power of Women and the Subversion of the Community*; Sophie Lewis, *Full Surrogacy Now*; Maria Mies, *Patriarchy and Accumulation on a World Scale*.

17. The US government began tracking the fertility rate in 1909 and measures the number of births per thousand women between the ages of fifteen and forty-four.

18. Phillips makes a startling proposition: "In *The Road*, the future seems outdated in more ways than one—everything that McCarthy describes might well have happened many years ago, say sometime in the mid-1980s" ("'He Ought Not Have Done It,'" 185). Nothing in the novel implies that the man and the boy are wandering through a post-1990s world—there are no pagers, cell phones, or smart phones, for instance.

19. In the moment when the man and the boy first discover the house with the human-stocked cellar, *The Road* indicates that its narrator has at least a little historical knowledge. Andrew Hoberek draws attention to the way the novel's setting connotes a "regionally specific history," which he reads as "embedded in the word 'chattel' and in the resonance of the ship's holds and the cargo they contain—of the treatment of human beings as property." He continues, "In the slippage from chattel to cattle, we can see the quite organized forms of cannibalism McCarthy depicts in the novel not as Hobbesian throwbacks but as perverse extensions of regional tradition" ("Cormac McCarthy and the Aesthetics of Exhaustion," 489).

20. Many nutrients are required to support the development of a fetus into a baby, and a succession of pregnancies for one person can lead to health problems like maternal depletion syndrome. McCarthy's novel labors under the realistic impracticality of using childbirth for food, since malnutrition results in the cessation of the menstrual cycle. I am indebted to an anonymous reader for this insight.

21. In fact, McCarthy's *Blood Meridian, or The Evening Redness in the West*

(1985) provides a useful touchstone to connect the 1980s frontier-bound post-apocalyptic novel with both the actual frontier of the mid-nineteenth century and the fantasies about space and a restored United States that permeate Brin's and Robinson's titles.

22. Dan Sinykin describes McCarthy's career as a successful attempt to marry literary and genre fiction, with the pinnacle being *The Road* ("The Conglomerate Era," 480–82).

23. I owe this insightful formulation to an anonymous reader.

24. This final novel in the trilogy was planned though never published. Gerry Canavan writes that in the archives of Butler's letters and work (held at the Huntington Library) are "dozens and dozens of false starts for the novel, petering out after twenty pages or thirty pages, others after just two or three; this cycle of narrative failure is recorded over hundreds of pages of discarded drafts" (*Octavia E. Butler*, 144). Butler died before she could muster these branching versions of her work into a singular form.

Chapter 7. Automobility Regression

1. Peter Hitchcock argues that "in general, oil dependency is not just an economic attachment but appears as a kind of cognitive compulsion that mightily prohibits alternatives to its utility as a commodity and as an array of cultural signifiers" ("Oil in an American Imaginary," 82). For more on what has been described as an energy unconscious, see Stephanie LeMenager, *Living Oil*; Graeme Macdonald, "Improbability Drives"; Vivason Soni, "Energy"; Patricia Yaeger, "Editor's Column."

2. See Brent Ryan Bellamy, "Flying Cars, Dino-Power, and Energy in SF."

3. Note that I made the final edits before submitting this manuscript to the publisher during the first months of social isolation during the COVID-19 pandemic. These lines in particular resonate differently for me reading them in the spring of 2020 than they did when I first wrote them. Much of this book could contain endnotes such as this one. Instead, I leave this single remark about the current global crisis caused by COVID-19: not one of these books imagined an apocalyptic event during which we would need to isolate ourselves to protect the most vulnerable among us. Indeed, protecting the most vulnerable is not typically a move of post-apocalyptic fiction.

4. See Roger Zelazny, *Damnation Alley*; George Miller, *Mad Max*, *Mad Max: Fury Road*, and *Mad Max 2*; George Miller and George Ogilvie, *Mad Max: Beyond Thunderdome*.

5. For a discussion of real-world energy infrastructures under threat, see Gretchen Bakke, *The Grid*.

6. For just-in-time production, see David Harvey, *The Condition of Post-*

modernity; Jeffery Nealon, *Post-Postmodernism*. For the green revolution, see Fredric Jameson, "Periodizing the 60s."

7. See Deborah Cowen, *The Deadly Life of Logistics*.

8. Macdonald has identified a consistent tendency of energy-speculative futures: "Consciously or otherwise, it is significant that the fictions of future energy-scarce scenarios contain salient caution about an almost-post-carbon future of 'alternatives' that does not necessarily herald a renewables utopia." Crucially, he argues that "in doing so they reveal the *nature* of any society as bound-up with a specific energy mode and particular system of social power" ("Research Note," 14; emphasis in the original).

9. Automobility regression is meant to be a play on the Library of Congress subject heading "Regression (Civilization)," the latter was used to classify certain early post-apocalyptic texts.

10. Kunstler's book is part of a series that also contains *The Witch of Hebron*, *A History of the Future*, and *The Harrows of Spring*.

11. The development of ways to ship oil around the world greatly disrupted the political capacities developed and deployed by coal miners. Timothy Mitchell imagines the difference between coal's "dendritic networks," full of "branches" and "choke points," and the way oil flows almost like current through "an electrical grid, where there is more than one possible path and the flow of energy can switch to avoid blockages or overcome breakdowns" (*Carbon Democracy*, 38). Coal's movement could be blockaded, but oil's could not. Mitchell neatly demonstrates the profound impact of oil on every aspect of social life.

12. Andreas Malm writes, "No piece of coal or drop of oil has yet turned itself into fuel, and no humans have yet engaged in systematic large-scale extraction of either to satisfy subsistence needs: fossil fuels necessitate waged or forced labor—the power of some to direct the labor of others—as conditions of their very existence" (*Fossil Capital* 19). See also Matthew Huber, *Lifeblood*.

13. For example, Earle says: "I prepared to smoke trout that I had left from the evening's fishing because they'd be worth something in trade and for breakfast I had plenty of eggs and the brown bread Jane Ann brought me. We didn't have a lot of things, but we had plenty of eggs. Half the people in town kept chickens, and rabbits too, which was the reason I didn't. Much of the year we had plenty of milk, and butter as well, though milk was more difficult to keep in high summer because we lacked refrigeration. Butter in a covered crock would keep on a sideboard for a week or more, even in hot weather. Many farmers made cheeses and traded for them, and Bill Schroeder, who ran the creamer, made several kinds" (Kunstler, *World Made by Hand*, 22).

14. Typically airports are located outside of a city core; have all entrances controlled at ground level and elevated for a view from the waiting lounge; and

contain plenty of washroom space, wide concourse halls, and many food preparation areas. Depending on the particular apocalyptic event, it makes sense for a story to be set in an airport.

15. For a further discussion of this difference see Amitav Ghosh, "Petrofiction."

16. This dilemma raises the very material problem of fossil fuels, what David McDermott Hughes calls oil's missed utopian moment, which he locates in the shifting relationship between fossil fuels—kerosene, coal, crude oil, and gasoline—and labor in mid-nineteenth-century Trinidad (*Energy without Conscience*, 41–60). Looking ahead, this relationship develops and finds repetitions in the twentieth century: for instance, the building of suburbs, automobiles, and highway infrastructure with energy-laden reserves of oil that could have instead been used to ensure a future with renewable energy.

17. For more on Crusoe as a post-apocalyptic figure, see Heather J. Hicks, *The Post-Apocalyptic Novel in the Twenty-First Century*.

18. If there is anything that seems science fictional about Varley's post-apocalyptic foray, it has to be the wood-fired engines, yet though such engines are not as powerful as ones that run on gas, they do work. A 2011 YouTube video features this description: "Running our entire place off of gasified white oak chunks and running the gas into a 1972-25Kw Onan 30 EK genset through a simple homemade carburetor" (Engineer775, "The Wood Gas Generator Runs the Whole Farm!"). Wood-fired combustion is a real technology, and it seems that some people who embrace a culture of disaster preparation, known colloquially as preppers, are very interested in it. It goes without saying that the creator of the YouTube video was fortunate to have a homestead and the gear, practical knowledge, and time required to accomplish this feat of engineering. Essentially, they have retrofitted a gasoline engine to run off of wood gas by installing a hopper and wood burner, with the fumes directed into the combustion engine.

19. See Brent Ryan Bellamy, "*Neuromancer*."

20. See William Gibson et al., "The Science in Science Fiction."

21. Buell tracks the connections of uneven development to fossil capital's felt unevenness: "oil has become an obsessive point of reference in and clear determinant over the daily lives of many, either victimizing them directly and cruelly as with Shell in Nigeria, or Texaco in Ecuador, or making them increasingly feel that their developed-world normalities are a shaky house of cards" ("A Short History of Oil Cultures," 70).

22. Catton posits that "today mankind is locked into stealing ravenously from the future," situating a coming catastrophe as the consequence of the good times had in the present (*Overshoot*, 3).

23. Buell mentions several post-apocalyptic novels in passing as he concludes

his analysis ("A Short History of Oil Cultures 82–83), including Butler's *Parable of the Sower* and Xenogenesis trilogy, Kazuo Ishiguro's *Never Let Me Go* (2005), McCarthy's *The Road*, Sarah Hale's *The Carhullan Army* (2007), Kunstler's *World Made by Hand*, and Andreas Eschbach's *Ausgebrannt* (2009).

Conclusion: Remainders of the American Century

1. Whitehead's paragraph about New York City offers a narrative version of the history provided by Samuel Zipp (*Manhattan Projects*). Zipp describes these projects as the efforts in the 1960s to remake the city, a process he refers to as "the rise of a world city and the decline into urban crisis" (ibid., 29).

2. *Zone One* features a special type of zombie that has given up. Skels resemble a typical zombie—hungry for human flesh, in a state of decomposition, more dangerous in groups, and vicious—while the stragglers are less typical. The latter constitute Whitehead's contribution to the zombie plot: stragglers just stand, sit or lie, and stare. They are skels that have thoroughly checked out. They often return to a fixed place, perhaps one still meaningful to some recess of their muscle or blood memory, and just wait.

3. The Sad and Rabid Puppies' lists included the space opera author Alistair Reynolds, who requested that he be removed. See David Barnett, "Hugo Awards Shortlist Dominated by Rightwing Campaign"; Katy Waldman, "How Sci-Fi's Hugo Awards Got Their Own Full-Blown Gamergate."

4. For Fredric Jameson, the answer to the "universal ideological conviction that no alternative is possible" is "the Utopian form itself"—not because it posits some image of a new harmonious world, but because that form asserts that a different world is possible "by forcing us to think the break itself" (*Archaeologies of the Future*, 232).

5. See Christina Sharpe, *In the Wake*.

Bibliography

Abbott, Carl. *Frontiers Past and Future: Science Fiction and the American West*. University Press of Kansas, 2006.

Abrams, Elliott, Gary Bauer, William J. Bennett, Jeb Bush, Dick Cheney, Eliot A. Cohen, Midge Decter, et al. "Statement of Principles." In *The United States and Iraq since 1990: Brief History with Documents*, edited by Robert K. Brigham, 91. Wiley-Blackwell, 2014.

Abrams, M. H. *A Glossary of Literary Terms*. 7th ed. Harcourt Brace College Publishers, 1999.

Adams, John Joseph. "Post-Apocalyptic Science Fiction." *Internet Review of Science Fiction*, January 2004. https://web.archive.org/web/20170417094257/http://www.irosf.com:80/q/zine/article/10013.

Adiutori, Vincent. "*The Road* Is Mapped: Cormac McCarthy's Modernist Irony." *Mediations* 28, no.1 (Fall 2014): 3–18.

Akomolafe, Bayo. "I, Coronavirus. Mother, Monster, Activist." April 7, 2020. https://bayoakomolafe.net/project/i-coronavirus-mother-monster-activist/.

Aldiss, Brian W., and David Wingrove. *Trillion Year Spree: The History of Science Fiction*. Atheneum, 1986.

Althusser, Louis. *For Marx*. Translated by Ben Brewster. Verso, 2005.

Amazon Publishing. "Work with Us." Accessed July 22, 2020. https://amazonpublishing.amazon.com/work-with-us.html.

American Booksellers Association. "Independent Bookstores Are Thriving." Accessed July 21, 2020. https://www.bookweb.org/for-the-record.

Anderson, Benedict. *Imagined Communities: Reflections on the Origin and Spread of Nationalism*. Verso, 2006.

Anderson, Kevin J., and Doug Beason. *Ill Wind*. Forge, 1995.

Anderson, Perry. "Homeland." *New Left Review* 81 (May–June 2013): 5–32.

Apter, Emily. *Against World Literature: On the Politics of Untranslatability*. Verso, 2013.

———. "Untranslatables: A World System." *New Literary History* 39, nos. 3–4 (2009): 581–98.

Armstrong, Nancy. "The Future *in* and *of* the Novel." *Novel* 44, no.1 (Spring 2011): 8–10.

Arrighi, Giovanni. *Adam Smith in Beijing: Lineages of the Twenty-First Century*. Verso, 2007.

———. *The Long Twentieth Century: Money, Power and the Origins of our Times*. Verso, 2010.

Arrighi, Giovanni, and Beverly J. Silver. Introduction to *Chaos and Governance in the Modern World System*, 1–36. University of Minnesota Press, 1999.

Atwood, Margaret. *The Handmaid's Tale*. McClelland and Stewart, 1985.

———. *Oryx and Crake*. Seal Books, 2003.

———. *The Year of the Flood*. McClelland and Stewart, 2009.

Auster, Paul. *In the Country of Last Things*. Penguin Books, 1988.

Austin, J. L. *How to Do Things with Words*. Oxford University Press, 1962.

Bakke, Gretchen. *The Grid: The Fraying Wires between Americans and Our Energy Future*. Bloomsbury, 2016.

Barba Guerrero, Paula. "A Vulnerable Sense of Place: Re-Adapting Post-Apocalyptic Dystopia in Octavia Butler's *Parable of the Sower* and Colson Whitehead's *Zone One*." *Revista de Estudios Norteamericanos* 23 (2019): 45–70.

Barnes, Steve. *Lion's Blood*. Warner Books, 2002.

———. *Zulu Heart*. Warner Books, 2003.

Barnett, David. "Hugo Awards Shortlist Dominated by Rightwing Campaign." *Guardian*, April 26, 2016. https://www.theguardian.com/books/2016/apr/26/hugo-awards-shortlist-rightwing-campaign-sad-rabid-puppies.

Baucom, Ian. *Specters of the Atlantic: Finance Capital, Slavery, and the Philosophy of History*. Duke University Press, 2007.

Beckett, Samuel. *Endgame*. Faber and Faber, 2009.

Bell, Madison Smartt. "A Writer's View of Cormac McCarthy." In *Myth, Legend, Dust: Critical Response to Cormac McCarthy*, edited by Rick Wallach, 1–12. Manchester University Press, 2000.

Bellamy, Brent Ryan. "Figuring Terminal Crisis in Steven Amsterdam's *Things We Didn't See Coming*." *Mediations* 28, no. 1 (Fall 2014): 19–34.

———. "Flying Cars, Dino-Power, and Energy in SF." *Strange Horizons*, January 25, 2016. http://strangehorizons.com/non-fiction/articles/flying-cars-dino-power-and-energy-in-sf/.

———. "*Neuromancer*: The Cultural Logic of Late Fossil Capital?" *Open Library of Humanities* 5, no. 1 (September 2019): 1–26.

———. " . . . or Bust: Science fiction and the Bomb, 1945–1960." In *The Cambridge History of Science Fiction*, edited by Gerry Canavan and Eric Carl Link, 218–31. Cambridge University Press, 2019.

———. "Reading Kim Stanley Robinson's Three Californias Triptych as Petrofiction." *Western American Literature* 51, no. 4 (Winter 2017): 409–27.

———. "Violent (Non-)Labour: On the Social Reproduction of the Clone in Carola Dibbell's *The Only Ones*." *Canadian Review of American Studies* 50, no. 2 (2020): 257–75.

———. "A Working Bibliography: U.S. Post-Apocalyptic Fiction and Cultural

Production." June 6, 2013. http://brentryanbellamy.com/2013/06/a-working-bibliography-u-s-post-apocalyptic-fiction-and-cultural-production/.

Benanav, Aaron, and John Clegg. "Misery and Debt: On the Logic and History of Surplus Populations and Surplus Capital." In *Contemporary Marxist Theory: A Reader*, edited by Andrew Pendakis, Jeff Diamanti, Nicholas Brown, Josh Robinson, and Imre Szeman, 585–608. Bloomsbury, 2014.

Berger, James. *After the End: Representations of the Post-Apocalypse*. University of Minnesota Press, 1999.

———. "'The Voice of the Bridegroom and the Bride Shall be Heard No More': Apocalypse, Critique, and Procreation." *Frame* 26, no. 1 (May 2013): 125–39.

Berlant, Lauren. *Cruel Optimism*. Duke University Press, 2011.

Bong Joon-ho, dir. *Parasite*. BarunsOn E&A, 2019.

———. *Snowpiercer*. Weinstein Company, 2013.

Booker, M. Keith. *Monsters, Mushroom Clouds, and the Cold War: American Science Fiction and the Roots of Postmodernism, 1946–1964*. Greenwood Press, 2001.

Booker, M. Keith, and Anne-Marie Thomas. *The Science Fiction Handbook*. Wiley-Blackwell, 2009.

Bould, Mark. "The Ships Landed Long Ago: Afrofuturism and Black SF." *Science Fiction Studies* 34, no. 2 (July 2007): 177–86.

Bowker. "Self-Publishing in the United States, 2007–2012: Print and Ebook." Accessed July 30, 2020. http://media.bowker.com/documents/self publishingpubcounts_2007_2012.pdf.

———. "Self-Publishing in the United States, 2008–2013: Print vs. Ebook." 2014. http://media.bowker.com/documents/bowker_selfpublishing _report2013.pdf.

Boyle, Danny, dir. *28 Days Later*. DNA Films, 2002.

Brackett, Leigh. *The Long Tomorrow*. Ballantine Books, 1986.

Braudel, Fernand. *Civilization and Capitalism*. Vol. 3: *The Perspective of the World*. Harper and Row, 1984.

Brenner, Robert. *The Economics of Global Turbulence: The Advanced Capitalist Economies from Long Boom to Long Downturn, 1945–2005*. New Left Review, 2004.

Breznican, Anthony. "Exclusive: Stephen King's *The Stand* Comes to Life Again." *Vanity Fair*, May 20, 2020. https://www.vanityfair.com/hollywood/2020/05/stephen-kings-the-stand-exclusive-first-look.

Brin, David. *The Postman*. Bantam Books, 1985.

Brooks, Albert. *2030: The Real Story of What Happens to America*. St. Martin's Griffin, 2011.

Brooks, Max. *World War Z*. Three Rivers Press, 2006.

Brouillette, Sarah. "Corporate Publishing and Canonization: *Neuromancer* and Science-Fiction Publishing in the 1970s and Early 1980s." *Book History* 5 (2002): 187–208.

Brouillette, Sarah, and David Thomas. "First Responses." Comparative Literature Studies 53, no. 3 (2016): 505–34.

Buell, Frederick. "Post-Apocalypse: A New U.S. Cultural Dominant." *Frame* 26, no. 1 (May 2013): 9–30.

———. "A Short History of Oil Cultures; or, The Marriage of Catastrophe and Exuberance." In *Oil Culture*, edited by Ross Barrett and Daniel Worden, 69–88. University of Minnesota Press, 2014.

Burgess, Helen J. "'Road of Giants': Nostalgia and the Ruins of the Superhighway in Kim Stanley Robinson's Three Californias Trilogy." *Science Fiction Studies* 33 (2006): 275–90.

Burton, LeVar. *Aftermath*. Vista, 1997.

Butler, Octavia E. *Lilith's Brood*. Grand Central Publishing, 2007.

———. *Parable of the Sower*. Grand Central Publishing, 2007.

———. *Parable of the Talents*. Grand Central Publishing, 2007.

Caffentzis, George. *In Letters of Blood and Fire: Work, Machines, and the Crisis of Capitalism*. PM Press, 2013.

Calvin, Rich. "Gender and the Apocalypse." *Los Angeles Review of Books*, May 30, 2015. https://lareviewofbooks.org/article/gender-and-the-apocalypse/#!.

Campbell, Joseph. *The Hero with a Thousand Faces*. Princeton University Press, 1972.

Canavan, Gerry. *Octavia E. Butler*. University of Illinois Press, 2016.

———. "Peak Oil after Hydrofracking." In *Materialism and the Critique of Energy*, edited by Brent Ryan Bellamy and Jeff Diamanti, 289–314. MCM Prime Press, 2018.

———. "Science Fiction without the Future." *American Book Review* 33, no. 3 (March–April 2012): 11–12.

Cant, John. "Appendix Two: The Road." In John Cant, *Cormac McCarthy and the Myth of American Exceptionalism*, 266–80. Routledge, 2008.

Caracciolo, Marco. "Negative Strategies and World Disruption in Postapocalyptic Fiction." *Style* 52, no. 3 (2018): 222–41.

Carr, Terry. "Introduction to *Neuromancer*." In William Gibson, *Neuromancer*, vii–viii. Ace Books, 1984.

Carrington, André. *Speculative Blackness: The Future of Race in Science Fiction*. University of Minnesota Press, 2016.

———. "The Unbearable Whiteness of Science Fiction." May 13, 2016. https://www.opendemocracy.net/en/transformation/whiteness-of-science-fiction/.

Carrington, Damian. "Arctic Stronghold of World's Seeds Flooded after Permafrost Melts." *Guardian*, May 19, 2017. https://www.theguardian.com/environment/2017/may/19/arctic-stronghold-of-worlds-seeds-flooded-after-permafrost-melts.

Carson, Rachel. *Silent Spring and Other Writings on the Environment*. Edited by Sandra Steingraber. Library of America, 2018.

Catton, William R., Jr. *Overshoot: The Ecological Basis of Revolutionary Change*. University of Illinois Press, 1982.

Cetinic, Marija. "House and Field: The Aesthetics of Saturation." *Mediations* 28, no. 1 (Fall 2014): 35–44.

Chabon, Michael. "Dark Adventure: On Cormac McCarthy's *The Road*." In Michael Chabon, *Maps and Legends: Reading and Writing along the Borderlands*, 95–108. McSweeney's Books, 2008.

Chantrill, Christopher. "Defense Spending." Accessed July 27, 2020. https://www.usgovernmentspending.com/defense_spending.

Charnas, Suzy McKee. *Motherlines*. Berkley/Putnam, 1978.

———. "Suzy McKee Charnas Interview, Part 2, from SnackReads." Interview by Josh Gentry. April 26, 2013. https://www.youtube.com/watch?v=Uay-bULF-tg.

———. *Walk to the End of the World*. Ballantine Books, 1974.

Clover, Joshua. *Riot. Strike. Riot. The Era of New Uprisings*. Verso, 2016.

Cooper, Lydia R. "'There Is No God and We Are His Prophets': Heroism and Prophetic Narrative in *The Road*." In Lydia R. Cooper, *No More Heroes: Narrative Perspective and Morality in Cormac McCarthy*, 132–60. Louisiana State University Press, 2011.

Cooper, Merian C., and Ernest B. Schoedsack, dirs. *King Kong*. Radio Pictures, 1933.

Cowen, Deborah. *The Deadly Life of Logistics: Mapping Violence in Global Trade*. University of Minnesota Press, 2014.

Coyle, Anne. "Morels and Morals: Hope in the Postapocalyptic *The Road*." In *Critical Insights: Cormac McCarthy*, edited by David N. Cremean, 271–87. Salem Press, 2013.

Crawford, Neta C. "Pentagon Fuel Use, Climate Change, and the Costs of War." Watson Institute, Brown University, June 12, 2019. https://watson.brown.edu/costsofwar/files/cow/imce/papers/2019/Pentagon%20Fuel%20Use,%20Climate%20Change%20and%20the%20Costs%20of%20War%20Final.pdf.

Cronin, Justin. *City of Mirrors*. Ballantine Books, 2016.

———. *The Passage*. Ballantine Books, 2010.

———. *The Twelve*. Ballantine Books, 2012.

Cumings, Bruce. "Still the American Century." *Review of International Studies* 25 (December 1999): 271–99.

Curtis, Claire P. *Postapocalyptic Fiction and the Social Contract: "We'll Not Go Home Again."* Lexington Books, 2010.

Dahlin, Robert. "Plenty of Product—but Tougher Competition." *Publishers Weekly*, September 8, 1997, 42–48.

Dalla Costa, Mariarosa, and Selma James. *The Power of Women and the Subversion of the Community*. Falling Wall Press, 1975.

Darlage, Dale. "*Farnham's Freehold.*" 2011. https://www.sfsite.com/08a/ff349.htm.

De Cristofaro, Diletta. *The Contemporary Post-Apocalyptic Novel*. Bloomsbury, 2019.

———. "Critical Temporalities: *Station Eleven* and the Contemporary Post-Apocalyptic Novel." *Open Library of Humanities* 4, no. 2 (2018). https://olh.openlibhums.org/articles/10.16995/olh.206/.

DeGraw, Sharon. *The Subject of Race in American Science Fiction*. Routledge, 2007.

Delany, Samuel R. "About 5,750 Words." In Samuel R. Delany, *The Jewel-Hinged Jaw: Notes on the Language of Science Fiction*, 1–16. Wesleyan University Press, 2009.

———. *Dhalgren*. Vintage Books, 2001.

———. "Racism and Science Fiction." *New York Review of Science Fiction*, August 1998. https://www.nyrsf.com/racism-and-science-fiction-.html.

DeNiro, Alan. *Total Oblivion, More or Less*. Spectra Ballantine Books, 2009.

Derrida, Jacques. "No Apocalypse, Not Now (Full Speed Ahead, Seven Missives, Seven Missiles)." *Diacritics* 14, no. 2 (Summer 1984): 20–31.

Derrida, Jacques, and Antoine Spire. "'Others Are Secret Because They Are Other.'" In Jacques Derrida, *Paper Machine*, translated by Rachel Bowlby, 136–63, Stanford University Press, 2005.

Dibbell, Carola. *The Only Ones*. Two-Dollar Radio, 2015.

Dick, Philip K. *Dr. Bloodmoney, or How We Got Along after the Bomb*. Ace Books, 1965.

———. *The Man Who Japed*. Vintage Books, 2002.

———. *The Penultimate Truth*. Belmont Books, 1964.

———. *The World Jones Made*. Ace Books, 1956.

———. *Vulcan's Hammer*. Ace Books, 1960.

Donnelly, Ignatius. *Caesar's Column*. BiblioBazaar, 2010.

Donnelly, Thomas, Donald Kagan, and Gary Schmitt. *Rebuilding America's Defenses: Strategy, Forces and Resources for a New Century*. Project for the New American Century, 2000.

Doyle, Briohny. "The Postapocalyptic Imagination." *Thesis Eleven* 131, no. 1 (December 2015): 99–113.

Du Bois, W.E.B. "The Comet." In *The Big Book of Science Fiction: The Ultimate Collection*, edited by Ann VanderMeer and Jeff VanderMeer, 53–61. Vintage Books, 2016.

Dyer, Richard. "The Matter of Whiteness." In *White Privilege: Essential Readings on the Other Side of Racism*, edited by Paula Rothenberg, 9–14. Worth Publishers, 2005.

Eco, Umberto. "At the Roots of the Modern Concept of Symbol." *Social Research* 52, no. 2 (Summer 1985): 383–402.

Edelman, Lee. *No Future: Queer Theory and the Death Drive*. Duke University Press, 2004.

Ekman, Stefan, and Audrey Isabel Taylor. "Notes toward a Critical Approach to Worlds and World-Building." *Fafnir* 3, no. 3 (2016): 7–18.

Elison, Meg. *The Book of Etta*. 47 North, 2017.

———. *The Book of Flora*. 47 North, 2019.

———. *The Book of the Unnamed Midwife*. 47 North, 2016.

Ellis, Jay. "Another Sense of Ending: The Keynote Address to the Knoxville Conference." *Cormac McCarthy Journal* 6, no. 1 (2008): 22–38.

Engineer775. "The Wood Gas Generator Runs the Whole Farm!" February 5, 2011. https://youtu.be/yYGKn12Weu4.

Epp, Michael. "What Is Living and What Is Dead in the U.S. Declaration of Independence, or, National Treasure and the State of Public Texts." *ESC* 41, nos. 2–3 (2015): 191–208.

Evans, Rebecca M. "The Best of Times, the Worst of Times, the End of Times? The Uses and Abuses of Environmental Apocalypse." *ASAP/Journal* 3, no. 3 (2018): 501–22.

Federici, Silvia. *Caliban and the Witch: Women, the Body, and Primitive Accumulation*. Autonomedia, 2004.

Finch, Laura, and Jessica Hurley. "Philadelphia." In Laura Finch and Jessica Hurley, *From the Bomb to the Crash: Geographies of Disaster in the American Century*. Accessed April 16, 2015. http://fromthebombtothecrash.squarespace.com/content-2.

Fisher, Phillip. *Hard Facts: Setting and Form in the American Novel*. Oxford University Press, 1985.

Fitting, Peter. "You're History, Buddy: Postapocalyptic Visions in Recent Science Fiction Films." In *Fights of Fancy: Armed Conflict in Science Fiction and Fantasy*, edited by George Edgar Slusser and Eric S. Rabkin, 114–31. University of Georgia Press, 1993.

Fleischer, Richard, dir. *Soylent Green*. Metro-Goldwyn-Mayer, 1973.

Floyd, Kevin. "Automatic Subjects: Gendered Labour and Abstract Life." *Historical Materialism* 24, no. 2 (2016): 61–86.

Fowler, Alastair. "The Life and Death of Literary Forms." In "Form and Its Alternatives," special issue, *New Literary History* 2, no. 2 (Winter 1971): 199–216.

Frank, Pat. *Alas, Babylon*. Harper Perennial Modern Classics, 2005.

Franklin, H. Bruce. *Robert A. Heinlein: America as Science Fiction*. Oxford University Press, 1980.

———. *War Stars: The Superweapon and the American Imagination*. University of Massachusetts Press, 2008.

Freedman, Carl. *Critical Theory and Science Fiction*. Wesleyan University Press, 2000.

Friedman, Lisa. "What Is the Green New Deal? A Climate Proposal, Explained," *New York Times*, February 21, 2019. https://www.nytimes.com/2019/02/21/climate/green-new-deal-questions-answers.html.

Frye, Stephen. "Histories, Novels, Ideas: Cormac McCarthy and the Art of Philosophy." In *The Cambridge Companion to Cormac McCarthy*, edited by Stephen Frye, 3–11. Cambridge University Press, 2013.

Fulton, R. E. "Donald A. Wollheim's Authoritative Universe: Editors, Readers, and the Construction of the Science Fiction Paperback, 1926–1969." *Book History* 19 (2016): 349–83.

Garforth, Lisa. "Green Utopias: Beyond Apocalypse, Progress, and Pastoral." *Utopian Studies* 16, no. 3 (2005): 393–427.

Ghosh, Amitav. *The Great Derangement: Climate Change and the Unthinkable*. University of Chicago Press, 2016.

———. "Petrofiction: The Oil Encounter and the Novel." In Amitav Ghosh, *Incendiary Circumstances: A Chronicle of the Turmoil of Our Times*, 138–51. Houghton Mifflin, 2005.

Gibson, William. *Neuromancer*. Ace Books, 1984.

Gibson, William, David Brin, and Anne Simon. Interviewed by Brooke Gladstone. "The Science in Science Fiction." *Talk of the Nation*, November 30, 1999. https://www.npr.org/2018/10/22/1067220/the-science-in-science-fiction.

Glass, Loren. *Counterculture Colophon: Grove Press, the "Evergreen Review," and the Incorporation of the Avant-Garde*. Stanford University Press, 2013.

Godfrey, Laura Gruber. "'The World He'd Lost': Geography and 'Green' Memory in Cormac McCarthy's *The Road*." *Critique* 52, no. 2 (2011): 163–75.

Gretlund, Jan Nordby. "Cormac McCarthy and the American Literary Tradition." In *Intertextual and Interdisciplinary Approaches to Cormac

McCarthy, edited by Nicholas Monk, 41–51. Routledge, 2011. Routledge, 2011.

Gross, Lawrence. "The Comic Vision of Anishinaabe Culture and Religion." *American Indian Quarterly* 26, no. 3 (2002): 436–59.

Gwinner, Donovan. "'Everything Uncoupled from Its Shoring': Quandaries of Epistemology and Ethics in *The Road*." In *Cormac McCarthy:* All the Pretty Horses, No Country for Old Men, The Road, edited by Sara L. Spurgeon, 137–56. Continuum, 2011.

Habermas, Jürgen. "Towards a Communication-Concept of Rational Collective Will Formation. A Thought-Experiment." *Ratio Juris* 2, no. 2 (July 1989): 144–54.

Hägglund, Martin. *Radical Atheism: Derrida and the Time of Life*. Stanford University Press, 2008.

Haraway, Donna. "Situated Knowledges: The Science Question in Feminism and the Privilege of Partial Perspective." *Feminist Studies* 14, no. 3 (Autumn 1988): 575–99.

Harrison, Harry. *Make Room! Make Room!* Doubleday, 1966.

Harvey, David. *The Condition of Postmodernity: An Inquiry into the Conditions of Cultural Change*. Wiley, 1992.

———. *The New Imperialism*. Oxford University Press, 2005.

Haslam, Jason. *Gender, Race, and American Science Fiction: Reflections on Fantastic Identities*. Routledge, 2015.

Hay, John. *Postapocalyptic Fantasies in Antebellum American Literature*. Cambridge University Press, 2017.

Heer, Jeet. "A Famous Science Fiction Writer's Descent into Libertarian Madness." *New Republic*, June 8, 2014. https://newrepublic.com/article/118048/william-pattersons-robert-heinlein-biography-hagiography.

Heffernan, Teresa. *Post-Apocalyptic Culture*. University of Toronto Press, 2008.

Heinlein, Robert A. *Farnham's Freehold*. Berkley Books, 1982.

Heise, Ursula K. "Reduced Ecologies: Science Fiction and the Meanings of Biological Scarcity." *European Journal of English Studies* 16, no. 2 (August 2012): 99–112.

Heller, Peter. *The Dog Stars*. Alfred A. Knopf, 2012.

Hicks, Heather J. *The Post-Apocalyptic Novel in the Twenty-First Century: Modernity beyond Salvage*. Palgrave Macmillan, 2016.

High, Steven. *Industrial Sunset: The Making of North America's Rest Belt, 1969–1984*. University of Toronto Press, 2003.

Hillcoat, John, dir. *The Road*. Dimension Films, 2009.

Hitchcock, Peter. "Oil in an American Imaginary." *New Formations* 69 (Summer 2010): 81–97.

Hoberek, Andrew. "Cormac McCarthy and the Aesthetics of Exhaustion." *American Literary History* 23, no. 3 (July 2011): 483–99.

———. "Living with PASD." *Contemporary Literature* 53, no. 2 (2012): 406–13.

Hobsbawm, Eric. *The Age of Capital: 1848–1875*. Abacus, 1995.

———. *The Age of Revolution: 1779–1848*. Vintage Books, 1996.

Hoffelder, Nate. "Permuted Press Drops Print Production and Delays Release Schedule, Demands Authors Pay to Get Out of Contracts." *Digital Reader*, October 15, 2014. https://the-digital-reader.com/2014/10/15/permuted-press-drops-print-production-delays-release-schedule-demands-authors-pay-get-contracts/.

Hoffert, Barbara. "Publishers Are Looking at You!" *Library Journal* 16, no. 3 (February 15, 1991): 146–54.

Hofstadter, Richard. "The Paranoid Style in American Politics." *Harper's*, November 1964. https://harpers.org/archive/1964/11/the-paranoid-style-in-american-politics/.

Hollinger, Veronica. "Genre vs. Mode." In *The Oxford Handbook of Science Fiction*, edited by Rob Latham, 139–51. Oxford University Press, 2014.

hooks, bell. *Black Looks: Race and Representation*. Between the Lines, 1992.

Horkheimer, Max, and Theodor W. Adorno. *Dialectic of Enlightenment: Philosophical Fragments*. Edited by Gunzelin Schmid Noerr and translated by Edmund Jephcott. Stanford University Press, 2002.

Howey, Hugh. "The 7K Report." Author Earnings, February 12, 2014. web.archive.org/web/20140304095256/http://authorearnings.com/the-report/.

———. *Wool*. Simon and Schuster, 2012.

Huber, Matthew T. *Lifeblood: Oil, Freedom, and the Forces of Capital*. University of Minnesota Press, 2013.

Hughes, David McDermott. *Energy without Conscience: Oil, Climate Change, and Complicity*. Duke University Press, 2017.

Hurley, Jessica. "Still Writing Backwards: Literature after the End of the World." *Frame* 26, no. 1 (May 2013): 61–76.

Hurley, Natasha. "Reproduction/Non-Reproduction." *Jeunesse* 7, no. 2 (Winter 2015): 148–61.

Innis, Harold. *A History of the Canadian Pacific Railway*. Hardwood Press, 2012.

Internet Speculative Fiction Database. "Publisher: Ace Books." Accessed July 27, 2020. http://www.isfdb.org/cgi-bin/publisher.cgi?37.

———. "Summary Bibliography: Philip K. Dick." Accessed July 30, 2020. http://www.isfdb.org/cgi-bin/ea.cgi?23.

Isfeld, Gordon. "Canadians' Household Debt Climbs to Highest in G7 in

World-Beating Borrowing Spree." *Financial Post*, January 19, 2016. https://financialpost.com/investing/outlook/canadians-household-debt-highest-in-g7-with-crunch-on-brink-of-historic-levels-pbo-warns.

James, P. D. *The Children of Men*. Vintage Canada, 2005.

Jameson, Fredric. *Archaeologies of the Future: The Desire Called Utopia and Other Science Fictions*. Verso, 2005.

———. "On the Power of the Negative." *Mediations* 28, no. 1 (Fall 2014): 71–74.

———. "Periodizing the 60s." In Fredric Jameson, *Ideologies of Theory*, 483–515. Verso, 2008.

———. *The Political Unconscious*. Cornell University Press, 1981.

———. "Postmodernism and the Market." In Fredric Jameson, *Postmodernism, or, The Cultural Logic of Late Capitalism*, 260–78. Duke University Press, 1991.

———. "Towards a New Awareness of Genre." *Science Fiction Studies* 9 (1982): 322–24.

Jemisin, N. K. *The Fifth Season*. Orbit, 2015.

———. *The Obelisk Gate*. Orbit, 2016.

———. *The Stone Sky*. Orbit, 2017.

Jerng, Mark C. *Racial Worldmaking*. Fordham University Press, 2017.

Josephs, Allen. "The Quest for God in *The Road*." In *The Cambridge Companion to Cormac McCarthy*, edited by Stephen Frye, 133–45. Cambridge University Press, 2013.

Joyce, Stephen. "Convergence Publishing and Prestige Niches." In Stephen Joyce, *Transmedia Storytelling and the Apocalypse*, 121–41. Palgrave Macmillan, 2018.

Katerberg, William Henry. *Future West: Utopia and Apocalypse in Frontier Science Fiction*. University Press of Kansas, 2008.

Keene, Brian. "Permuted Press: A New Age of Fuckery." Brian Keene's Bullshit Tumblr, 2015. https://briankeene.tumblr.com/post/100071459539/permuted-press-a-new-age-of-fuckery.

Kermode, Frank. *The Sense of an Ending: Studies in the Theory of Fiction*. Oxford University Press, 2000.

Ketterer, David. *New Worlds for Old: The Apocalyptic Imagination, Science Fiction, and American Literature*. Anchor Books, 1974.

Kilgore, De Witt Douglas. *Astrofuturism: Science, Race, and Visions of Utopia in Space*. University of Pennsylvania Press, 2003.

———. "Difference Engine: Aliens, Robots, and Other Racial Matters in the History of Science Fiction." *Science Fiction Studies* 37, no. 1 (2010): 16–22.

King, Stephen. *Danse Macabre*. Everest House, 1981.

———. *The Stand*. Signet, 1991.

———. "The Stand Inspiration." Accessed July 27, 2020. https://stephenking.com/library/novel/stand_the_inspiration.html.

Klein, Naomi. *The Shock Doctrine: The Rise of Disaster Capitalism*. Random House Canada, 2007.

Kollin, Susan. "'Barren, Silent, Godless': Ecodisaster and the Post-Abundant Landscape in *The Road*." In *Cormac McCarthy:* All the Pretty Horses, No Country for Old Men, The Road, edited by Sara L. Spurgeon, 157–71. Continuum, 2011.

Kuhne, David. "Gender Roles after the Collapse: Women in American Post-Apocalyptic Fiction." *CCTE Studies* 77 (2012): 22–28.

Kunsa, Ashley. "'Maps of the World in Its Becoming': Post-Apocalyptic Naming in Cormac McCarthy's *The Road*." *Journal of Modern Literature* 33, no. 1 (Fall 2009): 57–74.

Kunstler, James Howard. "Farewell to the Drive-In Utopia." *Salmagundi* 168–69 (Fall 2010–Winter 2011): 82–96.

———. *The Harrows of Spring*. Grove Atlantic, 2016.

———. *A History of the Future*. Grove Atlantic, 2014.

———. *The Long Emergency: Surviving the Converging Catastrophes of the Twenty-First Century*. Atlantic Monthly Press, 2005.

———. *The Witch of Hebron*. Grove Atlantic, 2010.

———. *World Made by Hand*. Grove Atlantic, 2008.

La Berge, Leigh Claire. "A Market Correction in the Humanities—What Are You Going to Do with That?" *Los Angeles Review of Books*, August 26, 2019. https://lareviewofbooks.org/article/a-market-correction-in-the-humanities-what-are-you-going-to-do-with-that/.

———. *Scandals and Abstraction: Financial Fictions of the Long 1980s*. Oxford University Press, 2015.

Lane-McKinley, Madeline, and Marija Cetinic. "Theses on Postpartum." *GUTS*, May 22, 2015. http://gutsmagazine.ca/theses-on-postpartum/.

Latimer, Heather. *Reproductive Acts: Sexual Politics in North American Fiction and Film*. McGill-Queen's University Press, 2013.

Lavender, Isiah, III. *Race in American Science Fiction*. Indiana University Press, 2011.

Lawson, Carol. "Behind the Best Sellers: Stephen King." *New York Times*, September 23, 1979. http://movies2.nytimes.com/books/97/03/09/lifetimes/kin-v-behind.html.

Le Guin, Ursula K. *The Dispossessed*. Avon, 1974.

———. *The Left Hand of Darkness*. Gollancz, 2017.

LeFranc, Genevieve. "A Century of Defense Spending in the United States."

July 22, 2015. https://dailyreckoning.com/a-century-of-defense-spending-in-the-united-states/.

LeMenager, Stephanie. *Living Oil: Petroleum Culture in the American Century*. Oxford University Press, 2014.

Lenin, Vladimir Ilyich. "Preface to the French and German Editions." In *Imperialism, the Highest Stage of Capitalism*, Accessed May 27, 2020. https://www.marxists.org/archive/lenin/works/1916/imp-hsc/pref02.htm.

Lepucki, Edan. *California*. Little, Brown and Company, 2014.

Levey, Nick. "Post-Press Literature: Self-Published Authors in the Literary Field." *Post45*, February 3, 2016. https://post45.org/2016/02/post-press-literature-self-published-authors-in-the-literary-field-3/.

Lewis, Sophie. *Full Surrogacy Now: Feminism against the Family*. Verso, 2019.

Lindgren Leavenworth, Maria, and Van Leavenworth. "Fragmented Fiction: Storyworld Construction and the Quest for Meaning in Justin Cronin's *The Passage*." *Fafnir* 4, no. 2 (2017): 22–33.

Linkon, Sherry Lee. *The Half-Life of Deindustrialization: Working-Class Writing about Economic Restructuring*. University of Michigan Press, 2018.

Lipsitz, George. "The Possessive Investment in Whiteness: Racialized Social Democracy and the 'White' Problem in American Studies." *American Quarterly* 47, no .3 (September 1995): 369–87.

London, Jack. *The Scarlet Plague*. Macmillan Company, 1915.

Lott, Eric. *Love and Theft: Blackface Minstrelsy and the American Working Class*. Oxford University Press, 1993.

Luce, Diane C. "The Painterly Eye: Waterscapes in Cormac McCarthy's *The Road*." In *Intertextual and Interdisciplinary Approaches to Cormac McCarthy*, edited by Nicholas Monk, 68–89. Routledge, 2011.

Luce, Henry. "The American Century." *Life*, February 17, 1941, 10.

Luckhurst, Roger. "The Many Deaths of Science Fiction: A Polemic." *Science Fiction Studies* 21, no. 1 (March 1994): 35–50.

Lukács, Georg. *The Historical Novel*. Pelican, 1981.

Lutz, Catherine. *The Bases of Empire: The Global Struggle against U.S. Military Posts*. New York University Press, 2009.

Macdonald, Graeme. "Improbability Drives: The Energy of Science Fiction." *Paradoxa* 26 (Fall 2014): 111–44.

———. "Research Note: The Resources of Fiction." *Reviews in Cultural Theory* 4, no. 2 (2013: 1–24).

Machosky, Brenda. *Structures of Appearing: Allegory and the Work of Literature*. Fordham University Press, 2012.

Malik, Rachel. "Horizons of the Publishable: Publishing in/as Literary Studies." *ELH* 75, no. 3 (Fall 2008): 707–35.

Malm, Andreas. *Fossil Capital: The Rise of Steam Power and the Roots of Global Warming.* Verso, 2016.

Mandel, Emily St. John. *Station Eleven.* Harper Avenue, 2014.

Manjikian, Mary. *Apocalypse and Post-Politics: The Romance of the End.* Lexington Books, 2012.

Mantell, Suzanne. "My One and Only." *Publishers Weekly,* September 20, 2004, S16–19.

Marx, Karl. *Capital: A Critique of Political Economy, Volume One.* Translated by Ben Fowkes, Penguin Books, 1990.

Matheson, Richard. *I Am Legend.* Nelson Doubleday, 1954.

McCarthy, Cormac. *Blood Meridian, or the Evening Redness in the West.* Random House, 1985.

———. *The Road.* Vintage Books, 2006.

McClanahan, Annie. *Dead Pledges: Debt, Crisis, and Twenty-First-Century Culture.* Stanford University Press, 2017.

McGiveron, Rafeeq O. "Heinlein's Inhabited Solar System, 1940–1952." *Science Fiction Studies* 23, no. 2 (July 1996): 245–52.

McGurl, Mark. "Everything and Less." *Modern Language Quarterly* 77, no. 3 (2016): 447–71.

———. *The Program Era: Postwar Fiction and the Rise of Creative Writing.* Harvard University Press, 2011.

Mehren, Elizabeth. "Some Dare Call It Romance: In a New Breed of Novel, Violence Is Rife and Heroes Always Win; Even Rambo Might Be Smitten." *Los Angeles Times,* July 29, 1988. https://www.latimes.com/archives/la-xpm-1988-07-29-vw-7997-story.html.

Melamed, Jodi. *Represent and Destroy: Rationalizing Violence in the New Racial Capitalism.* University of Minnesota Press, 2011.

Merril, Judith. *The Shadow on the Hearth.* Doubleday, 1950.

Mies, Maria. *Patriarchy and Accumulation on a World Scale: Women in the International Division of Labour.* Zed Books, 2014.

Mikics, David. *A New Handbook of Literary Terms.* Yale University Press, 2007.

Miles, Ron. "Gold Eagle Is Shutting Down." December 4, 2014. http://www.jamesaxler.com/Forums/tabid/238/aft/1334/Default.aspx.

Miller, George, dir. *Mad Max.* Kennedy Miller Productions, 1979.

———. *Mad Max: Fury Road.* Warner Bros., 2015.

———. *Mad Max 2: The Road Warrior.* Kennedy Miller Productions, 1981.

Miller, George, and George Ogilvie, dirs. *Mad Max: Beyond Thunderdome.* Kennedy Miller Productions, 1985.

Miller, T. S. "Slow Apocalypse by John Varley." *Strange Horizons*, January 28, 2013. http://strangehorizons.com/non-fiction/reviews/slow-apocalypse-by-john-varley/.

Miller, Walter, Jr. *A Canticle for Leibowitz*. EOS, 2006.

Milner, Andrew. *Locating Science Fiction*. Liverpool University Press, 2012.

Minio-Paluello, Mika, and James Marriot. *The Oil Road: Journeys from the Caspian Sea to the City of London*. Verso, 2013.

Mitchell, Timothy. *Carbon Democracy: Political Power in the Age of Oil*. Verso, 2013.

Monbiot, George. "Civilisation Ends with a Shutdown of Human Concern. Are We There Already?" *Guardian*, October 29, 2007. https://www.theguardian.com/commentisfree/2007/oct/30/comment.books.

Mond, Ian. "Ian Mond Reviews *The Book of Flora* by Meg Elison." *Locus*, June 21, 2019. https://locusmag.com/2019/06/ian-mond-reviews-the-book-of-flora-by-meg-elison/.

Montgomery, Maxine Lavon. *The Apocalypse in African-American Fiction*. University Press of Florida, 1996.

Moran, Alexander. "The Genrefication of Contemporary American Fiction." *Textual Practice*, 33, no. 2 (2019): 229–44.

Morrison, Toni. *Playing in the Dark: Whiteness and the Literary Imagination*. Vintage Books, 2015.

Moylan, Tom. "'Utopia Is When Our Lives Matter': Reading Kim Stanley Robinson's *Pacific Edge*." *Utopian Studies* 6, no. 2 (1995): 1–24.

Nawotka, Edward. "Down Economy Pushes University Press Remainders." *Publishers Weekly*, March 16, 2009, 8.

Nealon, Jeffery. *Post-Postmodernism, Or, the Cultural Logic of Just-In-Time Capitalism*. Stanford University Press, 2012.

Neel, Phillip A. *Hinterland: America's New Landscape of Class Conflict*. Reaktion Books, 2018.

Nilges, Mathias. "Neoliberalism and the Time of the Novel." *Textual Practice* 29, no. 2 (February 2015): 357–77.

Nolan, Christopher, dir. *Inception*. Warner Bros. Pictures, 2010.

———. *Interstellar*. Paramount Pictures, 2014.

Noys, Benjamin. "Afro-Pessimism Reading List." *academia.edu*. Accessed August 16, 2017. https://www.academia.edu/20191147/Afro-pessimism_Reading_List.

O'Donnell, Kevin, Jr. "How Thor Power Hammered Publishing." 1993. https://www.sfwa.org/2005/01/05/how-thor-power-hammered-publishing/.

Olmsted, Kathryn. "A Conspiracy So Dense: The Dubious Half-Life of

Richard Hofstadter's 'Paranoid Style.'" *Baffler*, November 2018. https://thebaffler.com/salvos/a-conspiracy-so-dense-olmsted.

Orwell, George. *Nineteen Eighty-Four*. Penguin Books, 2008.

Otto, Eric C. *Green Speculations: Science Fiction and Transformative Environmentalism*. Ohio State University Press, 2012.

Owens, Louis, and Hector Torres. "Dialogic Structure and Levels of Discourse in Steinbeck's *The Grapes of Wrath*." *Arizona Quarterly* 45, no. 4 (Winter 1989): 75–94.

Paik, Peter Y. *From Utopia to Apocalypse: Science Fiction and the Politics of Catastrophe*. University of Minnesota Press, 2010.

Panshin, Alexei. *Heinlein in Dimension: A Critical Analysis*. Advent, 1968.

Park, Madison. "US Fertility Rate Falls to Lowest on Record." CBSN Philly, August 11, 2016. https://www.cnn.com/2019/07/24/health/fertility-rate-births-2018-cdc-study/index.html.

Park, Phoebe. "Kenya's $13 Billion Railway Project Is Taking Shape." May 15, 2016. https://www.cnn.com/2016/05/15/africa/kenya-railway-east-africa/index.html.

Parvulescu, Anca. "Reproduction and Queer Theory: Between Lee Edelman's *No Future* and J. M. Coetzee's *Slow Man*." *PMLA* 132, no. 1 (January 2017): 86–100.

Patton, Paul. "McCarthy's Fire." In *Styles of Extinction: Cormac McCarthy's The Road*, edited by Julian Murphet and Mark Steven, 131–43. Continuum, 2012.

Peckinpah, Sam, dir. *The Wild Bunch*. Warner Brothers, 1969.

Permuted Press. "About." Accessed August 21, 2019. https://permutedpress.com/about.

Phillips, Dana. "'He Ought Not Have Done It': McCarthy and Apocalypse." In *Cormac McCarthy: All the Pretty Horses, No Country for Old Men, The Road*, edited by Sara L. Spurgeon, 172–88. Continuum, 2011.

Piercy, Marge. *Woman on the Edge of Time*. Alfred A. Knopf, 1976.

Pitetti, Connor. "Uses of the End of the World: Apocalypse and Postapocalypse as Narrative Modes." *Science Fiction Studies* 44, no. 3 (2017): 437–54.

Platt, Charles. "The Vanishing Midlist." *Interzone* 29 (May–June 1989): 49–51 and 72.

"Post-, prefix." *Oxford English Dictionary Online*. Accessed July 27, 2020. https://www-oed-com.proxy1.lib.trentu.ca/view/Entry/148402?redirectedFrom=post-apocalyptic#eid28952233.

Proudhon, Pierre-Joseph. *What Is Property? An Inquiry into the Principle of Right and of Government*. Accessed July 24, 2020. https://www.marxists.org/reference/subject/economics/proudhon/property/.

Rabkin, Eric S. "Introduction: Why Destroy the World?" In *The End of the World*, edited by Eric S. Rabkin, Martin H. Greenberg, and Joseph D. Olander, vii–xv. Southern Illinois University Press, 1983.

Rabkin, Eric S., Martin H. Greenberg, and Joseph D. Olander, eds. *The End of the World*. Southern Illinois University Press, 1983.

Rieder, John. *Colonialism and the Emergence of Science Fiction*. Wesleyan University Press, 2008.

———. *Science Fiction and the Mass Cultural Genre System*. Wesleyan University Press, 2017.

Robinson, Kim Stanley. *The Gold Coast*. Orb, 2013.

———. "The Novels of Phillip K. Dick." PhD diss., University of San Diego, 1982.

———. *Pacific Edge*. Orb, 2013.

———. *The Wild Shore*. Orb, 2013.

Roemer, Kenneth. *The Obsolete Necessity: America in Utopian Writings, 1888–1900*. UMI Bell and Howell, 1998.

Ronda, Margaret. *Remainders: American Poetry at Nature's End*. Stanford University Press, 2018.

Rosen, Jeremy. "Introduction to Ecologies of Neoliberal Publishing." April 8, 2020. http://post45.org/2020/04/introduction-to-ecologies-of-neoliberal-publishing/.

———. "Penguin Random House, Co-Opted Values, and Contemporary Cli-Fi." April 8, 2020. http://post45.org/2020/04/penguin-random-house-co-opted-valuesand-contemporary-cli-fi/.

Rosenthal, Morris. "Sale of Remainders, Review Copies and Deep Discount Books on Amazon." Accessed July 29, 2020. http://fonerbooks.blogspot.com/2005/09/sale-of-remainders-review-copies-and.html.

Roser, Max, and Mohamed Nagdy. "Military Spending." *Our World in Data*. Accessed July 28, 2020. https://ourworldindata.org/military-spending.

Roshwald, Mordecai. *Level 7*. University of Wisconsin Press, 2004.

Russ, Joanna. *The Female Man*. Bantam Books, 1975.

Sambrook, A. J. "A Romantic Theme: The Last Man." *Forum for Modern Language Studies* 2, no. 1 (January 1966): 25–33.

Sargent, Lyman Tower. *British and Utopian Literature, 1516–1985*. Hall, 1988.

Saxton, Alexander. "*Caesar's Column*: The Dialogue of Utopia and Catastrophe." *American Quarterly* 19, no. 2 (Summer 1967): 224–38.

Schaffner, Franklin J., dir. *Planet of the Apes*. Twentieth Century Fox, 1968.

Scheper-Hughes, Nancy. "The Last Commodity: Post-Human Ethics and the Global Traffic in 'Fresh' Organs." In *Global Assemblages: Technology,*

Politics, and Ethics as Anthropological Problems, edited by Aihwa Ong and Stephen J. Collier, 145–67. Blackwell, 2005.

Scherrer, Christoph. "Reproducing Hegemony: US Finance Capital and the 2008 Crisis." *Cultural Policy Studies* 5, no. 3 (October 2011): 219–46.

Schneider-Mayerson, Matthew. *Peak Oil: Apocalyptic Environmentalism and Libertarian Political Culture*. University of Chicago Press, 2015.

———. "What Almost Was: Politics of the Contemporary Alternate History Novel." *American Studies* 50, nos. 3–4 (Fall–Winter 2009): 63–83.

Schumpeter, Joseph A. *The Theory of Economic Development: An Inquiry into Profits, Capital, Credit, Interest, and the Business Cycle*. Translated by Redvers Opie. Transaction Publishers, 2004.

Scott, George C., dir. *Rage*. Warner Brothers, 1972.

Seed, David. *Science Fiction and the Cold War: Literature and Film*. Edinburgh University Press, 1999.

———. *Under the Shadow*. Kent State University Press, 2013.

Sharp, Patrick B. *Savage Perils: Racial Frontiers and Nuclear Apocalypse in American Culture*. University of Oklahoma Press, 2012.

Sharpe, Christina Elizabeth. *In the Wake: On Blackness and Being*. Duke University Press, 2007.

Sheldon, Rebekah. *The Child to Come: Life after Human Catastrophe*. University of Minnesota Press, 2016.

Shelley, Mary. *The Last Man*. Oxford University Press, 2008.

Shklovsky, Viktor. *Theory of Prose*. Translated by Benjamin Sher. Dalkey Archive Press, 1991.

Shute, Neville. *On the Beach*. William Morrow, 1957.

Shyamalan, M. Knight, dir. *After Earth*. Columbia Pictures, 2013.

Sinker, Mark. "Loving the Alien—*Black Science Fiction*." *Wire* 96 (February 1992): 30–33.

Sinykin, Dan N. "The Conglomerate Era: Publishing, Authorship, and Literary Form, 1965–2007." *Contemporary Literature* 58, no. 4 (2017): 462–91.

Slusser, George Edgar. *Robert A. Heinlein: Stranger in His Own Land*. Borgo, 1976.

Søfting, Inger-Anne. "Between Dystopia and Utopia: The Post-Apocalyptic Discourse of Cormac McCarthy's *The Road*." *English Studies* 94, no. 6 (2013): 704–13.

Solnit, Rebecca. *A Paradise Built in Hell: The Extraordinary Communities That Arise in Disaster*. Viking, 2009.

Soni, Vivason. "Energy." In *Fueling Culture: 101 Words for Energy and Environment*, edited by Imre Szeman, Jennifer Wenzel, and Patricia Yaeger, 132–35. Fordham University Press, 2017.

Sorenson, Leif. "Against the Post-Apocalyptic: Narrative Closure in Colson Whitehead's *Zone One*." *Contemporary Literature* 55, no. 3 (2014): 559–92.

Spahr, Juliana, and Stephanie Young. "The Program Era and the Mainly White Room." *Los Angeles Review of Books*, September 20, 2015. https://lareviewofbooks.org/article/the-program-era-and-the-mainly-white-room/.

Srinivasan, Roopa, Manish Tiwari, and Sandeep Silas, eds. *Our Indian Railway: Themes in India's Railway History*. Foundation Books, 2006.

Steinbeck, John. *The Grapes of Wrath*. Penguin, 2006.

Steven, Mark, and Julian Murphet. "Introduction: 'The Charred Ruins of a Library.'" In *Styles of Extinction: Cormac McCarthy's* The Road, edited by Julian Murphet and Mark Steven, 1–8. Continuum, 2012.

Stewart, George R. *Earth Abides*. Gollancz, 1999.

Sullivan, Nell. "Gender in McCarthy's Fiction." In *Critical Insights: Cormac McCarthy*, edited by David N. Cremean, 198–217. Salem Press, 2013.

———. "The Good Guys: McCarthy's *The Road* as Post-9/11 Male Sentimental Novel." *Genre* 46, no. 1 (2013): 79–101.

Suvin, Darko. "On the Poetics of the Science Fiction Genre." *College English* 34, no. 3 (1972): 372–82.

Taylor, Aubrey Isabel. *Patricia A. McKillip and the Art of Fantasy World-Building*. McFarland.

Taylor, Matthew, and Jonathan Watts. "Revealed: The 20 Firms behind a Third of All Carbon Emissions." *Guardian*, October 9, 2019. https://www.theguardian.com/environment/2019/oct/09/revealed-20-firms-third-carbon-emissions.

Tebbel, John. *A History of Book Publishing in the United States*. Vol. 3: *The Golden Age between the Two Wars, 1920–1940*. R. R. Bowker, 1978.

Tepper, Sheri S. *The Gate to Women's Country*. Bantam Books, 1989.

"This Week's Bestsellers: September 16, 2013." *Publisher's Weekly*, September 13, 2013. https://www.publishersweekly.com/pw/by-topic/industry-news/bookselling/article/59097-this-week-s-bestsellers-september-16-2013.html.

Thompson, John B. *Merchants of Culture: The Publishing Business in the Twenty-First Century*. Plume, 2012.

"Tim LaHaye, 'Left Behind' Co-Author and Evangelical Leader, Passes at 90." July 25, 2016. https://www.tyndale.com/news/tim-lahaye-left-behind-co-author-and-evangelical-leader-passes-at-90.

Trimble, S. *Undead Ends: Stories of Apocalypse*. Rutgers University Press, 2019.

Turner, Fredrick Jackson. *The Significance of the Frontier in American*

History. October 14, 2007. http://www.gutenberg.org/files/22994/22994-h/22994-h.htm.

U.S. Energy Information Administration. "The U.S. Leads Global Petroleum and Natural Gas Production with Record Growth in 2018." August 20, 2019. https://www.eia.gov/todayinenergy/detail.php?id=40973#:~:text=The%20United%20States%20surpassed%20Russia,world's%20largest%20producer%20of%20petroleum.

Varley, John. *Slow Apocalypse*. Ace Books, 2012.

Vine, David. *Base Nation: How U.S. Military Bases Abroad Harm America and the World*. Metropolitan Books, 2015.

———. "The United States Probably Has More Foreign Military Bases Than Any Other People, Nation, or Empire in History: And It's Doing Us More Harm Than Good." *Nation*, September 14, 2015. https://www.thenation.com/article/the-united-states-probably-has-more-foreign-military-bases-than-any-other-people-nation-or-empire-in-history/.

Wagner, Brian. *Disturbing the Peace: Black Culture and the Police Power after Slavery*. Harvard University Press, 2009.

Waldman, Katy. "How Sci-Fi's Hugo Awards Got Their Own Full-Blown Gamergate." *Slate*, April 8, 2015. https://slate.com/culture/2015/04/2015-hugo-awards-how-the-sad-and-rabid-puppies-took-over-the-sci-fi-nominations.html.

Warwick Research Collective. *Combined and Uneven Development: Towards a New Theory of World-Literature*. Liverpool University Press, 2015.

Watkins, Claire Vaye. *Gold Famed Citrus*. Riverhead Books, 2015.

Watkins, Susan. *Contemporary Women's Post-Apocalyptic Fiction*. Springer, 2020.

———. "Future Shock: Rewriting the Apocalypse in Contemporary Women's Fiction." *Lit* 23, no. 2 (April 2012) 119–37.

Wegner, Phillip E. *Life between Two Deaths, 1989–2001: U.S. Culture in the Long Nineties*. Duke University Press, 2009.

Wells, H. G. *The World Set Free*. Tantor Media, 2009.

White, Hayden. *Metahistory: The Historical Imagination in Nineteenth-Century Europe*. Johns Hopkins University Press, 1973.

———. "The Question of Narrative in Contemporary Historical Theory." In Hayden White, *The Content of the Form: Narrative Discourse and Historical Representation*, 26–57. Paperback ed. Johns Hopkins University Press, 1990.

Whitehead, Colson. *Zone One*. Doubleday, 2011.

Whyte, Kyle Powys. "Our Ancestors' Dystopia Now: Indigenous Conservation and the Anthropocene." In *Routledge Companion to the Environmental*

Humanities, edited by Ursula Heise, Jon Christensen, and Michelle Niemann, 270–81. Routledge, 2017.

Williams, Evan Calder. *Combined and Uneven Apocalypse*. Zero Books, 2011.

Williams, Paul. *Race, Ethnicity and Nuclear War: Representations of Nuclear Weapons and Post-Apocalyptic Worlds*. Liverpool University Press, 2011.

Williams, Raymond. *Marxism and Literature*. Oxford University Press. 1977.

Williams, Rhys. "Recognizing Cognition: On Suvin, Miéville, and the Utopian Impulse in the Contemporary Fantastic." *Science Fiction Studies* 41 (2014): 617–33.

Wilson, Robert Charles. *Julian Comstock: A Story of 22nd-Century America*. Tor, 2009.

Wolfe, Gary K. "The Remaking of Zero: Beginning after the End." In *The End of the World*, edited by Eric S. Rabkin, Martin H. Greenberg, and Joseph D. Olander, 1–19. Southern Illinois University Press, 1983.

Wolf-Meyer, Matthew. "Apocalypse, Ideology, America: Science Fiction and the Myth of the Post-Apocalyptic Everyday." *Rhizomes*, no. 8 (Spring 2004). http://www.rhizomes.net/issue8/wolfmeyer.htm.

Woodson, Linda. "McCarthy's Heroes and the Will to Truth." In *The Cambridge Companion to Cormac McCarthy*, edited by Stephen Frye, 15–26. Cambridge University Press, 2013.

Wren, M. K. *A Gift on the Shore*. Ballantine Books, 1990.

Wyndham, John. *The Day of the Triffids*. Doubleday, 1951.

Yaeger, Patricia. "Editor's Column: Literature in the Ages of Wood, Tallow, Coal, Whale Oil, Gasoline, Atomic Power, and Other Energy Sources." *PMLA* 126, no. 2 (2011): 305–10.

Yeates, Robert. "Gender and Ethnicity in Post-Apocalyptic Suburbia." *Journal of the Fantastic in the Arts* 27, no. 3 (2016): 411–34.

Zelazny, Roger. *Damnation Alley*. J. Boylston and Company, 2015.

Zipp, Samuel. *Manhattan Projects: The Rise and Fall of Urban Renewal in New York*. Oxford University Press, 2010.

Žižek, Slavoj. *Living in the End Times*. Verso, 2010.

———. *The Sublime Object of Ideology*. Verso, 2009.

Index

28 Days Later, 61

Abbot, Carl, 103–104, 107
Ace publishing, 76, 78–79; Ace Special series, 82–83. *See also* publishing industry
Adorno, Theodor, 197
After Earth, 62
Aftermath, 26, 206; and the apocalypse, 152–153; and biotechnology, 148–149; and genre, 147–148; and multiculturalism, 148–149
Alas, Babylon, 27, 182, 187, 198; and infrastructure, 186; and nuclear war, 33–34, 134; and oil, 174–175. *See also* Frank, Pat
Aldiss, Brian W., 137
Amazon, 91, 92, 94–95. *See also* publishing industry
Anderson Benedict, 104, 111
Anderson, Kevin J. and Doug Beason: *Ill Wind*, 194
Anderson, Perry, 118
apocalypse: as description, 59–60, 67; energy apocalypse, 27; as event, 69; religious, 32–33, 56–58, 59; temporality of, 56–57, 69, 161–162; uneven, 20–21, 43, 57, 135, 152–153, 196, 207
archive: destruction of, 18–19, 42–45
Arendt, Hannah, 115–116
Armstrong, Nancy, 167–168
Arrighi, Giovanni, 11–14, 16, 97, 122
atomic bomb. *See* nuclear war
Atwood, Margaret: MaddAddam Trilogy, 92–93, 96; *Oryx and Crake*, 7–8, 92; *The Year of the Flood*, 92–93
Auster, Paul, 84; *In the Country of Last Things*, 4–5
Austin, J.L., 112
Axler, James, 86, 90–91

Ballantine Books, 80. *See also* publishing industry
Bantam Books, 81–82, 83. *See also* publishing industry
Bear, Greg: *Blood Music*, 84
Beckett, Samuel: *Endgame*, 58
Bell, Madison Smartt, 159
Berger, James, 20, 58–60, 153
Berlant, Lauren, 9–10
Berman, Mitch: *Time Capsule*, 83
Bould, Mark, 140, 151
Bourdieu, Pierre, 5
Boyett, Steven R.: *Ariel*, 83
Brackett, Leigh, 20, 25. See also *Long Tomorrow, The*
Brenner, Robert, 13–14, 165
Brin, David. See *Postman, The*
Brooks, Albert: *2030*, 194
Brooks, Max: *World War Z*, 93–94
Brouillette, Sarah, 81, 95–96
Brunner, John: *The Traveler in Black*, 79
Buell, Frederick, 76, 196–198
Burton, LeVar. See *Aftermath*
Butler, Octavia E., 21, 151, 156; *Clay's Arc*, 21; *Earthseed*, 76; *Parable of the Sower*, 22, 27, 147, 175–177, 188, 198; *Parable of the Talents*, 2–3; Parables series, 96, 170–171;

263

Wild Seed, 83; Xenogenesis trilogy, 23–24, 62, 84

Canavan, Gerry, 178
Canticle for Leibowitz, A, 31, 34–35, 50–51; and the catalogue, 42, 45; and community, 42, 45; and the enclave, 42–46, 49–50. *See also* Miller Jr., Walter
Carr, Terry, 79, 82–83
Carrington, André, 140
Carson, Rachel: *Silent Spring*, 35
catalogue, the, 103; in *Earth Abides*, 36–38, 45, 49, 193–194; in *Slow Apocalypse*, 193–194. *See also* post-apocalypse, tropes of
Cetinic, Marija, 11–12, 17
Chabon, Michael, 92, 158, 160–161
Charnas, Suzy McKee, 20; *Motherlines*, 53–54, 80; *Walk to the End of the World*, 80
circulation, 110–112, 116; of books, 24–25, 74–75; of characters, 41–42, 122–125; of commodities, 93, 174–175, 179; of knowledge, 43–46, 93; of literary tropes, 22–24, 35–36, 50–51, 92–94; of zombies, 93, 203–204
cities, 20, 39–42, 134–135, 181–182, 201–202
Cohen, Neil A.: *Welcome to Nuke Jersey*, 87
Cold War, the, 14, 32, 46–47, 71–72, 104
community, 103; in *The Long Tomorrow*, 39–42, 45, 49, 180; imagined communities, 104–105, 111; in *The Postman*, 110–114; and race, 130–134; in *The Stand*, 68–69, 71–72; in *World Made by Hand*, 180–182. *See also* post-apocalypse, tropes of
Cooper, James Fenimore, 64
Cooper, Lydia R., 159
Corlett, Anne: *The Space Between the Stars*, 77
crisis, 2, 9–10, 57–59; racialized, 152–153; of reproduction, 164–167
Cumings, Bruce, 12
Curtis, Claire P., 114

Darlage, Dale, 139
De Cristofaro, Diletta, 189
defamiliarization, 64–65, 185–186. *See also* inversion
DeGraw, Sharon, 145–146
Delany, Samuel R., 20, 137, 149, 151; *Bridge of Lost Desire*, 84; Nevèrÿon series, 81–82
DeNiro, Alan: *Total Oblivion, More or Less*, 7–8
Derrida, Jacques, 18–19
Dibbell, Carola: *The Only Ones*, 4–5
Dick, Philip K., 78–79; *The Man Who Japed*, 74–76
Dog Stars, The, 27, 93, 155, 198, 206; and oil, 190–193
Donnelly, Ignatius: *Caesar's Column*, 3–4
Doubleday, 79, 83, 85, 92–93, 97. *See also* publishing industry
Douglass, Frederick, 142
Doyle, Briohny, 58, 189
Dreiser, Thomas, 64
Du Bois, W.E.B.: "The Comet," 27, 132–133, 170
Dyer, Richard, 134

Earth Abides, 31, 34–35, 50–51, 155; and the catalogue, 36–38, 45, 49,

193–194; and post-apocalyptic tropes, 61; and race, 130–132. *See also* Stewart, George R.
Eco, Umberto, 5
Edelman, Lee, 156
El Akkad, Omar: *American War*, 77
enclave, 103; in *A Canticle for Leibowitz*, 42–46, 49–50. *See also* post-apocalypse, tropes of
energy, culture of, 172–173, 189, 197; energy apocalypse, 27, 172–174 (see also *Alas, Babylon*; *Dog Stars, The*; *Parable of the Sower*; *Slow Apocalypse, The*; *Station Eleven*; *World Made by Hand*); and human labor, 178–179, 184, 186–187, 191; and mobility, 174–176, 188, 192, 195; nuclear power, 40–42, 43; and US hegemony, 172

Farnham's Freehold, 26, 155; apocalypse in, 136–137; and defamiliarization, 137, 138, 140–147; and the last man, 49, 136; and masculinity, 138–139; and racism, 138; and science fiction, 139–141; and slavery, 141–147, 206. *See also* Heinlein, Robert
Federici, Silvia, 116
Festinger, Leon, 56–57
feudalism/neofeudalism, 65–66, 112, 115, 121, 181
Finch, Laura, 134–135
Fisher, Phillip, 64
Fitting, Peter, 20
Floyd, Kevin, 150–151
Fowler, Alastair, 6
Frank, Pat, 25. See also *Alas, Babylon*
Franklin, H. Bruce, 12–13, 27, 33–34, 137

Freedman, Carl, 64
frontier, the, 26, 107–108, 115, 118–120, 124; as post-apocalyptic trope, 103–106, 128–129
future, 7–8, 116–117, 127–129, 203; no future, 156, 160–162, 178; reduced future, 1, 52–55, 62, 68–70, 72–73; 103, 127–129, 172–173, 189–190; and reproduction, 155–157

Gate to Women's Country, The, 26, 83; and future reduction, 66, 69, 72–73; and gender, 65, 67–68, 71; and neofeudalism, 65–66; and reproduction, 66–67
gender, 19–21, 65, 67–68, 71, 72–73, 159–160, 183–184. *See also* masculinity, reproduction
genre fiction, 86–88, 90, 93–94. *See also* literary fiction
Gibson, William, 121; *Neuromancer*, 60, 82
Godfrey, Laura Gruber, 159
Gold Eagle Books, 86–87, 90, 97. *See also* publishing industry

Hägglund, Martin, 18
Harrison, Harry: *Make Room! Make Room!*, 54
Harvey, David, 115–116
Hay, John, 55–56
Heer, Jeet, 137–138
Heffernan, Teresa, 56, 58
Heinlein, Robert, 137–138. *See also Farnham's Freehold*
Heller, Peter. See *Dog Stars, The*
Herbert, Frank: *The White Plague*, 84
Hicks, Heather J., 57–58
historical change, 8–10, 59, 64–65, 133

Hoberek, Andrew, 92
Hobsbawm, Eric, 124
Hollinger, Veronica, 3, 6–7
hooks, bell, 142–143
Horkheimer, Max, 197
Hoskin, Rik, 86
Howey, Hugh: *Wool*, 93–94
Hurley, Jessica, 45–46, 134–135
Hurley, Natasha, 164–165

I Am Legend, 31, 34–35, 50–51, 134, 136; and last man, 46–49, 50, 204; and masculinity, 48–49; and race, 46, 48–49. *See also* Matheson, Richard
individual versus collective, 2–3, 39, 45, 48, 112, 125–126, 148–149, 165, 181–182, 204
infrastructure, 185–190; in *Alas, Babylon*, 186; and bookselling, 91; in *Earth Abides*, 36; malls, 80–81, 86; and oil, 173–175; in *The Postman*, 112–113; as remainder, 18, 21–22, 36, 109–110; in *Station Eleven*, 186; in *Slow Apocalypse*, 193; in *The Wild Shore*, 124
inversion, 136–138, 140–147. *See also* defamiliarization

Jacobs, Harriet Ann, 142
James, Laurence, 86
James, P.D.: *Children of Men*, 156
Jameson, Frederic, 8–9, 45, 54, 62–63, 65, 84–85
Jemisin, N.K., 27; Broken Earth Trilogy, 205–206; *The Stone Sky*, 77
Jerng, Mark, 133
Joyce, Stephen, 77, 202

Katerberg, William H., 104
Kermode, Frank, 56–57, 59
King, Stephen, 84; *Carrie*, 84. See also *Stand, The*
Kunstler, James Howard: *Long Emergency, The*, 178. See also *World Made by Hand*

Lanier, Sterling E.: *Hiero's Journey*, 83; *The Unforsaken Hiero*, 83
last man, 46–49, 103, in *Farnham's Freehold*, 136; in *I Am Legend*, 46–49, 50, 204; in *the Road*, 49, 170. *See also* post-apocalypse, tropes of
Lavender III, Isiah, 138
Le Guin, Ursula K, 71, 84; *A Wizard of Earthsea*, 79; *The Left Hand of Darkness*, 79
Left Behind series, 88, 90–91
Lepucki, Edan: *California*, 156
Levey, Nick, 94
liberal subjectivity, 68, 105, 107, 116–121, 126
literary fiction, 76–78, 85, 92–93, 158, 169. *See also* genre fiction
London, Jack, *The Scarlet Plague*, 39, 155
Long Tomorrow, The, 31, 34–35, 50–51, 127; and community, 39–42, 45, 49, 180. *See also* Brackett, Leigh
Lord of the Rings, 71
Lott, Eric, 150

Machovsky, Brenda, 5
Malik, Rachel, 87
Mandel, Emily St. John, 77. *See also Station Eleven*
Manjikian, Mary, 11

Martelle, Craig: End Times Alaska series, 87
masculinity, 19–21, 27, 46–49, 138–139; as post-apocalyptic trope, 48–49. *See also* gender, reproduction
Matheson, Richard, 25. See also *I Am Legend*
McCarthy, Cormac. See *Road, The*
McGiveron, Rafeeq O., 137
McGurl, Mark, 92–94, 97
Mehren, Elizabeth, 86
Melamed, Jodi, 150
Merril, Judith, 20; *Shadows on the Hearth*, 4–5
Miller Jr., Walter, 25. See also *Canticle for Leibowitz*
Miller, T.S., 195
mode: of apocalypse, 56–58; as literary technique, 3–11; of production, 7–8, 12–14, 39–42, 66, 97, 119–121, 149–151, 179–184
Monbiot, George, 159, 166
Montgomery, Maxine Lavon, 152–153
Moore, Deborah D.: Journals series, 87
Moore, Ward: *Lot and Lot's Daughter*, 76
More, Thomas, 45
Morris, William, 45
Morrison, Toni, 134

neoliberalism, 1, 117–121
Nogha, Misha, 121
nuclear power, 40–42, 43. *See also* energy
nuclear war, 18–19, 32–34, 44, 53, 59, 65, 70, 74, 78, 122, 134, 136, 152

O'Donnell, Jr., Kevin, 89
Orwell, George: *Nineteen Eighty-Four*, 60
Owens, Lewis, 37–38

Palmer, David R.: *Emergence*, 83
Panshin, Alexei, 145; *Rite of Passage*, 79
Park, Madison, 164
Patton, Paul, 159
Permuted Press, 87, 91, 97. *See also* publishing industry
petroculture. *See* energy, culture of
Phillips, Dana, 159
Piercy, Marge, 20, 71
Pitetti, Connor, 58
Planet of the Apes, 60
Platt, Charles, 81
Pohl, Frederick and Jack Williamson: *Land's End*, 84
Pohl, Frederick and Jerry Pournelle: *Lucifer's Hammer*, 84
Postman, The, 26, 83, 104–106, 206; and apocalypse, 106, 147–148, 179; and community, 110–114; conflict between narrator and character, 108–110, 114, 116–117, 126; and the decline of US hegemony, 108–109; and the frontier, 105–106; and the future, 127–129; and the last man, 49; and restoration of the United States, 106–107, 112–113, 116–117, 127–129; and science fiction, 114–115, 128; and spatialization, 107–108, 169; and technology, 113–115
post-apocalypse: as allegory, 3–11, 23, 97; and ethical reading, 157–160; as genre fiction, 1–2, 20, 76–79,

92–96; as mode, 3, 6–11, 19, 25–26, 42, 50, 59; and the real world, 7–8, 52, 54–55, 62–63, 70–71; as symbol, 3–11; temporality of, 4–5, 9, 18, 56–59, 63, 104–105, 111, 128–129, 160–162; tropes of, 22–23, 25, 34–51, 60–61, 204 (*see also* catalogue, the; community; enclave, the; last man); as white, 19–21, 26, 48–49, 132, 134–137, 149, 153, 183

Prochnau, William: *Trinity's Child*, 84

Project for the New American Century, 15–16, 207

Proudhon, Pierre-Joseph, 179

publishing industry, 20, 24–25; best sellers, 84–88; big-box bookstores, 86; consolidation of, 77; history of, 75–76, 204–205; mall bookstores, 81–82, 86, 91; midlist publishing, 78–84, 89–90; as risk averse, 77, 80–82; self-publishing, 77, 93–94, 96–99. *See also*, remainders, remaindered books

Rabkin, Eric S., 6

race, 19–21, 204; in *Aftermath*, 147, 148–150, 153; and community, 130–134; in *Farnham's Freehold*, 138; in *I Am Legend*, 46, 48–49; in *World Made by Hand*, 182–183. *See also* apocalypse, uneven; post-apocalypse, as white; slavery; white supremacy

Rae-Lee, Chang: *On Such a Full Sea*, 93, 95

Rage, 71

remainders: as books, 24–25, 26, 74–75; of capital, 151; definition of, 3, 18–25, 203; as infrastructure, 18, 21–22, 36, 109–110, 185–186, 187–190; as literary elements, 19, 22–24; of the nation, 107, 109, 112–113, 206; remaindered books, 75, 88–91, 96–99, 103; as social contract, 110–113; temporality of, 18–19, 21–22; as things, 19, 21–22, 109–110, 154–155, 180

reproduction, 26–27, 66–67; and capitalism, 163–165; and survival, 131–132, 156, 160–161, 162–171. *See also* gender, masculinity

Rieder, John, 5, 20–21

Road, The, 26–27, 92; and the environment, 159; ethical reading of, 157–160; and gender, 154–155, 159–160, 169–171; and last man, 49, 170; as literary fiction, 158; and remaindered books, 75; and reproduction, 163–169; and survival, 157, 162–164, 165–166, 206; and temporality, 160–162; and race, 170

Robinson, Kim Stanley: Three Californias triptych, 121, 127. *See also Wild Shore, The*

Rosen, Jeremy, 95–96

Rosenthal, Morris, 97–98

Roshwald, Mordecai: *Level 7*, 32–34

Russ, Joanna, 71; *And Chaos Died*, 79

Saxton, Alexander, 4–5

Scheper-Hughes, Nancy, 151

Schneider-Mayerson, Matthew, 178

science fiction: in *Aftermath*, 149; and the atomic bomb, 32–33; black SF, 135, 151; in *Farnham's Freehold*, 139–141; feminist SF, 65, 72–73, 81; and the future, 173–174; as genre, 22–24, 26, 53, 62–63; Golden Age of, 34; and multiculturalism, 149;

New Wave, 34, 65, 82–83, in *The Postman*, 114–115, 128; in *The Slow Apocalypse*, 194
settler-colonialism, 20, 23, 26, 105–106, 114, 118, 207
Shute, Neville: *On the Beach*, 53
Silverberg, Robert: *At Winter's End*, 84; *The Queen of Springtime*, 84
Sinker, Mark, 151
Sinykin, Dan, 76, 77, 85, 92
slavery, 26, 135, 136–147, 206
Slow Apocalypse, The, 27, 206; and the apocalypse, 195; and the catalogue, 193–194; and infrastructure, 193; and scarcity, 195–196, 198–199; and science fiction, 194
Slusser, Edgar, 137
Smith II, Philip E., 145
Søfting, Inger-Anne, 166, 168
Sorenson, Leif, 59
Sosnowski, David: *Happy Doomsday*, 95
spatialization, 57, 103–106, 107–108, 122–126; 161–162, 169
Spire, Antoine, 18
Stand, The, 26, 65, 68, 129, 134, 147–148; and community, 68–69, 71–72; and future reduction, 68–70; and the last man, 49; politics of, 70–72; publication history of, 85–86. *See also* King, Stephen
Station Eleven, 27, 198, 206; and the commodity form, 187; and infrastructure, 186; and remainders, 185–186, 187–190. *See also* Mandel, Emily St. John
Steinbeck, John: *The Grapes of Wrath*, 37–38

Stephenson, Neal, 121
Stewart, George R, 25. *See also Earth Abides*
Stowe, Harriet Beecher, 64
Sullivan, Nell, 159–160, 168–169
survival, 1–2, 31, 52, 108–109, 155–157; and reproduction, 131–132, 156, 160–161, 162–171
Suvin, Darko, 62

technology, 31, 39–46, 52, 66, 113–115; 124–125
Tepper, Sheri S. See *Gate to Women's Country, The*
Thomas, David, 95–96
Thompson, John B., 90, 92, 94
Thor Power Tool Company v. Commissioner of Internal Revenue, 88–89
Torres, Hector, 37–38
Toy, Randall, 87
trace, the, 18–19
Trump, Donald J., 3, 297
Tubb, E.C.: *The Space-Born*, 78
Turner, Frederick Jackson, 107–108, 112

US hegemony: end of, 1–2, 11–17, 55, 108–119; 122, 179, 203–207; and financialization, 11–12, 13, 14, 16–17; and military, 12–17, 122; and oil, 172–173; restoration of, 2–3, 15–17, 106–121, 124–126, 127–129

VanderMeer, Jeff: *Borne*, 77
Varley, John. See *Slow Apocalypse, The*
Vintage Books, 76. *See also* publishing industry
Vonnegut, Jr., Kurt, 84

Wagner, Brian, 143
Walking Dead, The, 61–62
Watkins, Claire Vaye: *Gold Fame Citrus*, 62, 93
Wegner, Phillip, 14–15
Weir, Andy: *The Martian*, 95
Westfahl, Gary, 145
white supremacy, 19–21, 131–132, 133, 135–136, 143–146. *See also* apocalypse, uneven; post-apocalypse, as white; race
Whitehead, Colson, 77; *Zone One*, 27, 93, 201–205
Wild Bunch, The, 105
Wild Shore, The, 26, 83, 104–106, 169, 194, 206; and collective decision making, 125–126; and end of US hegemony, 122; and the frontier, 105–106; and restoration of US hegemony, 124–126, 127–129; and spatialization, 122–126; and technology, 124–125; and the future, 127–129; *See also* Robinson, Kim Stanley
Williams, Paul O.: *The Fall of the Shell*, 83
Williams, Raymond, 203
Williams, Rhys, 64
Wolf-Meyer, Matthew, 39–40
Wolfe, Gary K., 52–53, 63, 72
world destroying, 6–7, 17–19, 25–26, 52–55, 61–65, 195. *See also* future, reduced future
World Made by Hand, 27, 194, 198; and community, 180–182; and gender, 183–184; politics of, 177–179, 184; and race, 182–183. *See also* Kunstler, James Howard
Wren, M.K.: *A Gift on the Shore*, 75
Wyndham, John: *The Day of the Triffids*, 61

Yaeger, Patricia, 185
Yates, John Van Ness and Joseph White Moulton: *History of the State of New York*, 55–56
Yeates, Robert, 48

Zelazny, Roger: *Damnation Alley*, 33–34
Žižek, Slavoj, 14, 48

About the Author

BRENT RYAN BELLAMY is an instructor in the English and cultural studies departments at Trent University and is co-editor of *An Ecotopian Lexicon* and *Materialism and the Critique of Energy*.